Achieving Universal Primary Education by 2015

A Chance for Every Child

Barbara Bruns, Alain Mingat, and Ramahatra Rakotomalala

THE WORLD BANK
Washington, D.C.

1818 H Street, NW
Washington, DC 20433
Telephone 202-473-1000
Internet www.worldbank.org
E-mail feedback@worldbank.org

1 2 3 4 06 05 04 03

The findings, interpretations, and conclusions expressed herein are those of the authors and do not necessarily reflect the views of the Board of Executive Directors of the World Bank or the governments they represent.

The World Bank does not guarantee the accuracy of the data included in this work. The boundaries, colors, denominations, and other information shown on any map in this work do not imply any judgment on the part of the World Bank concerning the legal status of any territory or the endorsement or acceptance of such boundaries.

ISBN 0-8213-5345-4

**Library of Congress Cataloging-in-Publication Data
has been applied for**

Cover photo: Students writing in a war-torn classroom, Baukau, East Timor. Photo by Alex Baluyut/World Bank Photo Library.

CONTENTS

BOXES

TABLES

FIGURES

ACKNOWLEDGMENTS

This study is the work of a team led by Alain Mingat and Barbara Bruns. Team members included Ramahatra Rakotomalala, who developed the simulation model used and carried out the simulations for the African countries; Ashutosh Dubey, who supervised the data collection and simulations for the countries outside Africa; Nicholas Wilson, Saida Mamedova, and Jose Carlos Orihuela, who developed the new database of primary completion rates; Jee-Peng Tan, who contributed to data collection and analysis for the African countries; and Andrew Clark and Hongyu Yang, who assisted in data collection and analysis. Dina Abu-Ghaida carried out a review of relevant literature. Julie Wagshal tirelessly supported the team and handled the report processing through all stages with superb efficiency. Many other colleagues, especially Emanuela di Groppello, Lianqin Wang, Michael Drabble, Douglas Lehman, and Nancy Vandycke, helped in collection of the country-level data. We are grateful to Catherine Sunshine for copyediting; to John Mosier and Al Barkat of Intermax, Inc. and the team at Dohatec New Media for outstanding work in developing the CD-ROM; and above all to Mark Ingebretsen for superb production assistance.

We are grateful to Eduard Bos of the World Bank for the population data used in this analysis, to Sanjeev Gupta and Erwin Tiongson of the International Monetary Fund for fiscal data, and to our colleague Don Bundy and his collaborators at the Imperial College, U.K., for data and assistance in analyzing the impact of HIV/AIDS on the costs of achieving universal primary education. Many other World Bank colleagues helped with the analysis of country-level results, including Philip Goldman, Alan Wright, Brigitte Duces, Michelle Riboud, Keith Hinchliffe, Gary Theisen, Hena Mukherjee, Amit Dar, Christine Allison, Paud Murphy, Bruce Jones, Alexandria Valerio, Safaa El Kogali, Benoit Millot, Regina Bendokat, Keiichi Ogawa, Ayesha Vawda, Ousmane Diagana, John Newman, Peter Moock, Chris Thomas, Chris Shaw, and Tanaporn Poshyananda. Colleagues at numerous bilateral agencies also generously shared existing data and aided with data collection in the field. Without all of their help, this work would not have been possible. Finally, we are indebted to the governments of the Netherlands and Norway, which generously supported this research. We are especially grateful to Evelyn Herfkens, then minister of development cooperation in the Netherlands, for hosting the April 2002 international conference on Education for All in Amsterdam, at which this work was first presented.

The research was carried out under the direct supervision of Ruth Kagia, Birger Fredriksen, and Josef Ritzen, and the team owes much to their vision in launching this exercise, their intellectual guidance throughout, and their unflagging support. The technical work was overseen by an advisory panel led by Shanta Devarajan and including Jamil Salmi, Maureen Lewis, Elizabeth King, Deon Filmer, Emmanuel Jimenez, and Margaret Miller, which contributed much to the conceptual framework and methodology. Discussions with a large number of other colleagues helped to sharpen our thinking—notably Hanke Koopman and

Jeannette Vogelaar of the Netherlands Cooperation Agency; Len Good, Tom Wallace, and Susan Moir at the Canadian International Development Agency (CIDA); Harry Hagan and Steve Packer at the U.K. Department for International Development (DFID); Clay Lowery, Brian Crowe, Stephen Krasner, Buff Mackenzie, and Greg Loos of the U.S. government; Michael Hofmann of the German Ministry for Cooperation and Development; Serge Tomasi, Paul Coustère, and Jean-Claude Balmès from the French Ministry of Foreign Affairs; Olaf Seim from the Norwegian Ministry of Foreign Affairs; Chris Colclough of Sussex University, U.K.; Sir John Daniel, Abimanyu Singh, and Khawla Shaheen at UNESCO; Cream Wright at UNICEF; Lant Pritchett at Harvard University; Nancy Birdsall and Steve Radelet at the Center for Global Development; Brian Ames at the International Monetary Fund; Gene Sperling of the Basic Education Coalition; Phil Twyford, Anne Jellema, Oliver Buston, and Patrick Watt of the Global Campaign for Education; and Luis Crouch, Carolyn Winter, Bob Prouty, Peter Buckland, Hans-Martin Boehmer, Sukai Prom-Jackson, Kin-Bing Wu, and Eric Swanson at the World Bank. Any data inconsistencies, conceptual flaws, or other errors, however, are the sole responsibility of the authors.

We dedicate this book to our spouses, Miguel, Hélène and Fara, and to our own school-aged children, Elena, Pedro, Bakoly and Mamisoa, who share our vision of a world in which every child has the chance to complete primary school.

ACRONYMS

AFR   Africa Region

AIDS   Acquired immune deficiency syndrome

DAC   Development Assistance Committee (of the OECD)

EAP   East Asia and the Pacific Region

ECA   Europe and Central Asia Region

EFA   Education for All

IBRD   International Bank for Reconstruction and Development (of the World Bank Group)

IDA   International Development Association (of the World Bank Group)

G-7   Group of Seven

G-8   Group of Eight

GDP   Gross domestic product

GER   Gross enrollment ratio

GNI   Gross national income

HIV   Human immunodeficiency virus

LCR   Latin America and the Caribbean Region

MDB   Multilateral development bank

MDG   Millennium Development Goal

MNA   Middle East and North Africa Region

MRY   Most recent year

MTEF   Medium-term Expenditure Framework

NER   Net enrollment ratio

NGO   Nongovernmental organization

OECD   Organisation for Economic Co-operation and Development

PCGDP   Per capita GDP

PCR	Primary completion rate
PRSC	Poverty Reduction Support Credit
PRSP	Poverty Reduction Strategy Paper
PTR	Pupil-teacher ratio
SAR	South Asia Region
SWAP	Sector-wide approach
UNAIDS	Joint United Nations Programme on HIV/AIDS
UNESCO	United Nations Educational, Scientific, and Cultural Organization
UNICEF	United Nations Children's Fund
UPC	Universal primary completion

Executive Summary

Few global goals have been as consistently and deeply supported as the notion that every child in every country should have the chance to complete at least a primary education. The 1990 World Conference on Education for All in Jomtien, Thailand set this goal to be achieved by 2000. The World Education Forum in Dakar in 2000 reaffirmed and extended the Jomtien commitment, bringing a welcome emphasis on schooling quality while acknowledging that universal primary completion had not yet been reached (box 1). Universal primary completion and gender equity in primary and secondary education were affirmed again in that same year as Millennium Development Goals (MDGs).

Education, and particularly primary education, is a goal in and of itself, but it is also a powerful driver of progress toward the other MDGs. More equitable distribution of education is correlated with lower poverty and inequality and faster economic growth (Birdsall and Londoño 1998). Greater education for girls has strong positive impacts on the health of infants and children, immunization rates, family nutrition, and the next generation's schooling attainment (World Bank 2001). New data from Africa show that education for girls and boys may be the single most effective preventive weapon against HIV/AIDS (World Bank 2002b). Primary education also contributes to better natural resource management, including conservation of the tropical rain forest (Godoy and Contreras 2001). Increasingly, however, research suggests that many of these positive externalities associated with primary education require that a minimum threshold of five or six years of schooling be attained—hence the importance of ensuring primary school completion, and not just primary school access.

Combined with sound macroeconomic policies, education is fundamental for the construction of globally competitive economies and democratic societies. Education is key to creating, applying, and spreading new ideas and technologies which in turn are critical for sustained growth; it augments cognitive and other skills, which in turn increase labor productivity. The expansion of educational opportunity is a "win-win" strategy that in most societies is far easier to implement than the redistribution of other assets such as land or capital. Ultimately, education builds what Amartya Sen (1999) calls "human capabilities"—the essential and individual power to reflect, make choices, seek a voice in society, and enjoy a better life. In short, education is one of the most powerful instruments known for reducing poverty and inequality and for laying the basis for sustained economic growth, sound governance, and effective institutions.

Yet the world remains far from the core Education for All (EFA) goal—universal primary school completion. This study assesses whether universal primary comple-

Box 1 Global "Education for All" Goals

DAKAR WORLD EDUCATION FORUM GOALS	MILLENNIUM DEVELOPMENT GOALS
Expand and improve comprehensive early childhood care and education, especially for the most vulnerable and disadvantaged children.	
Ensure that by 2015 all children, particularly girls, children in difficult circumstances, and those belonging to ethnic minorities, have access to and complete free and compulsory primary education of good quality.	Ensure that, by 2015, children everywhere, boys and girls alike, will be able to complete a full course of primary schooling.
Ensure that the learning needs of young people and adults are met through equitable access to appropriate learning and life skills programs.	
Achieve a 50 percent improvement in levels of adult literacy by 2015, especially for women, and equitable access to basic and continuing education for all adults.	
Eliminate gender disparities in primary and secondary education by 2005, and achieve gender equality in education by 2015, with a focus on ensuring girls' full and equal access to and achievement in basic education of good quality.	Eliminate gender disparity in primary and secondary education, preferably by 2005, and at all levels of education no later than 2015.
Improve all aspects of the quality of education and ensure excellence of all so that recognized and measurable learning outcomes are achieved by all, especially in literacy, numeracy, and essential life skills.	

tion can be achieved by 2015, the target date set by the Millennium Development Goals. Specifically, it asks:

- How close is the world to achieving the millennium goal of universal primary completion?
- Is it achievable by 2015?
- If so, what would be required to achieve it, in terms of both education policy reform and incremental domestic and international financing?

A new World Bank database developed for this study shows that over the 1990s the average rate of primary school completion in the developing world (on a country-weighted basis) improved only from 72 to 77 percent, far short of the progress needed to ensure achievement of the education MDG of universal primary completion. On a population-weighted basis, buoyed by China's high reported completion rate, the global picture looks slightly better, rising from 73 to 81 percent over the decade.

On either basis, however, the global average masks large regional differences in both the distance from the MDG and the progress made over the last decade, as can be seen from figures 1 and 2. Sub-Saharan Africa has the lowest completion rate by far, with barely half of all school-age children completing primary school; it is followed by South Asia, with an average completion rate of about 70 percent. The Middle East and North Africa showed a disturbing pattern of stagnation over the 1990s, with the average completion rate remaining around 74 percent. The Europe and Central Asia region (92 percent) is closest to the goal of universal primary completion, followed by Latin America and the Caribbean (85 percent) and East Asia and the Pacific (84 percent).

Moreover, within every region, trends at the country level diverge sharply, with rapid progress registered in some countries, stagnation in others, and declines elsewhere. For example, while the global average completion rate for girls improved

FIGURE 1 Primary Completion Progress in Africa, Middle East and North Africa, and South Asia Regions, 1990–2015, Country-Weighted

Primary completion rate (percent)

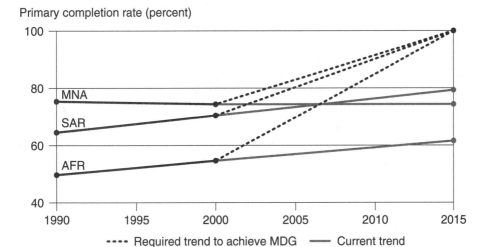

---- Required trend to achieve MDG ——— Current trend

Source: Annex figure B.5.

Primary Completion Progress in Europe and Central Asia, East Asia and the Pacific, and Latin America and the Caribbean Regions, 1990–2015, Country-Weighted

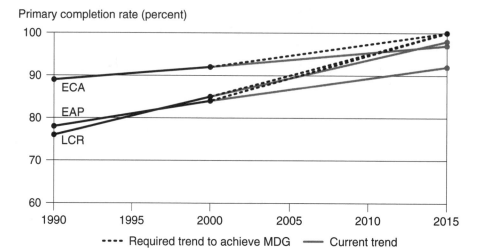

Source: Annex figure B.5.

more than that for boys over the 1990s, it still lags that of boys, at 76 percent compared to 85 percent. Serious gender disparities are evident in at least 13 countries, where girls' completion rates trail those of boys by more than 10 percentage points. While countries such as Tunisia, Bangladesh, and Sri Lanka have made impressive progress in narrowing the gender gap, in other countries it has widened, or narrowed only because of declines in boys' completion rates rather than improvement in girls'.

Overall, though, the trends over the 1990s provide some encouraging evidence that where political will is strong, effective reforms are adopted, and international support is adequate, dramatic progress in increasing primary completion rates is possible. A significant number of countries, from Brazil and Nicaragua in Latin America to Cambodia in East Asia to South Africa and The Gambia in Africa, registered improvements in the primary completion rate of 20 percentage points or more in less than a decade. This holds out hope that any developing country whose completion rate is currently 70 percent or higher could meet the MDG by 2015, provided it can achieve and sustain the rate of improvement registered by these high-performing countries.

On the other hand, progress is clearly fragile. Thirteen middle-income and 15 low-income countries saw their completion rates stagnate or decline over the 1990s. The case of Afghanistan (which dropped from an already low 22 percent in 1990 to an estimated 8 percent in 1999) is obvious and dramatic. But other countries losing significant ground include Zambia, the Republic of Congo, Albania, Cameroon, Kenya, Madagascar, Qatar, Iraq, the United Arab Emirates, Bahrain, and Venezuela.

At the trend rate of progress achieved over the 1990s, by 2015 the global primary completion rate will not exceed 83 percent. On a population-weighted basis, the world would come closer to achieving the MDG, with about 9 out of every 10 children globally completing primary school. But, as figures 1 and 2 indicate, underlying this global average would be a wide gulf in performance across regions. Ultimately, the MDG will not be attained unless every child in every country has the chance to complete primary school, and change will have to happen at the level of national education systems in order to reach the goal. Therefore, the focus of this analysis is the country-by-country prospects for reaching universal primary completion (UPC) by 2015.

According to the best available estimates, 37 of 155 developing countries have achieved or have virtually achieved universal primary completion and another 32 are "on track" to reach the goal on trend rates of progress achieved over the 1990s (table 1). Some 86 countries, however, are at risk of not reaching the goal unless progress is accelerated. They include countries that are making good progress but will fall short of the goal because their completion rates started from a very low base, as well as countries with higher completion rates that have registered declining trends or stagnation during the 1990s; these 43 countries are labeled "off track." Another 27 countries must be considered "seriously off track": on current trends, their completion rates will not exceed even 50 percent by 2015. Of the 70 countries that are off track or seriously off track, 51 are low-income countries.

Table 1

Prospects for Universal Primary Completion by 2015

Progress Rating	Low-Income Countries[a]	Middle-Income Countries[b]	All Developing Countries
On track	22	47	69
Achieved UPC	11	26	37
On track to achieve UPC by 2015	11	21	32
Off track	51	19	70
Off track to achieve UPC by 2015	28	15	43
Seriously off track	23	4	27
No data available	9	7	16
At risk, subtotal	60	26	86
Total	82	73	155

a. Countries eligible for lending from the International Development Association (IDA) and "blend" countries eligible for IDA and IBRD lending, plus non-member low-income countries such as the Democratic People's Republic of Korea.
b. Countries eligible for lending from the International Bank for Reconstruction and Development (IBRD), plus non-member middle-income developing countries.

Finally, there are 16 countries for which no data are available, and at least some of these, such as Somalia, Liberia, and Myanmar, are very likely at risk as well.

This picture is not encouraging. But a significant share of the at-risk countries *could* reach the goal, if they could match the average rate of progress of 3 percentage points per year observed in the best-performing countries over the 1990s. At this rate of progress, *all* of the middle-income and more than two-thirds of the low-income at-risk countries would reach the MDG. This goal is achievable and should be the focus of country policy and international assistance.

However, the countries lagging furthest behind—many in Sub-Saharan Africa, and many countries scarred by conflict—would need to improve at even faster rates, for which there is little historical precedent. Some of these countries are making impressive progress in extremely difficult contexts. But it is clear that the worldwide attainment of universal primary completion by 2015 will require an even stronger combination of political will, sustained and deep reform, faster diffusion of best practices, and intensified financial effort than has been marshaled to date.

What Will It Take to Achieve Universal Primary Completion by 2015?

To answer this question, we focused on the 55 largest low-income[1] countries in the world, which are home to 75 percent of all children out of school globally. These are countries whose fragile domestic resource base and institutional weaknesses make them the priority arena for a global effort to support the achievement of universal primary completion.

Building on pioneering work by Colclough and Lewin (1993) and other researchers,[2] we analyzed primary completion rates and gross enrollments as a function of characteristics of the education system that have long been identified as key: the resources allocated to primary education; average teacher salaries and unit costs; spending on complementary non-teacher-salary items; average class size (pupil-teacher ratio); and average rate of grade repetition. Even in this relatively small sample, there was enormous variance across countries in the fiscal commitment to primary education and in these indicators of the structure and costs of their education service delivery, as can be seen from table 2.

The sample exhibited great variance in system outcomes as well, with primary completion rates ranging from 20 to 100 percent, and gross enrollment ratios ranging from 30 to 120 percent. Very notable in figure 3 is the variance in the relationship between schooling enrollments and completion rates, which provides a strong argument for the importance of tracking primary completion directly.

The diagonal line in the graph represents perfect one-to-one mapping between the gross enrollment ratio (GER) and the primary completion rate (PCR), but very

---

1. Countries with gross national income (GNI) per capita of US$885 or less in 2000.
2. See, for example, Mehrotra (1998), Colclough and Al-Samarrai (2000), and Delamonica, Mehrotra, and Vandemoortele (2001).

Table 2

Benchmarks for Primary Education Efficiency and Quality

Variable	Sample Range in 1999/2000	SAMPLE MEAN IN 1999/2000		2015 Benchmarks
		Adjusted Sample	Highest-Completion Countries	
Service delivery				
Average annual teacher salary (as multiple of per capita GDP)	0.6–9.6	4.0	3.3	3.5
Pupil-teacher ratio	13:1–79:1	44:1	39:1	40:1
Spending on inputs other than teachers (as percentage of primary education recurrent spending)	0.1–45.0	24.4	26.0	33
Average repetition rate (percent)	0–36.1	15.8	9.5	10 or lower
System financing				
Government revenues (as percentage of GDP)[a]	8.0–55.7	19.7	20.7	14/16/18[b]
Education recurrent spending (as percentage of government revenues)	3.2–32.6	17.3	18.2	20
Primary education recurrent spending (as percentage of total education recurrent spending)	26.0–66.3	48.6	47.6	50[c]
Private enrollments (as percentage of total)	0–77.0	9.4	7.3	10

a. Government current revenues, excluding grants.
b. Staggered targets proportional to per capita GDP.
c. For six-year primary cycle; otherwise prorated for length of cycle.

FIGURE 3 | **Primary School Completion Rates and Gross Enrollment Ratios in a Sample of Low-Income Countries, circa 1999/2000**

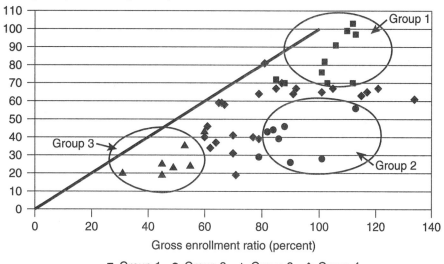

Primary completion rate (percent)

■ Group 1   ● Group 2   ▲ Group 3   ◆ Group 4

7

few of these low-income countries have achieved this. Instead, three stylized groupings may be observed, which we used to deepen the analysis:

Group 1 Relatively successful countries, with high GER (85 percent or above) and high PCR (70 percent or above).

Group 2 High inefficiency countries, with high GER (80 percent or above) but low PCR (60 percent or lower).

Group 3 Low coverage countries, with low GER and PCR (both 60 percent or lower).

Group 4 Countries falling in between the defined ranges, presenting milder versions of these patterns.

When education spending and service delivery characteristics were analyzed for the three stylized groups, several clear patterns emerged. The relatively successful countries in Group 1:

- Devote a higher share of their gross domestic product (GDP) to public primary education
- Have unit costs that fall in the middle of the range—not too high and not too low
- Pay teachers an average annual wage of about 3.3 times per capita GDP
- Have slightly higher spending on complementary, non-teacher-salary inputs
- Have an average pupil-teacher ratio of 39:1, and
- Have average repetition rates below 10 percent.

The Group 2 and Group 3 countries deviated widely from these average values, and in very distinct ways. Group 2 countries have significantly lower average spending and strikingly higher repetition—28 percent on average, compared to below 10 percent for Group 1. Group 3 countries have dramatically higher unit costs—about 70 percent higher than the other groups'—driven by very high average teacher salaries.

It appears from the experience of these Group 2 and 3 countries that deviating very far from the patterns observed in the more successful countries (for example, pupil-teacher ratios of 75:1 or 13:1, rather than 39:1 or 40:1) has forced their education systems into unhealthy adjustments and poor outcomes. The analysis suggests that the relatively balanced parameters observed in the Group 1 countries may offer a set of indicative benchmarks to guide service delivery and financing reforms. Bringing key service delivery and domestic financing parameters into line with benchmarks drawn from higher-performing countries offers a clear strategy for creating a higher-quality learning environment for children, associated with lower repetition, higher retention in school, and, consequently, a higher rate of primary completion.

Transparent parameters such as these also reveal each country's degree of domestic fiscal commitment to the goal of universal primary completion. Any global strategy for accelerating EFA progress must take this into account, encouraging more domestic effort where it is low, and taking care not to penalize countries currently showing stronger commitment.

These findings also imply that the road to universal primary completion for different countries will vary, depending on how their costs and structure of service delivery compare with the indicative benchmarks. For example, the high cost structure of Group 3 countries makes achieving universal primary completion prohibitively expensive; the high repetition and dropout rates of Group 2 countries make it virtually impossible. The inescapable conclusion—reaffirming what Colclough and Lewin (1993) posited a decade ago—is that the attainment of universal primary completion depends even more crucially on education system reform than on incremental financing.

COSTING THE MDG OF UNIVERSAL PRIMARY COMPLETION

It follows that the soundest basis for estimating the global financing requirements for achieving the education MDG is to aggregate these from country-level analysis that takes into account the reforms needed for a viable strategy in each country context. We used a simulation model to do this, estimating the costs of achieving universal primary completion in the 47 countries in our sample that have not yet achieved the goal, under different scenarios of gradual policy reform toward the benchmarks. Depending on each country's initial situation, a gradual process of either increase or decline in average teacher salaries, the pupil-teacher ratio, average repetition, and each of the other variables is programmed to occur between 2002 and 2015, at the same time as the evolution of student flows is projected in light of the latest data on population trends.

This framework focuses on the quality and quantity of primary education supply, but also recognizes that demand-side issues (household budget constraints, direct and opportunity costs of schooling, the social value attached to educating girls or children with disabilities, and so forth) are important determinants of school attendance and completion. Accordingly, our cost estimates assume that primary education is completely free to users (no tuition, book charges, teacher supplements, or contributions to construction from the community, for example), and we make explicit budgetary provisions for additional subsidies and incentives to overcome demand-side constraints for the most disadvantaged children, including a special provision for stipends to HIV/AIDS orphans. We assume these programs would be tailored to the specific country context. We assume a public sector responsibility for *financing* the bulk of primary schooling, but not necessarily public *provision*. Indeed, increased service delivery through community schools, alternative schools, nonprofit private schools, and schools run by nongovernmental organizations (NGOs) is in many developing countries a key strategy for achieving more efficient use of public resources and more equitable geographic coverage.

The gradual reforms in all parameters to 2015 influence the efficiency of student flows, the domestic resources available for primary education, and the progress toward universal primary completion, in effect producing 47 country-specific strategies for achieving the MDG. Under these scenarios, the countries analyzed would expand their education system coverage 30 percent by 2015 (with a doubling of enrollments in Africa). Average spending per student would more than double in real terms, reflecting the impact of economic growth on average teacher salaries, the significant increase in schooling quality implied by the benchmark allotment for non-salary inputs, and our provision for additional targeted support to AIDS orphans. Increased efficiency of student flows resulting from

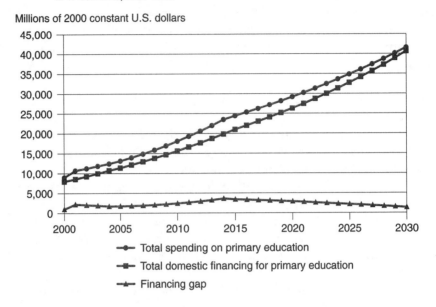

Figure 4 | Domestic and External Financing Required to Achieve the Education MDG in 47 Countries, 2001–2030

Millions of 2000 constant U.S. dollars

- —●— Total spending on primary education
- —■— Total domestic financing for primary education
- —▲— Financing gap

these quality improvements would substantially accelerate the progress toward universal primary completion by 2015. But even with increased fiscal effort in many of the countries in line with the targets for domestic resource mobilization, the simulations show that these countries, as a group, would not be able to achieve the goal without sustained and significant external financial support.

Over the period to 2015, we simulated an increase in these 47 countries' own financing for primary education from a base of about $8.5 billion in 2000 to about $21 billion per year in 2015.[3] Even this significant a domestic effort would not cover the total incremental costs of reaching the education MDG. Our simulations showed a financing gap over the period, rising from about $1.0 billion in the initial year to a peak of $3.6 billion in 2015 when full primary coverage and quality are achieved. At the peak, this financing gap represents 15 percent of total expenditures. Thereafter, the financing gap would decline steadily, to an estimated 3–5 percent of total expenditures in 2030.

As Table 3 shows, the bulk of the external support—more than 75 percent of the total, or close to $1.9 billion per year—would be needed in Africa. The simulations show that all 33 Sub-Saharan African countries in this low-income sample would face a financing gap in achieving universal primary completion. The external funding required would also represent a much larger share of their total financing needs—as high as 36% in the peak year of 2015, before declining to about 6% of total requirements by 2030.

---

3. Unless otherwise noted, dollar amounts in this book are 2000 constant U.S. dollars.

Table 3
....
Estimated Annual Financing Gap by Region
(millions of 2000 constant U.S. dollars)

Type of Financing	Africa	South Asia	Latin America and the Caribbean	East Asia and the Pacific	Middle East and North Africa	Europe and Central Asia	Total	Percentage of Total Financing Gap
Recurrent	1,127	97	14	30	21	34	1,323	55
Operation	841	97	14	30	21	34	1,037	43
AIDS	286	0	0	0	0	0	286	12
Capital	725	300	34	6	49	0	1,114	45
Total	1,852	397	48	36	70	34	2,437	100

Note: Numbers may not sum to totals because of rounding.

The four South Asian countries we studied would require about $397 million per year in external funding; the three low-income countries analyzed in Latin America and the Caribbean would face a gap of $48 million per year; two countries in East Asia would require external support of about $36 million per year; the one Middle Eastern country in the sample would need $70 million per year; and the three countries analyzed in the Europe and Central Asia region would have a combined financing gap of about $34 million per year.

An important finding is that about 55 percent of the external financing needed would be for recurrent budget support, and only 45 percent for capital support (new school construction). Since construction investments are generally easiest for donors to mobilize, we assume that *all* of the new construction needed in these countries would be financed externally. But the simulations make clear that an even larger volume of external support would be needed for recurrent budget requirements. Under our target parameters, virtually all countries in the sample would increase their domestic financing for EFA, and would finance 90 percent of the incremental recurrent costs of achieving the goal themselves. But the bigger constraint to achieving the goal will be the availability of external financing for recurrent expenses, not capital.

The financing gap estimated in this study is a lower-bound estimate of the global costs of attaining the education MDG, for several reasons. First and most crucially, our simulations in essence captured the incremental costs of *expanding* primary education systems in these countries to reach the goal by 2015. They did not capture the important needs—particularly in these very low income countries—for rehabilitation and upgrading of the current system. Our data set did not permit a detailed appraisal of the adequacy of existing classroom and administrative infra-structure or the adequacy of system functioning in each country, an appraisal that would be required to estimate the costs of needed upgrading, rehabilitation, and capacity building to complement the expansion costs we estimated. Given the precarious functioning of the education system in very many of the countries in our sample, it can be assumed that these needs are substantial. Because these investments are needed immediately, moreover, our simulation results for the first few years of the projection period particularly underestimate the true needs for external financing in these countries.

Second, although our sample included all of the most populous low-income countries—accounting for 94 percent of all children out of school in low-income developing countries—there are about 20 small low-income countries and several conflict-affected countries that were not analyzed. Moreover, we only estimated financing requirements through six grades of primary schooling; countries whose official primary cycle is longer than six years will face financing requirements that we did not capture. A full costing of the external needs would have to include all countries and reflect the full length of the primary cycle in each.

Third, this costing exercise simulated a reform path to the MDG for each country that assumed system reforms would be initiated immediately, and pursued steadily to 2015. In reality, there will be many cases where it is politically impossible to launch all needed reforms at the same time, where the pace of implementation will not always be linear, and where there is a need for the education system to deliver better service immediately, while key reforms—particularly on the resource mobilization side—may take longer to legislate and implement. To the extent that external assistance can facilitate such processes, transitional external financing requirements may be higher than the simulation estimates. However, the record on aid effectiveness also clearly points to the pitfalls of external assistance as a substitute for country commitment to needed reforms.

Finally, this costing exercise focused on the Millennium Development Goal of universal primary completion by 2015, and not on the full set of Education for All goals established at the Dakar conference. Developing countries are committed to pursuing all six Dakar goals, and the incremental costs to attain some of them—especially the elimination of gender disparities in secondary education, the achievement of a 50 percent improvement in adult literacy by 2015, and the expansion of early childhood care and education targeted to the most vulnerable children—will be significant. The financing framework introduced in the present study provides for balanced spending on *all* levels of education, and not only primary education, and would therefore provide some fiscal space for education systems to pursue the broader Dakar goals. But parallel efforts to the current study are needed for a full costing of the Education for All agenda, and especially to provide guidance on the "good practice" policies, service delivery parameters, and additional external financing that would be needed for developing countries to attain the Dakar goals in full.

ESTIMATING THE GLOBAL COSTS OF THE EDUCATION MDG

Despite these limitations, the current study does represent one of the most careful efforts to date to analyze and cost a strategy for attaining the education MDG of universal primary completion. In a world where both developing and developed countries face competing priorities and budget constraints, we insist on the importance of a global strategy—such as the one outlined here—that seeks to achieve the goal at minimum adequate cost, rather than "at any cost." In this vein, we tried to generate a plausible estimate of the likely costs of achieving the education MDG (through five or six years of schooling) in *all* developing and transition countries, building on our detailed analysis of 47 low-income countries.

"Scaling up" our analysis to include estimated needs for *rehabilitation* and *expansion of system infrastructure* (based on more comprehensive data for a smaller sample of countries) increased the total incremental costs of achieving universal primary completion by about $1.1 billion per year. Since our analysis showed financing needs for primary education already in excess of these countries' capacity to finance them domestically, all of these additional costs were added to the estimated external financing gap. This increased the overall financing gap for these 47 countries by roughly 45 percent, to about $3.5 billion per year. As the rehabilitation needs are all concentrated in the early years of the period, they would increase the external financing needs in those years especially dramatically.

Extending the estimate from the 47 countries we analyzed to the full group of 79 low-income countries increased the estimated financing gap by an additional 8 percent—a relatively modest amount, since our sample countries account for such a large share of the total school-age population in low-income countries.

Thus, the total incremental costs of achieving the education MDG (through five or six years of schooling) in all low-income countries, including all needs, would total an estimated $9.7 billion per year over the period to 2015, of which about $3.7 billion per year would need to come from official development assistance. This is about 50 percent higher than the $2.4 billion annual gap we projected.

Estimating the likely costs and financing gaps for the 47 middle-income countries that have not yet reached the MDG is more difficult, however. Although these countries are already much closer to the goal of universal completion, have more scope for domestic financing of primary education, and have more favorable demographic trends, their unit costs are much higher, due to lower pupil-teacher ratios and the higher dollar costs of teacher salaries and other inputs.

Based on current unit costs and enrollment data, but applying population and economic growth projections, we estimate that the incremental costs of reaching the education MDG in the middle-income countries would be in the range of $23-28 billion per year, compared to baseline spending on primary education estimated at about $80 billion in 2000.

However, this estimate is not strictly parallel to our estimate for the lower income countries, because it assumes no changes in service delivery efficiency or domestic financial commitment to the goal. Without country-by-country analysis, it is impossible to say how these population, cost, and financing factors would balance out, what the most appropriate reform trajectories for these countries would be, or what residual external financing needs would remain.

The one study so far that has applied our methodology (with regionally appropriate benchmark parameters) to 10 middle-income countries in Latin America and the Caribbean found that these countries should be able to finance the limited amount of school-level expansion needed to reach the primary education MDG, without an external gap, if they also adopt policies to improve the efficiency of student flows and devote reasonable domestic budget allocations to primary education (di Gropello, Dubey, and Winkler 2002). However, other studies—without assumptions on efficiency or financing reforms—have generated estimates of the financing gap for middle-income countries in the range of $4 billion per year.

We believe that, just as in the countries we analyzed, there is clear scope in middle-income countries to increase resource mobilization and improve efficiency in service delivery. Without careful country-by-country analysis of the type we have done, however, the most that can be said is that the incremental costs of reaching the education MDG in middle-income and transition countries could be as high as $23–28 billion per year, and, of this, the need for external financing might range between $1 billion (with appropriate policy reforms) to $4 billion, per year.

Summing these with our scaled-up estimates for the low-income countries results in a global estimate that roughly $33–38 billion per year in additional spending on primary education will be needed in developing countries between now and 2015 if the education MDG is to be met. This is the annual average of a spending increase that would take place gradually over the period, but it clearly connotes a significant challenge. The increase relative to current spending levels will be much higher for the low-income countries than for the middle-income and transition countries. We estimate that even with optimal policy reforms and strong domestic fiscal commitment to achieving the goal, countries themselves will not be able to generate the resources needed. We estimate that $5–7 billion of this total spending increase would need to come through external aid.

This estimate is anchored in careful country-by-country analysis. It is also shaped by an explicit focus on achieving the goal at minimum and sustainable global cost. But even this conservative estimate is many times higher than aid flows currently available for primary education, especially for the lowest income countries. It will take strong effort and commitment from development partners to mobilize this incremental funding, and equal effort from developing countries to use it well.

IMPLICATIONS FOR COUNTRIES AND DONORS

At the Monterrey conference on development finance in 2002, the donor community pledged increased development support channeled in a new and more selective framework to those countries with both sound policies and a willingness to be held accountable for clear results. At the Dakar conference in 2000, the donor community made a commitment that no developing country with a "credible plan" for achieving EFA would fall short of the 2015 goal for lack of external support. Our analysis suggests that a relatively small set of key parameters are important determinants of primary completion rate progress and therefore core elements of a "credible" or sound policy framework in education. Using these "indicative parameters" to guide education planning could bring increased technical rigor, transparency, and financial discipline to the process. Such a framework could help ensure that policy actions, new investments in school expansion, domestic resource mobilization, and external assistance all lead to progressive improvements in system functioning, measured against clear benchmarks.

However, this indicative framework is clearly not *sufficient* for a credible EFA plan, and must not be applied rigidly. First, the system-wide average values on which these parameters rest do not guarantee that the underlying distribution is efficient or equitable—particularly in large federalized education systems such as those of India or Nigeria. In India, for example, while the national average is 52 pupils per teacher, the pupil-teacher ratio is as low as 30:1 in some states and as high as 60:1 in others, reflecting serious disparities in education access and quality across the country. Addressing these regional disparities—which could not be captured in our simple simulation model—will clearly be costly and will require concerted action at the federal, state, and district levels. A credible EFA plan for any country must go beyond the national average benchmarks and also focus on subnational variance in education financing and service delivery.

Second, while the indicative benchmarks can provide a useful point of reference for all countries, there will be many cases where they are culturally, institutionally, or financially inappropriate. The ultimate value of this framework is as a guide to the direction of reform, not as a dictate regarding where it should end.

Third and most importantly, the indicative framework can help ensure that education systems have adequate overall resources and a healthy mix of core inputs. But it cannot guarantee the effective management of those resources. In a great many developing countries, achieving better management of education resources—at the central level, at the school level, and in the classroom—is as large a challenge as mobilizing more resources. Indeed, as primary education systems in many of these countries will more than double in size over the coming decade, the management challenges will become even more acute.

At the central level, ministries of education must achieve greater equity and efficiency in allocating financing and deploying personnel across different regions and across schools, as well as between administrative support services and school-level delivery. The share of resources absorbed into central administration in many systems is very high, with little value added for system quality or student learning. Across different regions, schools with similar enrollments often differ widely in the number of teachers and other resources deployed to them, with no formal rationale but with clear implications for quality and equity. Similarly, expenditure tracking analyses frequently find that only a fraction of the overall education resources allocated to schools actually reaches them, and often too late in the school year to be used productively. Finally, national systems to assess student learning and monitor progress at the classroom and school level are crucial for holding education actors accountable and stimulating system-wide improvement. Yet they exist in very few of the countries in our sample.

Management capacity at the school level is also crucial. The quality of school leadership makes the difference between an orderly environment where teachers perform and children can learn, and a chaotic environment marked by rampant absenteeism, poor school maintenance, disappearance of books and materials, and poor relations with parents and the community, as seen in all too many education systems. Simple and often costless actions such as assigning the best teachers to the early grades, adapting the school calendar to the needs of the community, and making sure that teachers show up on time and work a full week can greatly boost student attendance and learning. Effective management at the school level makes these happen.

And ultimately, it is management in the classroom that transforms education resources into student learning. Research shows that after controlling for student characteristics, learning outcomes can differ greatly even across equally resourced classrooms in the same school. What teachers do matters more for student learning than any other single factor. Teachers must use class time effectively; they must make creative use of learning materials; they must have the capacity to adapt their teaching practice to individual students' learning needs; and, above all, they must be motivated to devote time and hard work to proving that "every child can learn." In many developing countries, teachers' incentives, capacity, and practice are all greatly in need of strengthening.

Specific policies to address these management issues at all levels of the education system must equally be core elements of a credible EFA plan. But the first step toward a quality school system is to ensure adequate resources, allocated in an efficient balance against core system parameters. Without this, few other policy objectives or programs can be implemented or sustained.

Adopting this policy and financing framework would have several key implications for developing countries:

- The criteria for a "credible plan" would be less ambiguous and more technically rigorous.
- Countries' own commitments to EFA could be evaluated more transparently, as the allocation of a "fair share" of domestic fiscal resources to primary education.
- Steady improvement in service delivery parameters could be a quid pro quo for continued external support.
- The EFA process would be focused more sharply on key outcomes, especially the primary completion rate and student learning progress, and more accurate and timely measurement of these would be required.
- Countries and their partners would both be more clearly accountable for ensuring that external funding catalyzes tangible progress toward EFA and is not wasted in ineffective delivery systems.
- Countries' overall domestic resource mobilization and spending, not only education ministry spending, would become subject to EFA monitoring.

The implications for international development partners are equally strong. The simulation results show clearly that even with a maximum domestic effort, most low-income countries will not be able to achieve universal primary completion by 2015 without changes in both the level and nature of external support. Making good on the international community's commitment at Dakar would require development partners to take six basic steps.

First, they must significantly *increase donor funding for primary education*. The average external financing needed for just the 48 low-income countries we analyzed is about $2.5 billion per year between now and 2015—almost a tripling of current aid for primary education to these countries and about a fourfold increase in the level of donor support to the 33 Sub-Saharan African countries in the sample.

Second, donors should *ensure better targeting of "EFA priority" countries*. Current patterns of aid to education are not prioritizing countries in greatest need. The countries analyzed have an average primary completion rate of only 57 percent, yet receive only about 10–15 percent of current official development assistance going to education.

Third, the *mix of donor assistance should be changed*. Donors need to shift a larger share of external assistance to recurrent budget support. In turn, recipient countries need to show greater budgetary transparency and monitoring of outcomes.

Fourth, donors can *improve the efficiency of aid transfers*. A significant share of donor assistance typically supports technical assistance contracts, consultancies, seminars, study tours, and other expenditures that—no matter how valuable—do not count directly against the "core" resource requirements for EFA estimated in our simulations, about 55 percent of which would be for recurrent costs and notably for teacher salaries and appropriate demand-side interventions. Similarly, the unit construction costs we assumed (averaging about $8,000 per classroom for the sample) are far lower than those many donors report. Shifting to community-based construction of new schools and classrooms to lower unit costs is essential for reaching the MDG but will require flexibility on the part of donors.

Fifth, donors should *transfer funds via new mechanisms*. The stability and predictability of external assistance is crucial if countries are to take on recurrent expenditures (such as hiring of additional teachers) that are not easily compressed if external support fluctuates. On the other hand, it is not easy for bilateral donors, subject to their own political processes and budget constraints, to make long-term funding commitments. Greater use of pooled donor assistance and direct budget transfers in the context of sector-wide approaches (SWAPs) and other programmatic support could help match donor assistance more effectively to countries' core financing needs and ensure a more stable and predictable flow of funding.

Finally, there is an urgent need for *more effective monitoring of progress, increased research, and faster diffusion of knowledge about what works*. The costs of EFA monitoring, data collection, international research, and global and local activities to diffuse new knowledge are not included in the estimated financing gap, but these investments in the global public good should be considered core responsibilities of the international community. The road to EFA will for many countries be an enormous challenge. Accumulated country experience and international research can play an important role in smoothing it.

THE EFA FAST-TRACK INITIATIVE

Building on the above analysis, a new compact for primary education designed to accelerate global progress toward the education MDG was endorsed by the Development Committee of the World Bank and International Monetary Fund in April 2002 and by the G-8 in its action plan for education at the June 2002 summit in Kananaskis, Alberta, Canada. The new compact, called the EFA Fast-Track Initiative, is the first proposal to emerge since the Monterrey conference that aims at accelerating MDG progress using the Monterrey framework of increased development support in exchange for increased accountability for results. The new initiative is supported by all major bilateral donors for education and by UNESCO, UNICEF, the World Bank, and the regional development banks, all of which have jointly formed the EFA Fast-Track Partnership. At the heart of the Fast-Track Initiative are:

- A commitment by developing countries to accelerate efforts to achieve universal primary education cost-effectively, within an "EFA indicative framework" (box 2); and
- A commitment by donors to provide sustained incremental financing (as much as possible on a grant basis), where credible plans to accelerate progress in primary education exist.

> **Box 2**
>
> ## EFA Indicative Framework
> ....
>
> - Average annual teacher salary (as multiple of per capita GDP)
>
> - Pupil-teacher ratio
>
> - Share of recurrent spending on inputs other than teachers
>
> - Average repetition rate
>
> - Education share of government recurrent budget
>
> - Primary education share of education recurrent budget

In June 2002, a first set of 18 low-income countries was invited to join the initiative and to submit their EFA plans, including baseline indicative framework indicators and annual targets, for donor financing. The 18 countries (box 3) are diverse regionally and in terms of their proximity to universal primary completion; together, they account for an estimated 18 million children without access to education. This first set of countries was invited to consider committing to the Fast-Track Initiative on the basis of two simple and transparent criteria: (a) they have formally adopted national Poverty Reduction Strategy Papers (PRSPs) that integrate their education plans into overall national development priorities; and (b) they have education sector plans in place, agreed with the donors. The rationale for these two criteria is that having these elements in place should allow fast-track support to catalyze measurable progress more quickly. It should be noted that the Fast-Track Initiative is aimed at accelerating MDG progress in, and learning lessons from, countries that are currently on track to reach the goal as well as supporting countries that are off track.

A second set of five high-priority countries was also invited to join the initiative, but with a different status initially, as they did not yet meet the two criteria. These "Big Five" countries are deemed high priority because they account for the largest numbers of children without access to primary education globally—about 50 million of the 113 million children in total estimated to be out of school. The spirit of the Fast-Track Initiative is that country commitment to sound sector programs integrated into broader poverty reduction strategy as well as commitment to appropriate policy actions in line with the EFA indicative framework are important for effective use of development resources. "Analytical Fast-Track" support aims to help these countries reach that status. India is the first of the "Big Five" countries to meet the two criteria, and the government is considering participation in the FTI.

In countries with PRSPs and sector plans in place, the Fast-Track process involves a complementary in-country analysis to benchmark education system performance relative to the EFA indicative framework; to set appropriate annual targets for their country context; and to refine estimates of the external financing needs for accelerated progress in primary education, consistent with the implementation of appropriate reforms and the medium-term expenditure framework established in their PRSP. Although for the first set of countries these adjustments have been set out in "Fast-track proposals," it is expected that the process of identifying priority policy actions to align system functioning with the indicative framework benchmarks will increasingly be mainstreamed into the development of those plans in the first place and separate FTI proposals will not be needed. The first FTI proposals have represented a more comprehensive assessment of financing needs than we costed, as they include rehabilitation requirements. The estimated expansion needs, however, may be compared with the financing gap estimates presented here.

An important part of the process is also careful assessment of the physical and institutional capacity to execute increased primary education investment and expenditure. The Fast-Track Initiative implies a major expansion of the management challenge for systems that are generally perceived to be weakly managed today. But this cannot be an argument against such expansion; it simply means that attention to capacity building and institutional support must be an equal part of the partnership effort.

Finally, the estimated needs are compared with the pipeline of existing donor commitments for primary education in each country, including general budget support under Poverty Reduction Support Credits (PRSC) or other multisector programs. It should be recalled that the financing gaps estimated in the present study are gross financing gaps, with no adjustment for the current level of external assistance to the primary sector.

As of March 2003, ten of the first 18 countries invited to join the Fast-Track Initiative submitted proposals for consideration. The Fast-Track partners committed, upon verification of the estimated financing gaps against implementation plans, to ensure that these gaps are filled for the next three years, contingent on countries' continued progress in executing the accelerated program and improving sector functioning in line with their indicative framework targets. The partners also agreed to meet regularly to review implementation, harmonize their education assistance to Fast-Track countries, and decide on additional proposals. Intensified collaboration among donor representatives at the client country level is a key part of this process.

Box 3

First EFA Fast-Track Group, 2002

Albania
Bolivia
Burkina Faso
Ethiopia
The Gambia
Ghana
Guinea
Guyana
Honduras
Mauritania
Mozambique
Nicaragua
Niger
Tanzania
Uganda
Vietnam
Republic of Yemen
Zambia

Analytical Fast-Track Countries

Bangladesh
Democratic Republic of Congo
India
Nigeria
Pakistan

In addition to transparent annual monitoring of their progress against indicative framework targets, recipient countries also committed to monitoring key outcomes such as the net intake rate into first grade for girls and boys, the primary completion rate for girls and boys, and student learning achievement, although it is understood that these outcome indicators can be slow to reflect progress.

CONCLUSION

Universal primary completion is crucial for national economic and social advancement. It is a goal that all developing countries are committed to achieving by 2015, but one that will not be reached without a significant acceleration of current progress. Faster progress requires the bridging of substantial policy, capacity, and data gaps in many developing countries, in addition to financing gaps. The lack of external financing in some cases is not as binding as the constraints imposed by lack of capacity or the policy framework.

This study focuses on two of these gaps—the education policies that in many countries are needed for faster progress, and the incremental financing required to support this progress. The data we used did not permit us to analyze issues of institutional capacity in any depth, despite the obvious importance of capacity for the implementation of policies and investments and the attainment of desired outcomes. Nor does this study focus on the data gap per se, although the research was hampered by the limited, inconsistent, and outdated education statistics available in the countries analyzed, and the new primary completion database we developed is an effort to provide a better basis for monitoring MDG progress.

Our projections may be considered a minimum estimate of the incremental financing needed to achieve the MDG in the 48 low-income countries (including Afghanistan) currently furthest from the goal, within a framework of country commitment and gradual but effective policy reform. Although the $2.5 billion per year core external funding requirement we estimate is conservative, it is nonetheless many times higher than the current level of aid for primary education to these countries. Our conclusion is that both the policy and implementation challenge for low-income countries and the financing challenge for their development partners will be significant if the education MDG is to be met.

Finally, however important a goal it may be, primary completion is not the only challenge facing education systems in the developing world. Rather, it is just the first step toward a system of lifelong learning for all citizens, which is as relevant for the poorest countries as it is for the wealthiest. All countries, no matter how far they are today from universal primary completion, must simultaneously invest in and promote the balanced development of all levels of their education systems. In a globally integrated and highly competitive world economy, no country can any longer consider primary schooling a terminal level of education for its labor force. Indeed, it is important that expanded donor support for primary education under the EFA Fast-Track and other initiatives be matched by efforts to help countries expand lower secondary education, in anticipation of a growing wave of primary graduates.

But increasing the share of children who complete primary schooling is the essential first step. In a borderless world, where the gulf between the rich, educated, and empowered and the poor, stagnating, and powerless increasingly poses threats to all, the achievement of universal primary completion—like the other MDGs—is of global interest. The new EFA Fast-Track Initiative, if launched successfully and expanded steadily to reach all of the at-risk developing countries, offers the possibility of boosting rates of primary completion progress to the levels necessary to reach the goal. Few global goals have been as consistently and deeply supported as the notion that every child in every country should have the chance to complete primary school. With global effort, it could become a reality.

The Global Challenge of Education for All

1

One hundred eighty-nine countries have committed themselves to eight Millennium Development Goals aimed at eradicating extreme poverty and improving the welfare of their people by the year 2015 (box 1.1). The second of the goals is "Achieve universal primary education," with the specific target of ensuring that, "by 2015, children everywhere, boys and girls alike, will be able to complete a full course of primary schooling." It echoes a commitment made by many of the same countries in Jomtien, Thailand in 1990 to achieve universal primary education by the year 2000. The Jomtien commitment was reaffirmed and extended at the World Education Forum in Dakar in 2000 (box 1.2).

As the Dakar forum acknowledged, the Jomtien goal was not met. Many countries clearly remain far from the target. However, until now it has not been possible to assess where individual countries stand in relation to the target with any accuracy, for lack of internationally comparable data on primary completion rates. In the absence of such data, it has been difficult to evaluate the global prospects for reaching the target by 2015 or to estimate the incremental actions and financing that would be required. Given strong international interest in these issues, several previous studies have attempted to analyze the likelihood of the education MDG being met by projecting trends to the goal based on enrollment data rather than completion rates, and by employing a number of different methodologies for estimating the incremental costs. Resulting estimates of the incremental global financing requirements have varied widely, from approximately $7 billion to $15 billion annually.

This study seeks answers to three questions:

- *How close is the world to achieving the millennium goal of universal primary completion?*
- *Is it achievable by 2015? and*
- *If so, what would be required to achieve it, in terms of both education policy reform and incremental domestic and international financing?*

The approach here differs from all previous studies in that it is based on direct measurement of primary completion rates, rather than relying on conventionally available gross and net enrollment ratios, which are a poor proxy for schooling completion rates. We draw on the first effort to create an internationally standardized database of primary completion rates in 155 countries and trace the evolution of these rates from 1990 to the most recent year possible. (See chapter 2 for a definition of the completion rate, the methodology used to calculate it, and a discussion of data and technical issues.)

Using these new data, we examine the countries and regions in which the greatest progress has been registered since Jomtien and those in which completion rates have stagnated or declined. We analyze the prospects for reaching the MDG with no change in current trends.

Box 1.1 Millennium Development Goals

GOALS AND TARGETS	INDICATORS
GOAL 1: ERADICATE EXTREME POVERTY AND HUNGER	
TARGET 1. Halve, between 1990 and 2015, the proportion of people whose income is less than $1 a day.	1. Proportion of population below $1 per day 2. Poverty gap ratio (incidence x depth of poverty) 3. Share of poorest quintile in national consumption
TARGET 2. Halve, between 1990 and 2015, the proportion of people who suffer from hunger.	4. Prevalence of underweight children (under 5 years of age) 5. Proportion of population below minimum level of dietary energy consumption
GOAL 2: ACHIEVE UNIVERSAL PRIMARY EDUCATION	
TARGET 3. Ensure that, by 2015, children everywhere, boys and girls alike, will be able to complete a full course of primary schooling.	6. Net enrollment ratio in primary education 7. Proportion of pupils starting grade 1 who reach grade 5 8. Literacy rate of 15- to 24-year-olds
GOAL 3: PROMOTE GENDER EQUALITY AND EMPOWER WOMEN	
TARGET 4. Eliminate gender disparity in primary and secondary education preferably by 2005 and at all levels of education no later than 2015.	9. Ratio of girls to boys in primary, secondary, and tertiary education 10. Ratio of literate females to males among 15- to 24-year-olds 11. Share of women in wage employment in the nonagricultural sector 12. Proportion of seats held by women in national parliaments
GOAL 4: REDUCE CHILD MORTALITY.	
TARGET 5. Reduce by two-thirds, between 1990 and 2015, the under-5 mortality rate.	13. Under-5 mortality rate 14. Infant mortality rate 15. Proportion of 1-year-old children immunized against measles
GOAL 5: IMPROVE MATERNAL HEALTH	
TARGET 6. Reduce by three-quarters, between 1990 and 2015, the maternal mortality ratio.	16. Maternal mortality ratio 17. Proportion of births attended by skilled health personnel
GOAL 6: COMBAT HIV/AIDS, MALARIA, AND OTHER DISEASES	
TARGET 7. Have halted by 2015, and begun to reverse, the spread of HIV/AIDS.	18. HIV prevalence among 15- to 24-year-old pregnant women 19. Contraceptive prevalence rate 20. Number of children orphaned by HIV/AIDS
TARGET 8. Have halted by 2015, and begun to reverse, the incidence of malaria and other major diseases.	21. Prevalence and death rates associated with malaria 22. Proportion of population in malaria risk areas using effective malaria prevention and treatment measures 23. Prevalence and death rates associated with tuberculosis 24. Proportion of TB cases detected and cured under DOTS (Directly Observed Treatment Short Course)
GOAL 7: ENSURE ENVIRONMENTAL SUSTAINABILITY	
TARGET 9. Integrate the principles of sustainable development into country policies and programs and reverse the loss of environmental resources.	25. Proportion of land area covered by forest 26. Land area protected to maintain biological diversity 27. GDP per unit of energy use (as proxy for energy efficiency) 28. Carbon dioxide emissions (per capita) *(Plus two figures of global atmospheric pollution: ozone depletion and the accumulation of global warming gases)*
TARGET 10. Halve, by 2015, the proportion of people without sustainable access to safe drinking water.	29. Proportion of population with sustainable access to an improved water source
TARGET 11. By 2020, have achieved a significant improvement in the lives of at least 100 million slum dwellers.	30. Proportion of people with access to improved sanitation 31. Proportion of people with access to secure tenure *(Urban/rural disaggregation of several of the above indicators may be relevant for monitoring improvement in the lives of slum dwellers)*
GOAL 8: DEVELOP A GLOBAL PARTNERSHIP FOR DEVELOPMENT	

Box 1.2 Global "Education for All" Goals

DAKAR WORLD EDUCATION FORUM GOALS	MILLENNIUM DEVELOPMENT GOALS
Expand and improve comprehensive early childhood care and education, especially for the most vulnerable and disadvantaged children.	
Ensure that by 2015 all children, particularly girls, children in difficult circumstances, and those belonging to ethnic minorities, have access to and complete free and compulsory primary education of good quality.	Ensure that, by 2015, children everywhere, boys and girls alike, will be able to complete a full course of primary schooling.
Ensure that the learning needs of young people and adults are met through equitable access to appropriate learning and life skills programs.	
Achieve a 50 percent improvement in levels of adult literacy by 2015, especially for women, and equitable access to basic and continuing education for all adults.	
Eliminate gender disparities in primary and secondary education by 2005, and achieve gender equality in education by 2015, with a focus on ensuring girls' full and equal access to and achievement in basic education of good quality.	Eliminate gender disparity in primary and secondary education, preferably by 2005, and at all levels of education no later than 2015.
Improve all aspects of the quality of education and ensure excellence of all so that recognized and measurable learning outcomes are achieved by all, especially in literacy, numeracy, and essential life skills.	

Next, building on and extending the research of others, such as Colclough and Lewin (1993), Oxfam (Watkins 1999), and Delamonica, Mehrotra, and Vandemoortele (2001), we identify a set of key education policy and domestic financing parameters that can explain countries' differential MDG progress. We find that education systems in the low-income countries that have either achieved 100 percent primary completion or are relatively close have some basic features in common.

Finally, we ask: If those countries currently lagging behind were to reform key features of their education systems to more closely approximate the systems of more successful countries, could universal primary completion be achieved by

2015? And, if so, what would be the incremental domestic and international financing requirements under this scenario?

This study is the first attempt we know of to analyze the challenge of Education for All through both the development of a new monitoring indicator and direct collection of the most recent available educational enrollment and public finance data. Because of time limitations, the analysis concentrates on the 47 low-income countries with populations over 1 million[4] that have not yet achieved universal primary completion. A full estimate of the global cost of achieving the education MDG would have to include the countries not analyzed here. However, the countries we studied are home to 75 percent of all children out of school globally. These countries are far from the goal, with an average primary completion rate of only 57 percent, and their poverty, fragile domestic resource base, and institutional weakness make them priority claimants on international support. The bulk of the incremental external resources and effort for global achievement of universal primary completion will very clearly be needed here.

A major effort was made for this study to update the global picture of progress to date through the direct collection of data from a large number of developing countries. In cases where recent country data were not available or only partially available, we used published UNESCO data. In all cases, new data were checked for consistency against any available household survey data and UNESCO sources. The exercise pointed to serious issues of accuracy and consistency in education enrollment data for many countries, and in some cases required us to make estimates that diverged from official enrollment statistics when these were inconsistent with population, household survey, or past data, but always using consistency with other data as a guide.

Given the ambitious scope of this work and the relatively short time in which it was carried out, this study is only a small first step in what we hope will be a new analytical direction for EFA. The technical annexes and CD-ROM accompanying this volume include the simulation model and all of the raw data, sources, and assumptions used for the countries analyzed, as well as the country-by-country simulation results. We will have succeeded if this work inspires governments committed to Education for All as well as national and international education researchers to focus on primary completion rates, and to revisit the policy framework, country data, and simulations presented in this report. The road to EFA will for many countries be an enormous challenge. Accumulated country experience and expanded international research can play an important role in easing the way.

WHY IS UNIVERSAL PRIMARY EDUCATION SO IMPORTANT?

Education is one of the most powerful instruments known for reducing poverty and inequality and for laying the basis for sustained economic growth. It is fundamental for the construction of democratic societies and dynamic, globally competitive economies. For individuals and for nations, education is the key to creating, applying, and spreading knowledge.

---

4. Low-income countries were defined as IDA-eligible in 2001 (that is, countries with GNI per capita of $885 or less in 2000).

Primary education develops the capacity to learn, to read and use math, to acquire information, and to think critically about that information. Primary education is also the gateway to all higher levels of education that train the scientists, teachers, doctors, and other highly skilled professionals that every country, no matter how small or poor, requires. Microeconomic research has established unequivocally that education improves individual incomes; Psacharopoulos and Patrinos (2002) estimate an average global private return on primary education of 27 percent. Research also indicates the contributions of primary education to better natural resource management, including conservation of the tropical rain forest (Godoy and Contreras 2001) and more rapid technological adaptation and innovation. Broad-based education is associated with the faster diffusion of information in the economy, which is crucial for increased productivity among workers and citizens in traditional as well as modern sectors (Porter 1998; Hanushek and Kimko 2000).

When a large share of children do not complete primary education, the productivity of the labor force, the potential for knowledge-driven development, and the reservoir of human potential from which society and the economy can draw are all fundamentally constrained. As figure 1.1 shows, in several developing regions the average level of schooling of the labor force is still less than a complete primary education. At the start of the new millennium, adults average just 0.8 years of formal education in Mali and Niger, 1.1 years in Mozambique and Ethiopia, 2.0 years in Nepal, and 2.5 years in Bangladesh (Barro and Lee 2000).

Research strongly suggests that such low levels of human capital are fundamentally inadequate for sustained economic development, stable democratic institutions, or poverty reduction. Azariadis and Drazen (1990) were the first to postulate that countries may be trapped in a low-returns equilibrium until their

FIGURE 1.1 Average Educational Attainment of Adult Population by Region, 2000

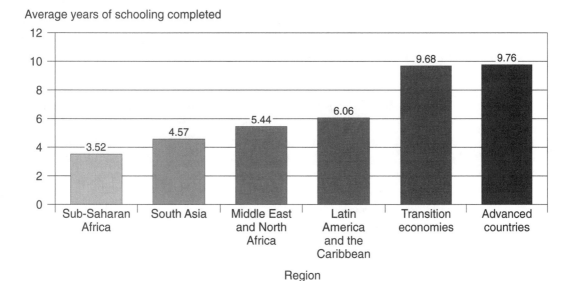

Source: Barro and Lee 2000.

level of human capital accumulation rises above six years of schooling. Once this threshold is passed, countries seem to achieve a higher steady-state macroeconomic growth path. The latest empirical studies on the question of the impact of education on economic growth all report a positive association (Barro 1999b; de la Fuente and Domenech 2000; Hanushek and Kimko 2000). On democratization, Barro (1999a) finds in a study of more than 100 countries between 1960 and 1995 that the propensity for democracy rises both with primary schooling and with a smaller gap between male and female primary attainment.

The role of primary education in reducing poverty and income inequality is even more strongly established than is its contribution to overall economic growth. Illiteracy is one of the strongest predictors of poverty, and unequal access to educational opportunity is one of the strongest correlates of income inequality. A large body of research points to the catalytic role of primary education, "the people's asset" (O'Connell and Birdsall 2001), for those individuals in society who are most likely to be poor: girls, ethnic minorities, orphans, people with disabilities, and people living in rural areas. Extending adequate-quality primary education to these vulnerable groups is crucial in order to equip them to contribute to and benefit from economic growth.

Data from the International Adult Literacy Survey (OECD and Statistics Canada 2000) indicate a high correlation between country levels of income inequality and inequality in the distribution of literacy, suggesting that more evenly spread levels of human capital are associated with greater income equality. Recent research by Birdsall and Londoño (1998) confirms that these factors are closely linked: more equitable distribution of education promotes faster economic growth as well as reducing inequality. Birdsall and Londoño have shown that the degree of inequality in the distribution of education has a strong and robust negative effect on growth, independent of the average level of education and also independent of factors such as trade openness and varying natural resource endowments. The implication is clear: the expansion of educational opportunity is one of the most powerful tools governments have to simultaneously promote income equality and growth—a "win-win" strategy that in most societies is far easier to implement than the redistribution of other assets such as land or capital.

Ultimately, the case for universal primary education goes beyond economic arguments. Education provides people with what Nobel laureate Amartya Sen (1999) calls "human capabilities"—the essential and individual power to reflect, make better choices, seek a voice in society, and enjoy a better life. Education, and particularly primary education, also promotes achievement of all of the other Millennium Development Goals: poverty reduction, gender equity, child health, maternal health, lower HIV/AIDS and other communicable diseases, and environmental sustainability.

Indeed, a substantial body of research documents that education—and especially education for girls—is one of the strongest drivers of improvement in fertility, health, and nutrition outcomes. Girls' education has documented impacts on infant and child mortality and enhanced family welfare. A recent study of 63 countries concluded that gains in women's education made the single largest contribution to declines in malnutrition during 1970–1995, accounting for 43 percent of the total progress (Smith and Haddad 2000). Another study, using data on 100 countries, found that an additional year of female education reduced total fertility rates on average by 0.23 births, while a three-year increase in the average educational level of women was associated with as much as one child less per woman. It also found that mothers who have completed primary education are 50 percent more likely to ensure that their infant children are immunized than mothers with no education (World Bank 2001).

And very recent research indicates that for girls and boys, education may be the single most effective preventive weapon against HIV/AIDS. New data from high seroprevalence countries show that the better educated have lower rates of infection, especially among younger people (Gregson, Waddell, and Chandiwana 2001; Kelly 2000; Vandemoortele and Delamonica 2000). In sum, progress toward the goal of universal primary education will unquestionably have strong complementary effects on achievement of the other millennium goals.

Universal primary completion is by no means the only challenge facing education systems across the world. It is only the first step toward the ultimate goal of lifelong learning for all citizens, which is as relevant for the poorest countries of the developing world as it is for the countries of the Organisation for Economic Co-operation and Development (OECD). All countries, no matter how far they are today from universal primary completion, must simultaneously invest in and promote the balanced development of all levels of their education systems. In a globally integrated and highly competitive world economy, no country can any longer consider primary schooling a terminal level of education for its labor force.

But increasing the share of children who complete primary schooling is the essential first step. In a borderless world, where the gulf between the rich, educated, and empowered and the poor, stagnating, and powerless increasingly poses threats to all, the achievement of universal primary completion is of global interest. This book lays out a strategy for accelerating progress toward that goal by 2015.

WHY UNIVERSAL PRIMARY EDUCATION MUST MEAN UNIVERSAL PRIMARY COMPLETION

To date, efforts to achieve Education for All have focused heavily on getting children enrolled in school, rather than on improving either completion rates or student learning outcomes. This is problematic for several reasons.

First, a growing body of research suggests that completion of at least five to six years of schooling is a critical threshold for sustainable mastery of basic competencies, such as literacy and basic numeracy. Literacy surveys conducted in African countries and elsewhere indicate that a high share of the adults who have completed less than five or six years of primary schooling remain functionally illiterate and innumerate for the rest of their lives (figure 1.2). The strong implication is that from a human capital perspective there is a substantial difference between getting all children enrolled in primary school and ensuring that all children complete the five- or six-year primary cycle. Especially striking in the data is the very limited impact on lifelong literacy from as many as three years of schooling. It is plausible that many of the other direct benefits and externalities of education are similarly

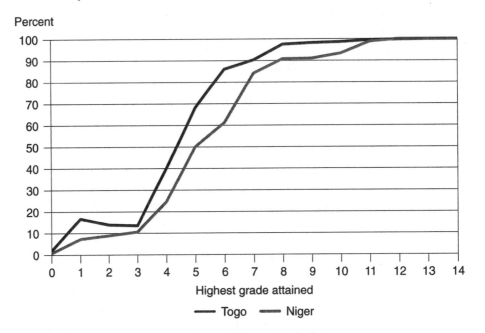

FIGURE 1.2 Proportion of Adults Who Can Read and Write Easily by Highest Grade Attained, Togo and Niger

Source: UNICEF Multiple Index Cluster Survey (MICS) data, 2000, and authors' estimates.

linked to the completion of a relatively high threshold number of five to six years of schooling, which in fact represents the length of the primary cycle in most countries. So, formulating the MDG target in terms of universal primary completion, rather than universal primary enrollment, makes strong sense from the standpoint of human capital formation.

Second, schooling *enrollment ratios,* whether on a gross or net basis, are poorly correlated with the rate of primary school completion. In virtually every developing country, the horizontal line of an average enrollment ratio masks the underlying reality of a curve-shaped schooling profile in which many more children begin school than complete it. Schooling profiles (such as those shown in figure 1.3) constructed from household survey or education enrollment data give a good picture of how access to schooling can differ from retention along the primary cycle for schooling cohorts in the recent past. These data show, for example, that in both Brazil and Indonesia in the late 1980s access to primary schooling was already fairly universal, with close to 100 percent of children starting grade 1. However, the pattern of retention in school was very different, resulting in only about 60 percent of children completing five grades in Brazil, compared to 90 percent in Indonesia.

A crucial issue from the standpoint of EFA monitoring is the fact that a single gross enrollment ratio, or even a single net enrollment ratio, can be consistent with a number of different schooling profiles. As a result, there is no consistent correlation between either gross or net enrollment ratios and the primary completion rate.

FIGURE 1.3 : Sample Schooling Profiles

Proportion of 15- to 19-year-olds who have completed each grade

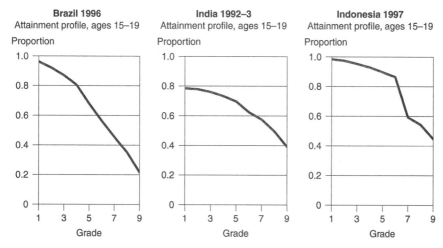

Source: Filmer and Pritchett 1999.

Figure 1.4 shows the substantial disparities between gross enrollment ratios and primary completion rates for a sample of developing countries. What is significant from an analytical standpoint is not so much that a disparity exists, but that there is no constant relationship underlying the gap.

FIGURE 1.4 : Primary Gross Enrollment Ratios and Completion Rates, Selected Countries, 1999

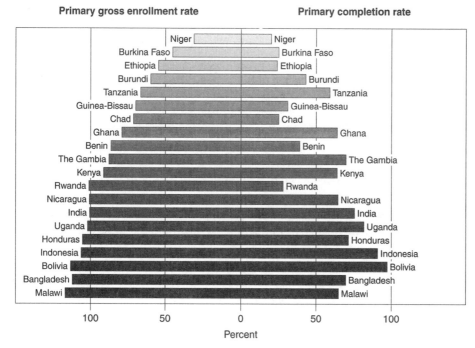

Source: Annex table A.2.

Disparities between the primary gross enrollment ratio and the completion rate arise for many reasons: children enter school early (below the official schooling age), or, more commonly in developing countries, they start school late. They may repeat grades. Another common pattern is that children drop out of school before the end of the year, because of their own or other family members' illness or their families' need for their labor, and return to reenroll in the same grade the following year. Finally, schools may be incomplete and not offer all grades locally. All these factors contribute to the fact that gross enrollment ratios are typically 10-60 percent higher than primary completion rates.

Important gender differences become evident in the comparison of GERs against completion rates, as well. In some countries, for example in the Caribbean, girls' GERs may be somewhat lower than those of boys but their completion rates higher. Elsewhere, as in several West African countries, girls' enrollments may show only a slight disparity with boys', but girls' completion rates are very significantly lower. Completion rate data greatly enhance understanding of the gender issues that exist in educational opportunity.

As important as analyzing the overall completion rate is decomposing it for different groups. In every country, completion rates are lowest for children from poor families and children in rural areas. Household survey data, as in figure 1.5, show how the schooling profile for children in the lowest income quintile can lag that of children from higher income groups. Moreover, in some countries, as noted, gender equity is also an issue, and completion rates are sharply lower for girls than for boys. In such countries the combined impact of family income and gender can produce a dramatic disparity between schooling completion rates for girls from the poorest families and boys from the wealthiest families—as in Nepal (figure 1.6).

As table 1.1 shows, even in countries where the current GER is close to 100 percent, the proportion of rural children, and especially rural girls, actually completing the primary cycle can be extremely low. It would be a tragedy for these vulnerable groups if countries such as Togo took 115 percent GER to mean that Education for All had been achieved.

Similar issues exist with respect to net enrollment ratios (NERs). Although one might expect net enrollment ratios, which exclude overage students, to be more closely correlated with primary completion rates, this is not the case. Table 1.2 provides an example of the variance in completion rates among countries with an identical 81 percent NER. Therefore, although the net enrollment ratio is useful for monitoring the proportion of the official school-age population that is not currently enrolled—the "out of school population"—it is not a good substitute for direct measure of the primary completion rate as the basic indicator of progress toward the education MDG.

In the search for something more reliable than gross enrollment ratios and in the absence of alternatives, the net enrollment ratio has in fact been proposed as the key indicator for monitoring progress toward the education MDG. But in addition to the fact that it does not capture actual primary completion, the net enrollment ratio presents another disadvantage: the target of 100 percent net enrollment in primary school is an unrealistic goal. It would require that every single child enter primary

FIGURE 1.5 | Schooling Profiles Disaggregated by Income

Proportion of 15- to 19-year-olds who have completed each grade

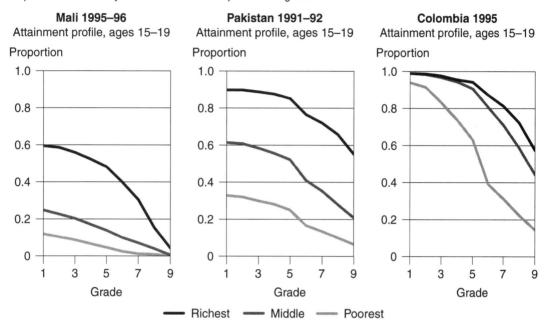

Mali 1995–96
Attainment profile, ages 15–19

Pakistan 1991–92
Attainment profile, ages 15–19

Colombia 1995
Attainment profile, ages 15–19

—— Richest   —— Middle   —— Poorest

Source: Filmer and Pritchett 1999.

FIGURE 1.6 | Schooling Profiles Disaggregated by Gender and Income

Proportion of 15- to 19-year-olds who have completed each grade

Nepal 2001
Attainment profile, ages 15–19

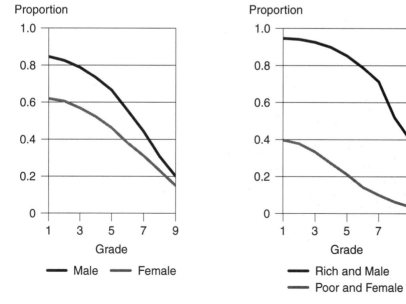

—— Male   —— Female

—— Rich and Male
—— Poor and Female

Source: Filmer 2000 and updates.

Table 1.1

Proportion of Children Completing Primary School: Regional Averages and Selected Countries

Region and Country	Primary Gross Enrollment Ratio (%)	PERCENTAGE OF AGE GROUP COMPLETING PRIMARY CYCLE		
		Total	Rural	Rural Girls
Africa	77	45	—	—
Niger	31	20	12	7
Burkina Faso	45	25	16	10
Guinea	62	34	25	11
Benin	86	39	27	14
Mauritania	88	46	42	38
Mozambique	78	36	21	14
Madagascar	90	26	12	11
Togo	115	68	57	46
South Asia	100	70	—	—
Latin America and the Caribbean	113	85	—	—
Middle East and North Africa	95	74	—	—

— Not available.

Source: Annex table A.2 and authors' estimates from World Bank education country status reports.

school at exactly the official schooling age, proceed through the cycle with zero repetition, and stay in school with no disruptions, resulting in a 100 percent on-time completion rate. If such a perfect cohort flow could be achieved, the net enrollment ratio would in fact be equal to the primary completion rate: both would be 100 percent. However, although virtually all children in OECD countries complete primary school, primary NERs rarely reach 100 percent. Indeed, the

Table 1.2

Comparison of Gross Enrollment Ratio, Net Enrollment Ratio, and Primary Completion Rate for Selected Countries, 2000

Country	Gross Enrollment Ratio	Net Enrollment Ratio	Primary Completion Rate (%)
El Salvador	111	81	80
Mongolia	92	81	66
Togo	115	81	68

Source: Annex table A.2 and UNESCO data.

average net enrollment ratio across the OECD is only 94 percent, and this ratio has been remarkably stable over the past 30 years of educational development in industrial countries (Brossard and Gacougnolle 2001).

What this net enrollment ratio tells us is that even in the most advanced countries, some children start school a little early or late, some may struggle to get through the primary curriculum, and some may be held back a grade at one point or another, but with the right support and, above all, a school system-wide ethos that "every child can learn," very close to 100 percent of children eventually complete primary schooling. This more flexible concept is a more realistic—and substantively meaningful—goal for developing countries as well. It puts the onus on school systems to prepare teachers with diverse pedagogical strategies to meet children's different learning needs. It requires school systems to allocate resources so that special support is provided to slower learners, children with physical or emotional disabilities, or children for whom consistent school attendance is jeopardized by poverty or family health crises. It requires school systems to put in place systems of learning assessment to ensure that children's grade progression actually reflects adequate mastery of the primary curriculum.

These are in fact the substantive goals of EFA. They should be measured by an indicator that captures a country's progress over time in delivering this kind of quality educational service to its children. That indicator should allow for the uneven path to primary school completion that is a reality for many children in the developing world, given constraints to on-time enrollment (if an overcrowded local school lacks places, for example) and constraints to stable attendance. The methodology proposed in this report for calculating a primary completion rate that provides a direct measure of the share of children who complete primary education (regardless of their age at completion) provides such an indicator. The next chapter analyzes international progress in improving primary completion rates over the decade of the 1990s, while subsequent chapters focus on the policies that underlie this progress. Important aspects of the story in many countries are policy reforms and pedagogical innovations to create primary schools that more flexibly meet the needs of children, both inside the classroom and outside of school.

The Global Scorecard: Progress since Jomtien

Shifting from primary enrollments to completion rates as the basic measure of MDG progress may seem like moving back the goal post in a game already lost. Universal primary completion is undeniably a more challenging goal than universal primary enrollment. Of 155 developing countries, about half have already built sufficient schools and places to educate 100 percent of their primary school-aged children. But only 37 of those countries today retain 100 percent of children in school through primary graduation. Unlike universal access, universal completion cannot be achieved without ensuring schooling quality, students' learning progress, and household demand for education—all of which are interlinked.

Nonetheless, countries from Brazil and Nicaragua in Latin America to Cambodia in East Asia to South Africa, Guinea, and The Gambia in Africa have proven over the 1990s that dramatic progress in increasing primary completion rates is possible—provided that political will is strong, effective reforms are adopted, and international support is adequate. Improvements of 20 percentage points in the primary completion rate in less than a decade—or more than 2 percentage points increase per year—have been registered in these countries and a number of others (annex tables B.3 and B.4).

On the other hand, progress is not automatic, nor is sustained status assured. In a troubling number of countries, primary completion rates have slid backwards since Jomtien. Thirteen middle-income and 15 low-income countries saw their completion rates stagnate or decline over the 1990s (annex tables B.5 and B.6). The case of Afghanistan (which dropped from an already low 22 percent in 1990 to an estimated 8 percent in 1999) is obvious and dramatic. But several middle-income Gulf states, Latin American countries such as Venezuela and Belize, and African countries such as Zambia, Republic of Congo, Cameroon, Kenya, and Madagascar have also lost ground.

Later in this chapter we explore global, regional, and country-by-country trends in primary completion rates more fully. But first, we turn to the definition of the primary completion rate and associated methodological issues: How it is calculated? How reliable is it as a statistic? And why hasn't it been compiled before?

WHAT IS THE PRIMARY COMPLETION RATE?

The primary completion rate (PCR) is a flow measure of the annual output of the primary education system. It is calculated as the total number of students successfully completing (or graduating from) the last year of primary school in a given year, divided by the total number of children of official graduation age in the population. It is an application of the OECD methodology for measuring secondary school completion rates to the primary level.

It should be emphasized that the primary completion rate is not the same as the "cohort survival rate" estimated by UNESCO. That indicator measures the survival to grade 5 among those children who enroll in school. But this has the important limitation of not reflecting the sometimes large share of children, especially in low-income countries, who do not have access to primary school.

The PCR measures the proportion of all children of official graduation age who complete primary school in a given year. As the numerator in the primary completion rate counts all children completing the final grade of primary school, it will typically include overage children who either started school late or have repeated one or more grades of primary school, but are now graduating successfully. In countries where there is some repetition yet the dropout rate is low, the primary completion rate can, in a particular year, exceed 100 percent. However, completion rates consistently above 100 percent can be assumed to reflect data weaknesses, in either reported enrollment statistics or age-specific population estimates.

The primary completion rate focuses on capturing the share of children who *ever* complete the cycle; it is not a measure of "on-time" primary completion. An on-time completion rate could also be calculated, by netting overage children out of the numerator. But data for this are not readily available. More fundamentally, though, the philosophy of this study is that the key number of policy interest to countries from a human capital standpoint is the share of children who eventually obtain a primary-level education.

It should be understood that even though overage children may appear in the numerator of the primary completion rate, they appear only once. Since children are counted only when they actually graduate from, or complete, the cycle, steady-state monitoring of the completion rate will give an accurate picture of trends over time in the average share of students in a population cohort who complete primary school. As school system flow distortions eventually decline, the share of overage or underage children will be reduced as well. However, as noted in chapter 1, they may never disappear altogether.

In education systems that are not in a steady state—that is, where either the size of the school-age population is changing or the coverage of the education system is expanding rapidly—the current primary completion rate may not be a good reflection of the likely future completion rate for the cohort now entering primary school. But if the primary completion rate is monitored over time it will reflect these trends and give a good sense of progress toward the MDG goal of universal primary completion. As such, it may be used to set meaningful targets.

DATA SOURCES AND METHODOLOGICAL ISSUES

Primary completion rates are calculated from the same two basic data sources used to compute gross and net enrollment ratios: (a) enrollment data from national ministries of education, and (b) United Nations population data.

The grade-specific enrollment data required for the primary completion rate are collected in all countries and published by the UNESCO Institute for Statistics. We used this database to calculate a baseline (1990) value of the PCR for all countries.

However, since developing the most up-to-date picture possible of where countries currently stand in relation to the MDG target was a priority of this exercise, we collected enrollment data for the most recent year possible directly from national education ministries, through World Bank task teams. In most cases, that meant the year 2000. When it was impossible to obtain more recent data, we relied on published UNESCO data, most often for 1997. In some cases, the only available data were for even earlier years.

The primary completion rate is both conceptually and practically a fairly straightforward education statistic. But there are some methodological and data issues. The first is the differing length of the primary cycle across countries (which also affects gross and net enrollment ratios). For this study, primary education is defined as UNESCO's ISCED (International Standard Classification of Education) Level 1: "the beginning of systematic apprenticeship of reading, writing and mathematics; the start of compulsory education; primary education; first stage of basic education."

As UNESCO notes, this stage in most countries is covered in a five- or six-year cycle. About 45 percent of countries have six-year, and another 13 percent of

Table 2.1
Length of the Primary Cycle in 155 Developing Countries, circa 2000

Years in Primary Cycle	Number of Countries	Percentage of Developing Countries	Typical Regions/Countries
3	2	1[a]	Russia, Armenia
4	26	18	Europe and Central Asia Africa
5	20	13	South Asia East Asia and the Pacific
6	70	45	Africa East Asia and the Pacific Latin America and the Caribbean Middle East and North Africa
7	21	14	Africa Latin America and the Caribbean
8	12	8	Europe and Central Asia Africa
9	2	1	Libya, Rep. of Yemen
10	2	1	Jordan, West Bank/Gaza

a. Less than 1 percent.

Source: UNESCO Institute for Statistics.

countries have five-year, primary cycles. But in 24 percent of countries, the official primary cycle is longer. As countries develop economically and educationally, the length of compulsory education is typically extended to the next cycle, which UNESCO defines as Level 2: "lower secondary education" or the "second stage of basic education." However, in many countries this integrated cycle of Levels 1 and 2 of compulsory education is called primary education.

In some countries this cycle is seven years, and in four countries it is nine or 10 years. Two of these four countries, the Republic of Yemen and Lebanon, have decided to consider the primary cycle as the first six years of schooling for EFA monitoring purposes. We have accordingly done so in this study.

About 20 percent of countries have a shorter primary cycle, usually four years. Many lusophone and former Soviet Union countries follow this pattern. In 2000, Armenia adopted a three-year primary cycle. The Russian Federation recently extended its three-year cycle by an additional year, effective 2003.

Our database calculates the primary completion rate based on the official cycle length in each country. Obviously, it is considerably easier to get 100 percent of children through three grades of primary school than through eight. But since gross enrollment and net enrollment ratios are also estimated on the basis of countries' official cycle length, this ensures that the primary completion rates are consistent and therefore comparable with those series.

A second issue arises from the fact that not all countries report the number of children completing primary school. Typically, this requires the collection of end-of-year enrollment data, and many low-income countries only report enrollments at the beginning of the year. For countries where actual primary graduates are reported, the primary completion rate estimate uses that number. In these cases, accounting for dropouts is not an issue, as students who drop out during the course of the year naturally do not appear in the end-of-year enrollment numbers.

For countries that do not report end-of-year enrollments, we calculated a "proxy primary completion rate" defined as follows:

> Proxy primary completion rate = (the total number of students in the final year of primary school, minus repeaters) divided by (the total number of children of official graduation age in the population).

The reasoning is that the repetition rate in the final year of primary schooling typically does not change dramatically from one year to the next, although steady improvement over time can occur. Thus, the share of children repeating the grade this year, having failed it the previous year, is a reasonable approximation of the share of students who are likely to fail the grade this year. Subtracting this number from the total number of children enrolled in the grade at the beginning of the year gives a reasonable approximation of the number of children who will successfully complete the grade and graduate from primary school in the current year.

When estimating a proxy primary completion rate, ideally one would also make an adjustment for students who drop out during the year. Where estimates of dropout existed, they were used. However, data on dropout rates in the final year of schooling typically were not available, and thus most of the proxy primary completion rates present an overstatement of the true primary completion rate, and should be taken as an upper-bound estimate. For a few countries in the sample, even recent data on repetition rates could not be obtained; for those countries, the proxy PCR further overstates the true primary completion rate.

The third and final issue concerns the population data used in the denominator of the primary completion rate. All population data used in this report were taken from the United Nations/World Bank population database used for all World Bank work, including the calculation of the World Development Indicators. This series is compiled for all countries from national census data, with regular review and adjustments of national data by a panel of international demographers using emerging demographic and household survey data, medical registries, and other agreed sources. This data series includes total population estimates, population estimates by age and gender, and projections through 2015. The age-specific population estimates for boys and girls needed for calculating the primary completion rate are readily available in this database.

This data series is the best internationally comparable set of population estimates available. However, there is a somewhat higher risk of error in the age-specific data used for the primary completion rate than in the overall population estimates, which may have discouraged the systematic estimation of PCRs in the past. And for countries that have not carried out national censuses for some time or have experienced war, mass migration, or other major dislocations, these estimates may not be very accurate even though they are the best available.

In sum, strenuous efforts have been made to develop an internationally consistent set of estimates of the primary completion rate in 155 developing countries. But this first set of primary completion rate and proxy estimates needs to be regarded as just that—an initial data set that can be improved greatly in terms of both robustness and timeliness if national governments and international partners work together to refine them.

Even a cursory review will point up many gaps in the data, particularly for small countries, earlier years, and gender breakdowns, and obvious anomalies and estimates that are suspect. There is work to be done to encourage countries to collect end-of-year data on the number of graduates, to allow true PCRs to be estimated for all countries. There is scope for more systematic quality assurance and maintenance of this database through collaboration with the UNESCO Institute for Statistics. And there is the prospect of improved population data becoming available soon, as more countries complete the detailed age-specific analysis of 2000 censuses or carry out new household surveys.

Thus, the PCR and proxy estimates in this report are only a point of departure. But they represent the most direct effort to date to measure progress toward the MDG target of universal primary completion and to provide a basis for future monitoring. Within the limitations of available data, the completion rates presented here reasonably capture the reality of primary education system coverage and student attainment in many of the 155 developing countries measured. With a collaborative international effort to improve the quality of this database, it could be an increasingly valuable tool.

Since Jomtien in 1990, the global average completion rate for the developing world has improved only from 72 to 77 percent (see Annex figure B.1). Underlying this average, as figure 2.1 shows, is substantial variance across regions in both the distance from UPC and the progress made over the 1990s. Sub-Saharan Africa has the lowest completion rate by far, with barely half of all school-age children completing primary school; it is followed by South Asia, with a regional average completion rate of about 70 percent. The Middle East and North Africa showed a disturbing pattern of stagnation over the 1990s, with the average completion rate remaining around 74 percent. The Europe and Central Asia region (92 percent) is closest to the goal, followed by Latin America and the Caribbean (85 percent) and East Asia and the Pacific (84 percent).

Table 2.2 presents changes in median completion rates, as well as regional means, because in many cases the means are skewed by a few extremely high- or low-performing countries, some of whose data are questionable. In Africa and Latin America, for example, the increase of only 3 percentage points in the regions' median completion rates over the period indicates that increases in their mean completion rates were driven by high numbers for a few countries. On the other hand, in South Asia the median completion rate improved from 50 to 67 percent

FIGURE 2.1 : **Primary Completion Progress by Region, 1990–2000, and Projected Trends (Country-Weighted)**

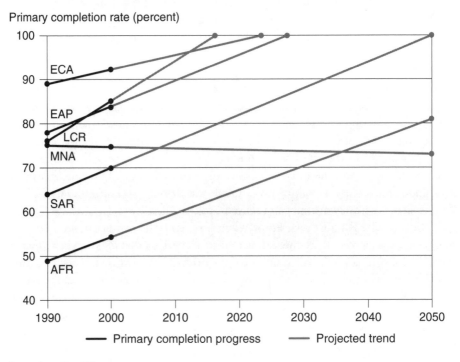

Primary completion rate (percent)

Source: Annex figure B.3.

Table 2.2
....
Primary Completion Progress by Region, 1990–2000, Country-Weighted

Region	1990			Most Recent Year[a]		
	Mean	Median	Range	Mean	Median	Range
Africa	49	42	11–135	55	45	19–117
East Asia and the Pacific	78	89	39–99	84	90	54–108
Europe and Central Asia	89	90	67–100	92	93	77–109
Latin America and the Caribbean	76	86	28–112	85	89	40–110
Middle East and North Africa	75	75	32–102	74	76	30–104
South Asia	64	50	22–111	70	67	8–112
All developing countries	72	81	11–135	77	83	8–117
IDA-eligible countries	50	45	11–112	62	64	8–117
IBRD-eligible countries	84	89	43–135	87	92	44–111

a. Usually 1999/2000.

over the decade—an impressive trend that is largely masked in the comparison of means by the dramatic decline in Afghanistan. Both the means and medians for low-income countries improved more than those for middle-income countries.

On a population-weighted basis (table 2.3) the global progress is more encouraging, with the global completion rate increasing from 73 to 81 percent over the decade. The population-weighted average is dramatically more positive for East Asia (97 percent compared with 84 percent on a country-weighted basis), reflecting the high reported completion rate in China. For the Middle East and North Africa, the population-weighted average of 83 percent is also significantly higher than the country-weighted average, influenced by Egypt's weight. For the remaining regions there is relatively little difference. But in Sub-Saharan Africa, the average completion rate of 51 percent on a population-weighted basis is even more discouraging than the country-weighted mean.

Globally, even though completion rates for girls improved more than those for boys over the decade, girls' average completion (76 percent) continues to lag that of boys (85 percent). Every region showed a significant increase in girls' completion rates, with the 14 percentage point improvement in Latin American countries the most impressive change. On the other hand, it is sobering that the population-weighted completion rate for boys actually declined in the Africa region over the decade, was stagnant in Europe and Central Asia, and was virtually stagnant in East Asia and in the Middle East and North Africa. Only the South Asia and Latin

Table 2.3
....
Primary Completion Progress by Region, 1990–2000, Population-Weighted

Region	1990			Most Recent Year[a]		
	Girls	Boys	Both	Girls	Boys	Both
Africa	43	57	50	46	56	51
East Asia and the Pacific	92	97	96	98	98	97
Europe and Central Asia	85	95	90	93	95	93
Latin America and the Caribbean	71	64	69	85	81	83
Middle East and North Africa	71	84	78	78	86	83
South Asia	59	77	68	63	84	74
All developing countries	65	79	73	76	85	81

a. Usually 1999/2000.

America regions showed a significant increase in the share of boys completing primary school. Latin America's increase of 17 percentage points over the decade was even stronger than the increase for girls in that region.

AFRICA

Data for African countries are presented in table 2.4, sorted from highest to lowest completion rate in the most recent year available. The first five countries listed have achieved universal primary completion according to available data and our working definition of universal completion as 95 percent or higher. South Africa has reached the goal since Jomtien. By contrast, Zambia, which had essentially achieved universal primary completion in 1990, has since then suffered a substantial decline to 83 percent (in 1995).

Both in 1990 and today, Sub-Saharan Africa is the region with the lowest average completion rate, at 55 percent. More than half the countries in the region for which data are available are less than halfway to the MDG target. The encouraging news, however, is that a substantial number of African countries have been able to increase completion rates over the 1990s, and some—such as Guinea, Eritrea, Mali, and Mauritania—have made truly impressive progress from very low starting levels. The Gambia, starting from a slightly higher base, has made even faster progress, with the primary completion rate increasing by more than 3 percentage points per year from 1991 to 2000. Malawi's rate of increase in the first half of the decade was extremely high, 4 percentage points per year, but it is doubtful that it has been sustained. On the other hand, Uganda's improvement (see box 2.1) may accelerate further over the next two years, as the wave of children who entered school following the elimination of fees in 1996 make their way to graduation from the seven-year system.

Box 2.1 **Primary Completion Progress in Uganda**

In 1990, only an estimated 39 percent of Ugandan children completed the seven-grade primary cycle. By 2001 that share was 65 percent and growing rapidly, as the result of a bold reform in 1996 that eliminated primary school tuition fees for up to four children per family. President Museveni's dramatic action removed a key obstacle for poor families and emphasized the importance of education.

The impact on demand for primary schooling was immediate and tremendous. In 1997 total primary school enrollments jumped from 3.4 million to 5.7 million children, with the greatest increases coming among girls and the poorest children. By 1999 the wealth bias that had characterized access to primary education was all but eliminated, and by 2000 there was virtually no gap between male and female net enrollment ratios (89.3 percent vs. 88.8 percent).

The primary system has had to scramble to deal with the swell in enrollments, however. Pupil-teacher ratios shot up from 40:1 to 60:1 by 1999, and unqualified teachers had to be deployed to many areas, until the Ministry of Education could ramp up the production of additional trained teachers. Input ratios for textbooks and materials also deteriorated. Although the government acted quickly to reallocate spending to primary education and to mobilize additional donor support, the loss of tuition income at the school level and the huge influx of new students led to palpable declines in schooling quality. With any large enrollment expansion, a decline in average student learning outcomes can be expected. But in Uganda, the drop has been precipitous: between 1996 and 1999, the share of students receiving a satisfactory score fell from 48 percent to 31 percent in mathematics, and from 92 percent to 56 percent on the English oral test.

Uganda's experience—and the earlier experience of Malawi with a similar elimination of tuition fees—provides strong evidence that schooling demand in low-income countries is more elastic than previously estimated. But Malawi, where schooling quality has continued to erode

Uganda: Primary GER and PCR, 1990–2001 (percent)

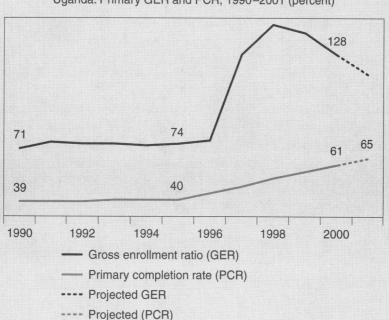

Box 2.1 continued

since the elimination of fees in 1995, has already provided sobering evidence that enrollment gains, and especially completion rate progress, will not persist if schooling quality does not meet minimum standards. For poor parents in particular, the opportunity costs of children's school attendance are high, and parents will not keep children in primary school through to completion unless they perceive that school conditions are minimally adequate, the curriculum content is relevant, and students are learning. The fiscal priority Uganda has given to primary education and the ministry's systematic actions since 1997 to improve quality have attracted substantial donor support, but there is still considerable progress to be made. Uganda's experience shows, however, that rapid progress in primary completion is possible, with bold actions to eliminate demand-side constraints where they exist and strong complementary attention to schooling quality.

Table 2.4

Africa: Changes in Primary Completion Rates during the 1990s

Country	Eligible for IDA/IBRD lending	Years in primary cycle	PRIMARY COMPLETION RATE							
			1990				MOST RECENT YEAR			
			Girls	Boys	Both	Year	Girls	Boys	Both	Year
Cape Verde	IDA	6	—	—	—	—	119	115	117	1997
Zimbabwe	IDA	7	94	100	97	1990	111	116	113	1997
Mauritius	IBRD	6	135	136	135	1990	108	115	111	1997
Botswana	IBRD	7	126	102	114	1990	107	96	102	1996
South Africa	IBRD	7	81	72	76	1990	100	95	98	1995
Namibia	IBRD	7	80	59	70	1990	94	86	90	1997
Zambia	IDA	7	84	110	97	1988	75	90	83	1995
Swaziland	IBRD	7	—	—	71	1990	85	78	81	1997
São Tomé and Principe	IDA	4	—	—	—	—	—	—	84	2001
Gabon	IBRD	6	77	66	71	1991	80	79	80	1995
Gambia, The	IDA	6	35	45	40	1991	—	—	70	2000
Lesotho	IDA	7	82	45	64	1990	83	55	69	1996
Nigeria	IDA	6	62	82	72	1990	61	73	67	2000
Uganda	IDA	7	30	49	39	1990	—	—	65	2001
Ghana	IDA	6	54	71	63	1990	—	—	64	1999
Togo	IDA	6	26	55	41	1990	52	73	63	1999
Tanzania	IDA	7	45	46	46	1989	60	58	59	1997
Kenya	IDA	8	57	69	63	1990	57	58	58	1995

Table 2.4 (continued)

Africa: Changes in Primary Completion Rates during the 1990s

Country	Eligible for IDA/IBRD lending	Years in primary cycle	PRIMARY COMPLETION RATE							
			1990				MOST RECENT YEAR			
			Girls	Boys	Both	Year	Girls	Boys	Both	Year
Malawi	IDA	8	22	38	30	1990	40	61	50	1995
Mauritania	IDA	6	26	41	34	1990	43	48	46	1998
Equatorial Guinea	IBRD	5	—	—	—	—	43	48	46	1993
Congo, Rep. of	IDA	6	55	68	61	1990	60	28	44	2000
Cameroon	IDA	6	52	61	57	1990	39	46	43	1999
Burundi	IDA	6	43	49	46	1990	—	—	43	1998
Senegal	IDA	6	35	56	45	1989	34	48	41	2000
Côte d'Ivoire	IDA	6	32	55	44	1990	33	48	40	1999
Congo, Dem. Rep. of	IDA	6	35	60	48	1990	34	45	40	2000
Benin	IDA	6	15	31	23	1990	30	47	39	1998
Mozambique	IDA	5	23	36	30	1990	22	50	36	1998
Eritrea	IDA	5	20	23	22	1991	31	40	35	1999
Sudan	IDA	8	—	—	—	—	33	38	35	1996
Guinea	IDA	6	9	24	16	1990	24	44	34	2000
Comoros	IDA	6	32	38	35	1991	34	32	33	1993
Sierra Leone	IDA	7	—	—	—	—	30	36	32	2000
Guinea-Bissau	IDA	6	12	21	16	1988	24	40	31	2000
Madagascar	IDA	5	35	33	34	1990	26	26	26	1998
Burkina Faso	IDA	6	14	24	19	1990	20	30	25	1998
Rwanda	IDA	6[a]	35	33	34	1990	27	30	28	2000
Ethiopia	IDA	6	18	25	22	1990	12	36	24	1999
Mali	IDA	6	9	14	11	1990	18	29	23	1998
Niger	IDA	6	13	23	18	1990	15	23	20	1998
Central African Republic	IDA	6	19	37	28	1990	—	—	19	2000
Chad	IDA	6	7	31	19	1990	9	29	19	2000
Angola	IDA	4	35	42	39	1990	—	—	—	—
Liberia	IDA	6	—	—	—	—	—	—	—	—
Seychelles	IBRD	6	—	—	—	—	—	—	—	—
Somalia	IDA	8	—	—	—	—	—	—	—	—

— Not available.

a. Rwanda 1990 data are for a seven-grade primary cycle; 2000 data are for the new six-grade cycle.

These examples provide clear evidence that a path of rapid and sustained improvement in primary completion rates can be achieved by countries no matter what their starting level of education system coverage, and no matter what their level of income per capita.

EAST ASIA AND THE PACIFIC

Five countries in the East Asia and Pacific region have achieved universal primary completion. But in general, the stellar pace of education progress seen in East Asian countries over the 1970s and 1980s has not been sustained since Jomtien. With the exception of Cambodia, which has registered tremendous improvement from a low base in the last several years, and to a lesser extent the Lao People's Democratic Republic, primary completion rates in the East Asia and Pacific region have largely stagnated or declined over the past decade (table 2.5). According to these estimates, none of the East Asian and Pacific countries that had yet to achieve universal primary completion as of Jomtien has done so since, except possibly Vietnam.

EUROPE AND CENTRAL ASIA

European and Central Asian developing countries inherited an extensive education infrastructure, and at the beginning of the transition in 1990 were characterized by virtually universal primary enrollments and the highest average primary completion rate of any region—89 percent. The most recent data (table 2.6) still show Europe and Central Asia (ECA) as the region closest to universal primary completion. Eleven of the 23 countries in the region for which data are available have achieved the goal and it can be considered within reach of all the ECA countries, most of which are also helped by a relatively short official primary cycle.

However, the region faces very significant quality issues, increasing evidence of demand constraints, and the challenge of adapting educational content and goals to the needs of more open societies and market economies. With the severe economic declines that accompanied transition, along with the social, demographic, and political upheaval the region has experienced, many countries have had great difficulty maintaining the inherited education infrastructure, let alone improving the quality of education delivered. Many of the former Soviet republics relied heavily on subsidies from Moscow to develop and maintain their education systems; the withdrawal of these, plus the sharp economic declines of the 1990s, have placed education systems in the region under stress.

The dislocations of the 1990s have had a particularly strong impact on the poorest countries, in Central Asia, the Caucuses, and the Balkans, all of which are now struggling to maintain a basic level of education services in the face of public finance constraints and institutional weaknesses. Very high officially reported enrollments and completion rates in several Central Asian countries—especially Kazakhstan, Turkmenistan, Kyrgyz Republic, and Uzbekistan—are not included in our database, as they are not corroborated by household survey data which reveal troubling declines in schooling attendance. Population data for many countries in the region are also problematic, in some cases based on censuses from 1980.

Available data show Armenia, Georgia, Moldova, and Tajikistan as the ECA countries farthest from the MDG, and of these, only Moldova appears to have

Table 2.5

East Asia and the Pacific: Changes in Primary Completion Rates during the 1990s

Country	Eligible for IDA/IBRD Lending	Years in Primary Cycle	PRIMARY COMPLETION RATE							
			1990				MOST RECENT YEAR			
			Girls	Boys	Both	Year	Girls	Boys	Both	Year
China	IBRD	5	95	107	99	1990	106	111	108	1996
Vietnam	IDA	5	—	—	—	—	98	104	101	2001
Samoa	IDA	8	—	—	—	—	92	105	99	1997
Korea, Rep. of	IBRD	6	96	96	96	1990	98	95	96	2000
Fiji	IBRD	6	—	—	—	—	93	97	95	1992
Philippines	IBRD	6	91	88	89	1989	—	—	92	1996
Indonesia	IDA	6	93	93	92	1990	92	90	91	2000
Thailand	IBRD	6	90	95	93	1990	—	—	90	2000
Malaysia	IBRD	6	91	91	91	1990	90	89	90	1994
Vanuatu	IDA	6	90	89	89	1990	81	92	86	1992
Mongolia	IDA	4	—	—	—	—	—	—	82	1998
Cambodia	IDA	6	32	46	39	1997	—	—	70	2001
Lao PDR	IDA	5	—	—	56	1995	64	73	69	2000
Solomon Islands	IDA	6	59	70	65	1990	54	77	66	1994
Papua New Guinea	IBRD	6	51	55	53	1990	53	64	59	1995
Timor-Leste, Dem. Rep.	IDA	6	—	—	—	—	53	55	54	2001
Kiribati	IDA	7	—	—	—	—	—	—	—	—
Korea, DPR	n. a.	4	—	—	—	—	—	—	—	—
Marshall Islands	IBRD	6	—	—	—	—	—	—	—	—
Micronesia, Fed. States of	IBRD	6	—	—	—	—	—	—	—	—
Myanmar	IDA	5	—	—	—	—	—	—	—	—
Palau	IBRD	8	—	—	—	—	—	—	—	—
Tonga	IDA	6	—	—	—	—	—	—	—	—

n. a. Not applicable.
— Not available.

registered progress over the 1990s. Albania's completion rate declined over the 1990s. Overall, the region is characterized by a growing gap in performance between states that are developing rapidly, such as the Baltic and Central European countries—with the Czech Republic, Latvia, Lithuania, and Hungary all showing completion rate progress—and those such as Albania, Armenia, Georgia, and the Central Asian countries, whose economic problems are increasingly reflected in the education sector.

Table 2.6
....
Europe and Central Asia: Changes in Primary Completion Rates during the 1990s

| | | | PRIMARY COMPLETION RATE | | | | | | | |
| | | | 1990 | | | | Most Recent Year | | | |
Country	Eligible for IDA/IBRD Lending	Years in Primary Cycle	Girls	Boys	Both	Year	Girls	Boys	Both	Year
Czech Republic	IBRD	4	86	92	89	1992	107	110	109	1995
Hungary	IBRD	4	90	97	93	1989	102	102	102	1995
Azerbaijan	IDA	4	—	—	—	—	101	99	100	1998
Romania	IBRD	4	91	100	96	1989	98	99	98	1996
Slovak Republic	IBRD	4	92	100	96	1992	97	96	97	1996
Poland	IBRD	8	98	102	100	1990	97	96	96	1995
Serbia and Montenegro	IDA	8	68	77	72	1990	—	—	96	2000
Russia	IBRD	3	—	—	—	—	—	—	96	2001
Croatia	IBRD	8	86	85	86	1992	96	95	96	2001
Lithuania	IBRD	4	84	92	88	1992	94	97	95	1996
Ukraine	IBRD	3	—	—	—	—	—	—	94[a]	2002
Belarus	IBRD	4	94	100	97	1992	92	95	93	1996
Turkey	IBRD	5	82	99	90	1990	89	95	92	1994
Bulgaria	IBRD	4	87	93	90	1990	92	92	92	1996
Macedonia, FYR	IBRD	8	84	94	89	1992	87	94	91	1996
Albania	IDA	8	92	102	97	1990	95	84	89	1995
Bosnia and Herzegovina	IDA	4	—	—	—	—	—	—	88	1999
Estonia	IBRD	6	91	95	93	1992	86	89	88	1995
Latvia	IBRD	4	75	77	76	1992	84	87	86	1996
Armenia	IDA	4	—	—	—	—	95	70	82	1996
Georgia	IDA	4	—	—	—	—	—	—	82	1998
Moldova	IDA	4	65	68	67	1991	—	—	79	1999
Tajikistan	IDA	4	—	—	—	—	75	80	77	1996
Kazakhstan	IBRD	4	—	—	—	—	—	—	—	—
Kyrgyz Republic	IDA	4	—	—	—	—	—	—	—	—
Slovenia	IBRD	4	93	106	99	1992	—	—	—	—
Turkmenistan	IBRD	4	—	—	—	—	—	—	—	—
Uzbekistan	IDA	4	—	—	—	—	—	—	—	—

— Not available.
a. Staff estimate.

LATIN AMERICA AND THE CARIBBEAN

Twelve of 30 countries in Latin America and the Caribbean have achieved UPC and three more countries are on the cusp of doing so. The remaining 15 countries have varied widely in their progress since Jomtien (table 2.7). Two countries, Nicaragua and Brazil, have raised primary completion rates by more than 20 percentage points over the decade, and for Brazil especially, with an eight-year primary system, this is truly impressive progress (box 2.2). Bolivia has similarly increased completion through an eight-grade primary system from 55 to 72 percent over the decade.

Only slightly less dramatic is the progress in El Salvador, Costa Rica, and Peru, all of which started with a higher base and increased their completion rates by more than 15 percentage points over the decade. Colombia has also shown significant improvement.

However, a few countries in Latin America have shown the reverse trend. Countries that appeared to have universal primary completion within close reach, such as Venezuela, Guyana, and Belize, have seen completion rates decline by as much as 8 percentage points over the decade. Ecuador and Honduras show basically stagnating trends.

Table 2.7

Latin America and the Caribbean: Changes in Primary Completion Rates during the 1990s

Country	Eligible for IDA/IBRD Lending	Years in Primary Cycle	PRIMARY COMPLETION RATE							
			1990				Most Recent Year			
			Girls	Boys	Both	Year	Girls	Boys	Both	Year
St. Kitts and Nevis	IBRD	6	—	—	—	—	104	115	110	2001
Grenada	IDA	7	—	—	—	—	104	107	106	2001
St. Lucia	IDA	7	106	117	112	1990	104	109	106	2001
Dominica	IDA	6	—	—	—	—	107	99	103	2000
Mexico	IBRD	6	89	88	89	1990	*93*	85	100	2000
Antigua and Barbuda	IBRD	7	—	—	—	—	—	—	*95–100*[a]	2000
Cuba	n. a.	6	—	—	—	—	—	—	*95–100*[a]	2001
Chile	IBRD	6	97	92	94	1990	—	—	99	2000
Uruguay	IBRD	6	98	93	95	1990	101	95	98	2000
Peru	IBRD	6	—	—	85	1988	—	—	98	2000
Ecuador	IBRD	6	98	99	99	1992	96	96	96	1999
Argentina	IBRD	7	—	—	—	—	95	91	96	2000
Jamaica	IBRD	6	94	87	90	1990	98	91	94	2000
Trinidad and Tobago	IBRD	5	93	95	94	1990	94	94	94	2000

Table 2.7 (continued)

Latin America and the Caribbean: Changes in Primary Completion Rates during the 1990s

Country	Eligible for IDA/IBRD Lending	Years in Primary Cycle	PRIMARY COMPLETION RATE							
			1990				MOST RECENT YEAR			
			Girls	Boys	Both	Year	Girls	Boys	Both	Year
Panama	IBRD	6	87	88	87	1990	—	—	94	2000
Costa Rica	IBRD	6	74	72	73	1990	—	—	89	2000
Guyana	IDA	6	93	90	92	1990	95	84	89	2000
Colombia	IBRD	5	83	61	72	1990	—	—	85	2000
St. Vincent	IDA	6	—	—	—	—	84	85	84	2001
Belize	IBRD	6	90	89	90	1990	83	81	82	1999
El Salvador	IBRD	6	62	59	61	1989	—	—	80	2000
Paraguay	IBRD	6	65	65	65	1990	—	—	78	2000
Venezuela	IBRD	5	96	87	91	1990	79	77	78	1999
Bolivia	IDA	8	—	—	55	1990	—	—	72	2000
Brazil	IBRD	8	54	42	48	1990	—	—	72	1999
Honduras	IDA	6	63	68	66	1991	—	—	67	2000
Nicaragua	IDA	6	50	40	45	1990	70	61	65	2000
Dominican Republic	IBRD	8	—	—	—	—	67	56	62	2000
Guatemala	IBRD	6	39	46	43	1991	—	—	52	2000
Haiti	IDA	6	27	29	28	1990	—	—	40	1997

n.a. Not applicable.
— Not available.
a. Staff estimate.

Box 2.2 **Primary Completion Progress in Brazil**

In the space of one decade, Brazil has increased the share of children who complete primary school from 48 to 72 percent, one of the 10 fastest rates of improvement observed in our global sample. How Brazil did it provides a good picture of how sensitive primary completion rates are to schooling quality, particularly for the poor.

Before 1990, entry to primary school was practically universal in Brazil (recall the schooling profile pictured in figure 1.3), but less than half of all children completed the eight-year cycle. Dropout was worst in the poor northeast region, and especially in rural schools. But after 1995, Brazilian education policy under Minister Paulo Renato Souza focused strongly on improving the quality of primary education overall, and especially for the poor.

Box 2.2 continued

First, Brazil passed a major constitutional change in the distribution of fiscal resources for education. The FUNDEF reform established a yearly per-pupil spending floor to ensure a minimum standard of education for all children. National tax revenues began to cross-subsidize the states and municipalities least able to mobilize their own fiscal resources for education, thereby reducing the gulf in teacher salaries and school quality between richer and poorer regions. Innovative programs also channeled increased resources directly to schools, so they could implement their own development plans.

Second, the federal ministry strengthened its role in norm setting and quality assurance. It established the first national student assessment system and developed new national curriculum guidelines that stressed problem solving, independent learning, and critical thinking. A national commission set new quality standards for textbooks and learning materials and the ministry made on-time delivery of adequate learning materials to schools a visible national priority. New legislation was passed to sort out the confused and overlapping roles of the federal, state, and municipal governments in primary education, with the federal ministry for the first time assuming clear responsibility for guaranteeing equity and quality.

Third, heavy emphasis was placed on upgrading teacher quality—and teacher motivation. Higher qualifications were set for teacher certification, and the hiring of teachers without competitive examination, part of old-style patronage politics, was disallowed. A federally funded in-service teacher training program, using cost-effective distance delivery and high-quality materials, helped raise the share of primary teachers with a complete secondary education. Teacher salaries and pensions were increased, and civil service reforms began to allow for dismissal based on performance.

Brazil: Primary Education Access by Income Quintile, 1992–2001

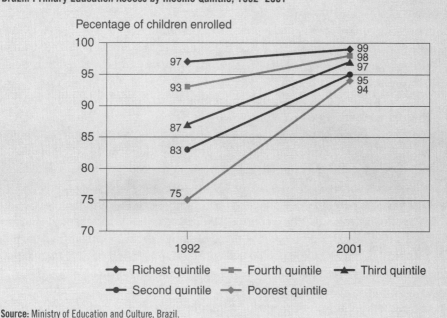

Pecentage of children enrolled

Richest quintile · Fourth quintile · Third quintile
Second quintile · Poorest quintile

Source: Ministry of Education and Culture, Brazil.

Box 2.2 continued

Fourth, innovative demand-side programs such as *bolsa escola*, which channels subsistence grants to low-income mothers whose children stay in school, and home visits from health agents who also check on school attendance helped send the message to very poor families that "every child belongs in school" and "every child can succeed."

In short, adequate and more equitable financing and a concerted program of quality improvements, efficiency enhancements, and demand-side interventions have combined in Brazil to raise the primary completion rate from 48 to 72 percent in the space of one decade. As the figure shows, the bulk of the progress has come from improvement in the quantity and quality of services delivered to children in the poorest income quintiles. Brazil's experience shows that with political commitment and comprehensive strategies, simultaneous rapid progress in educational quality and equity is possible.

Nonetheless, the major story in the region is the significant number of countries that have progressed rapidly, some from a very low base, suggesting that this region may have many lessons to share. Estimates for this region are also more reliable than for the other regions, as most Latin American and Caribbean countries report actual primary completion, and educational statistics are reasonably good.

In terms of gender equity, in Guatemala, El Salvador, St. Lucia, and Bolivia completion rates for girls lag those for boys, but an equally common pattern in Latin America is the opposite: boys' completion rates are lower than girls', sometimes significantly so, as in Uruguay, Jamaica, Mexico, and Nicaragua.

MIDDLE EAST AND NORTH AFRICA

Only two of the 19 countries in the Middle East and North Africa have achieved universal primary completion—Jordan and the Arab Republic of Egypt, whose statistics indicate a dramatic 22 percentage point improvement over the decade. In general, data for this region are of questionable quality and most of the completion rates are proxy rates.

The available data show substantial progress in Tunisia, which increased from 75 to 91 percent, as well as improvements in Kuwait, Algeria, Oman, Saudi Arabia, and Morocco, the last from a low base. Although the average completion rate for the region as a whole changed very little over the decade, this region more than any other is marked by great underlying variation at the country level (table 2.8). Fully half of the countries for which two data points exist show declining completion rates over the period.

Bahrain, which in 1990 reported 100 percent completion, has apparently suffered a decline to 91 percent since then. Although the data showing a tremendous drop in Qatar must be considered questionable, completion rates in Iraq, Syria, the Islamic Republic of Iran, and Djibouti all appear to have fallen.

Gender disparities in completion rates are evident in Morocco (47 percent completion for girls, 63 percent for boys), in Egypt (92 percent for girls, 104 percent for boys), in Djibouti (24 percent for girls, 36 percent for boys), and dramat-

Table 2.8
....

Middle East and North Africa: Changes in Primary Completion Rates during the 1990s

Country	Eligible for IDA/IBRD Lending	Years in Primary Cycle	PRIMARY COMPLETION RATE							
			1990				MOST RECENT YEAR			
			Girls	Boys	Both	Year	Girls	Boys	Both	Year
Jordan	IBRD	6	102	101	102	1990	106	102	104	2000
Egypt, Arab Rep.	IBRD	5	70	84	77	1990	92	104	99	1996
Iran, Islamic Rep.	IBRD	5	88	101	94	1990	89	95	92	1996
Bahrain	n.a.	6	101	100	101	1990	99	85	91	1996
Tunisia	IBRD	6	70	80	75	1990	90	93	91	1996
Algeria	IBRD	6	76	89	82	1990	88	93	91	1996
Syrian Arab Rep.	IBRD	6	92	103	98	1990	86	95	90	1996
United Arab Emirates	n.a.	6	98	90	94	1990	86	76	80	1996
Oman	n.a.	6	63	70	67	1989	76	76	76	1996
Kuwait	n.a.	4	55	57	56	1991	71	69	70	1996
Lebanon	IBRD	5	—	—	—	—	—	—	70	1996
Saudi Arabia	n.a.	6	56	64	60	1990	69	68	69	1996
Yemen, Rep.	IDA	6	—	—	—	—	38	77	58	2000
Iraq	IBRD	6	57	69	63	1990	52	63	57	1995
Morocco	IBRD	6	35	58	47	1991	47	63	55	1996
Qatar	n.a.	6	74	74	74	1990	43	45	44	1995
Djibouti	IDA	6	24	40	32	1990	24	36	30	1999
Libya	n.a.	9	—	—	—	—	—	—	—	—
West Bank/Gaza	IDA	10	—	—	—	—	—	—	—	—

n.a. Not applicable.
— Not available.

ically so in the Republic of Yemen (38 percent for girls, 77 percent for boys). Tunisia, on the other hand, has made clear progress in narrowing the gender gap over the decade, and Egypt and Morocco also appear to have made some progress. In a troubling number of cases in this region, however, gender parity has improved only because boys' completion rates have fallen.

SOUTH ASIA

The average primary completion rate for the South Asia region (70 percent) is the second lowest in the world, above only that of Africa. Even the higher population-weighted average of 74 percent still means that only three out of every four children

Table 2.9

South Asia: Changes in Primary Completion Rates during the 1990s

Country	Eligible for IDA/IBRD Lending	Years in Primary Cycle	PRIMARY COMPLETION RATE							
			1990				MOST RECENT YEAR			
			Girls	Boys	Both	Year	Girls	Boys	Both	Year
Maldives	IDA	5	111	111	111	1992	110	113	112	1993
Sri Lanka	IDA	5	94	106	100	1990	114	108	111	2001
India	IDA	5	61	78	70	1992	63	88	76	1999
Bangladesh	IDA	5	47	54	50	1990	72	68	70	2000
Nepal	IDA	5	29	67	49	1988	58	70	65	2000
Bhutan	IDA	7	—	—	—	—	—	—	59	2001
Pakistan	IDA	5	30	57	44	1989	—	—	59	2000
Afganistan	IDA	6	14	29	22	1989	0	15	8	1999

— Not available.

in the region complete a primary education, which for most of the countries is only a five-year system.

Two countries in the region have achieved universal primary completion: Sri Lanka and the Maldives (table 2.9). Three others have made very impressive progress: Nepal, Bhutan, and Bangladesh. Bangladesh has also made exceptional progress in gender equity, with girls' completion rates now apparently higher than boys'.

The largest country in the region, India, shows encouraging signs that strong efforts at educational improvement since the mid-1990s, especially at the state and district levels, are beginning to produce results. However, this rate of progress will need to be accelerated if the country that is home to the largest number of children out of school globally is to meet the MDG.

Trend analysis is not possible for Pakistan, but it is evident that the completion rate started the decade from a low base and with a substantial gender disparity and that progress has been minimal. The data also show the terrible erosion of primary education in Afghanistan during the 1990s, especially for girls. However, early reports for 2002 indicate a massive return of children to Afghan primary schools, with a very high share of them girls. Data for countries in this region are quite limited and, for most countries, of poor quality. Inconsistencies between official enrollment data and household surveys are not uncommon.

THE GLOBAL PROSPECTS FOR UNIVERSAL PRIMARY COMPLETION BY 2015

Figure 2.2 provides a graphic picture of global prospects for achieving the education MDG by 2015 on current trends. At the current rate of progress, by 2015 the

FIGURE 2.2 : **Global Progress in Primary Completion, 1990–2000 and Projected Trends (Country-Weighted)**

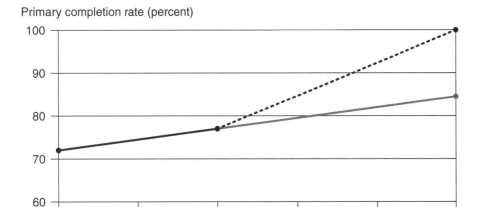

Primary completion rate (percent)

---- Required trend to achieve MDG ⎯⎯ Current trend

Source: Annex figure B.1.

global primary completion rate will not exceed 83 percent. On a population-weighted basis, the world will come closer to the MDG, with about nine out of every 10 children globally completing primary school (see annex figure B.2).

But as figures 2.3 and 2.4 show, these global averages substantially conceal the gulf that would exist across regions in 2015. Three regions—Europe and Central Asia, East Asia and the Pacific, and Latin America and the Caribbean—would come close to the goal, if not achieve it. Three other regions—South Asia, Middle East and North Africa, and Africa—would be left behind, and in the case of Africa, significantly behind. On current trends, in 2015 only 60 percent of all African children will complete a primary education.

Ultimately, the MDG will not be attained unless every child in every country has the chance to complete primary school, and change will have to happen at the level of national education systems in order to reach the goal. Therefore, the focus of this analysis is the country-by-country prospects for reaching universal primary completion by 2015.

Summary results of an exercise to project the country-by-country prospects for achieving the education MDG are shown in table 2.10. Among the world's 155 developing countries, the best available data indicate that 37 countries (including 11 low-income countries) have achieved universal primary completion. At the trend rates of progress registered over the 1990s, another 32 countries can also be expected to reach the goal. Even though, as the previous sections showed, primary completion rates clearly can go down as well as up, for the purposes of a baseline estimate we labeled as "on track" the countries whose past trends, if continued, would be sufficient to reach the goal. Thus, 69 countries (including 22 low-income ones) are likely to reach the goal by 2015.

The other 86 countries, however, are at risk of not reaching the goal. Forty-three of these countries, labeled "off track," are countries that are short of the goal

FIGURE 2.3  Primary Completion Progress in Europe and Central Asia, East Asia and the Pacific, and Latin America and the Caribbean Regions, 1990–2015, Country-Weighted

Primary completion rate (percent)

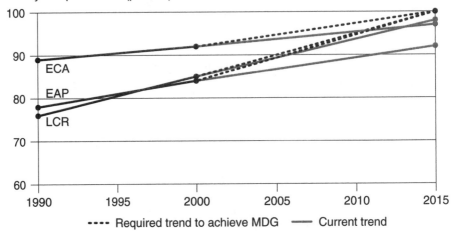

Source: Annex figure B.5.

FIGURE 2.4 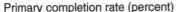 Primary Completion Progress in Africa, Middle East and North Africa, and South Asia Regions, 1990–2015, Country-Weighted

Primary completion rate (percent)

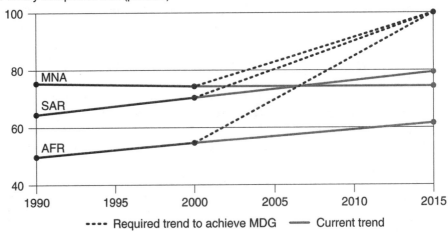

Source: Annex figure B.5.

but could be expected to reach it with a reasonable acceleration of progress or reversal of a mild declining trend. But another 27 countries, considered "seriously off track," will not even reach 50 percent primary completion by 2015 on current trends. Of these 70 off-track and seriously off track countries, 51 are low-income countries. A final set of 16 countries has no available data, including countries such

Table 2.10
....
Prospects for Universal Primary Completion by 2015

Progress Rating	Low-income Countries[a]	Middle-income Countries[b]	All Developing Countries
On track	22	47	69
Achieved UPC	11	26	37
On track to achieve UPC by 2015	11	21	32
Off track	51	19	70
Off track to achieve UPC by 2015	28	15	43
Seriously off track	23	4	27
No data available	9	7	16
At risk, subtotal	60	26	86
Total	82	73	155

a. IDA-eligible and "blend" countries (eligible for IDA and IBRD lending), plus non-member low-income countries such as Cuba.
b. IBRD-eligible plus non-member middle-income developing countries.

as Somalia, Liberia, and Libya. We consider this subgroup also at risk, for a total of 86 countries at risk of not achieving the MDG.

What would happen if all of the countries currently off track could accelerate their progress to achieve the trend improvement rate of 3 percentage points per year registered by the best-performing countries over the 1990s?[1] Although this would mean achieving and sustaining historically high rates of progress, there are three reasons why this scenario might be possible. First, in the context of a national commitment to the MDGs, countries might reassess their past performance and focus on accelerating it. Second, there is a growing number of success cases over the 1990s from which to learn. Third, linear projections of historical rate improvement in some cases lead to implausible projections, particularly in the case of declining trends (Qatar and Afghanistan would have primary completion rates below zero in 2015).

If all 70 of the off-track countries were able to increase their primary completion rates from 2003 to 2015 at an average rate of 3 percentage points per year, the world would come much closer to meeting the MDG target, but it would still fall short. Under this accelerated improvement scenario, however, all 19 of the middle-income countries—whether off track or seriously off track—would reach the goal. Thirty-five of the at-risk low-income countries would also meet the MDG. This scenario should be considered an achievable goal.

However, the 16 low-income countries that are furthest from the goal would need to achieve and sustain an even faster rate of progress in order to reach universal

---

1. This was calculated by finding the median of the trend improvement rates for the 10 best-performing IBRD countries and the 12 best-performing IDA countries, which represented the entire subset of countries averaging more than 2 percentage points per year improvement over the 1990s.

primary completion by 2015. Thirteen of the countries would need to raise primary completion rates by more than 4 percentage points per year; and three countries (including Afghanistan) would require a sustained increase of more than 5 percentage points per year. The prospects for these countries—heavily concentrated in Sub-Saharan Africa, many scarred by conflict—are sobering at best.

As can be seen from annex tables B.3 and B.4, only six countries have registered trend rates of improvement in the primary completion rate of more than 3 percentage points per year. In two of these cases, the trend was observed over less than a full decade, and in several cases, the data are somewhat questionable. In short, for the 16 countries furthest from the goal to reach it by 2015 will require completion rate progress at historically unprecedented rates.

But there is some basis for hope that the trend rates of primary completion progress *will* increase in coming years. A good number of developing countries have achieved dramatic gains in primary completion over the past decade. Faster diffusion of their experiences and knowledge about reform strategies that work may help countries at all levels of educational development to accelerate progress. In the next chapter, we analyze key features of the primary education systems in these higher performing countries, and the lessons they hold for countries at risk.

What Will It Take to Achieve Universal Primary Completion by 2015?

Chapter 2 showed that while a number of developing countries have already achieved universal primary completion and others are on track to do so by 2015, as many as 86 developing countries are at risk of not reaching the MDG on current trends. Sixty of these are very low income, or IDA-eligible, countries; 26 are middle-income countries. Any global strategy for achieving the MDG must find ways to help these at-risk countries accelerate progress.

A first step toward such a strategy is understanding what drives EFA success. Why have some countries achieved universal primary completion so much faster than others? Among those that haven't achieved it, why are some making more rapid progress? A growing body of international experience and research offers the potential for a deeper understanding of the determinants of EFA success. This chapter reviews and extends that work, based on analysis of primary completion.

DETERMINANTS OF EFA PROGRESS

For the 55 low-income countries with populations over 1 million for which sufficient data could be compiled, we compared primary gross enrollment ratios and primary completion rates in a scatter plot (figure 3.1).[1] The diagonal line in this figure, where the PCR equals the GER, represents a perfectly efficient student flow through the primary system, in a steady state. Since the completion rate obviously cannot exceed the gross enrollment ratio, all country observations fall below the line. The greater the distance from the line, the less efficient the cohort flow in that country. The closer to the origin a country falls, the lower its primary education coverage.

Figure 3.1 shows the wide range in primary completion rates across countries and equally wide disparities in the relationship between gross enrollments and primary completion. To deepen our understanding of the underlying determinants of high primary completion, we compared characteristics of the education systems in "successful" and less successful countries. To ensure that the sample of successful countries was regionally diverse and of a reasonable size (to avoid biasing the results

---

1. The starting sample included all 79 IDA-eligible countries with per capita GNI below $885 in 2000. Time limitations prevented us from analyzing the 16 low-income countries with populations below 1 million. Of the remaining 63 countries, we had to exclude Bosnia and Herzegovina, Liberia, Myanmar, Somalia, Sri Lanka, Serbia and Montenegro, Tajikistan, and Afghanistan for lack of data, although we used an alternative methodology to estimate the financing requirements for Afghanistan, as described in chapter 4. This left us with a sample of 55 countries, of which 8 have achieved or are close to UPC (defined here as completion rate through grade 5 or 6 over 90 percent) and 47 have not. See annex table A.1 for a full list of countries in the sample.

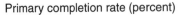

FIGURE 3.1 Primary School Completion Rates and Gross Enrollment Ratios in a Sample of Low-Income Countries, circa 1999/2000

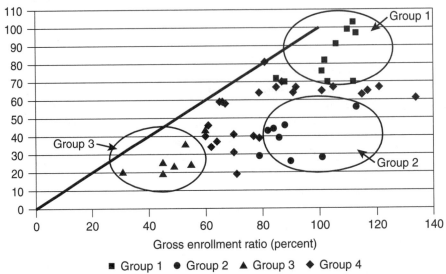

■ Group 1 ● Group 2 ▲ Group 3 ◆ Group 4

to the particular institutional features of any one region), we set a relative definition of EFA success as follows:

EFA success = GER 85 percent or above and PCR 70 percent or above.[2]

We called this set of high-performing countries Group 1. Given the wide range of GERs and PCRs in the sample, in order to sharpen the analysis we also set boundary parameters that separated the most extreme of the "unsuccessful" countries into two distinct, stylized groups:

- High inefficiency countries: GER 80 percent or above, but PCR 60 percent or lower. These countries were designated Group 2.
- Low coverage countries: GER and PCR both 60 percent or lower. This was Group 3.

When the sample was sorted on these boundaries, 10 countries fell into the category of relative EFA success (Group 1), 8 in high inefficiency (Group 2), and 7 in low coverage (Group 3). (For a full listing of the country groups see annex table A.3). Twenty-four countries fell in between the defined ranges (Group 4). Following Colclough and Lewin (1993), for each of the three groups we analyzed the domestic financing available for primary education; spending per student and key underlying cost factors; and the average repetition rate, which is a key driver of the

2. With "EFA success" defined as a completion rate over 90 percent, four of the eight countries in the sample that met the criterion were countries in Eastern Europe and Central Asia. Given the unique institutional legacy of these countries, it would bias the analysis of success factors if these countries retained this weight in the successful group. We omitted these countries from Group 1, but in order to get an adequate sample size had to set the criterion of (relative) EFA success as 70 percent completion rate or higher. European and Central Asian countries with estimated completion rates below 90 percent were retained in the simulation exercise, however. See annex table A.1.

Table 3.1

Key Education System Parameters for Adjusted Sample of 49 Countries, Grouped by Relative EFA Success

Variable	Group 1	Group 2	Group 3	Group 4	Sample Average
Number of countries	10	8	7	24	n.a.
Gross enrollment ratio (percent)	103	91	48	85	84
Primary completion rate (percent)	83	39	27	53	53
Government revenues (as percentage of GDP)[a]	20.7	21.3	17.1	19.5	19.7
Education recurrent spending					
as percentage of GDP	3.8	2.5	2.6	3.3	3.1
as percentage of government revenues	18.2	15.5	16.9	17.7	17.3
Primary education recurrent spending					
as percentage of GDP	1.7	1.3	1.3	1.4	1.5
as percentage of total education recurrent spending	47.6	52.4	50.8	47.2	48.6
Unit cost (as percentage of per capita GDP)	11.8	9.5	18.7	11.8	12.4
Average annual teacher salary (as multiple of per capita GDP)	3.3	3.4	6.9	3.5	4.0
Spending on inputs other than teachers (as percentage of primary education recurrent spending)	26.0	23.4	27.1	23.3	24.4
Pupil-teacher ratio	39:1	49:1	56:1	40:1	44:1
Private enrollments (as percentage of total)	7.3	10.5	7.7	10.4	9.4
Average repetition rate (percent)	9.5	27.8	19.5	13.3	15.8

n.a. Not applicable.
a. Government current revenues, excluding grants.

completion rate. The mean values are summarized in table 3.1. The full set of country-level data is found in annex tables A.2 through A.5.

These data show that the Group 1 (relative EFA success) countries:

• Devote a higher share of national resources to public primary education (1.7 percent of GDP compared with 1.3 percent of GDP in Groups 2 and 3)
• Exhibit about average unit costs (spending the equivalent of 11.8 percent of per capita GDP per public primary student, compared with the sample average of 12.4 percent)
• Pay annual teacher salaries averaging 3.3 times per capita GDP
• Spend slightly more than average of their recurrent budget on items other than teacher salaries
• Have a pupil-teacher ratio of about 39:1, considerably below the averages for Groups 2 and 3, and
• Have much lower repetition than the other groups (9.5 percent compared with the sample average of 15.2 percent).

Group 1's pattern may be summed up as: *healthy spending; reasonable unit costs, teacher salaries, and class size;* and *low repetition.* It is interesting to note that Group 1's higher spending on primary education derives mainly from higher spending on education as a share of the government budget, and not from higher tax revenues relative to GDP or a higher share of education spending for primary education. In fact, Group 1 devotes a lower share of education spending to the primary level than the other groups, most likely because its relatively high primary completion rates mean more demand for subsequent levels of the education system.

The countries in Group 2 have gross enrollment ratios close to those of Group 1, and also above the average for the sample. But their completion rates are only half as high as Group 1's and below the sample average. This dramatic gap between enrollments and completion is the principal stylized characteristic of Group 2. Group 2 has the highest revenue-GDP ratio in the sample, but its lower share of total public spending for education results in lower spending on primary education as a share of GDP than in Group 1, even though Group 2 countries devote a higher share of their education spending to the primary level.

Group 2's unit costs are the lowest of the sample, reflecting its higher pupil-teacher ratio (49:1, compared with Group 1's 39:1) and lower spending on non-salary items. But the defining characteristic of Group 2 is the average repetition rate of 28 percent—at any given moment, more than one of every four primary school children in these countries are repeating a grade. Thus, although unit costs are relatively low, the costs per graduate in these countries are very high.

The dropout rate in primary school, although not measured directly here, is clearly high in Group 2 countries, reflected in the fact that only 39 percent of children complete primary school, despite high access. The stylized pattern of Group 2 is therefore *inadequate spending on quality* and *excessive repetition*.

Group 3 countries are painfully far from EFA goals by any definition. The first defining characteristic of these countries is extremely low primary coverage. Less than half of all children in these countries have access to schooling, and only one child in four completes a primary education. Group 3 countries mobilize the lowest share of national resources in taxes of any of the groups, which translates into a low share of GDP for primary education, even though Group 3 countries' budget shares for education in general and for primary education in particular are close to those of the other groups.

A second defining characteristic of Group 3 countries is their dramatically higher unit costs—60–70 percent above unit costs in Groups 1 and 2. The underlying driver is also clear. Teacher salaries in Group 3 average almost seven times per capita GDP, about double the ratio of the other countries. The extremely high cost of teachers forces the education system to adjust with very high pupil-teacher ratios (56 students per teacher, compared with 39 in Group 1). Perhaps related to the very large class size, Group 3's repetition rates are also high—more than double those of Group 1, although still lower than in Group 2.

The stylized characterization of Group 3 is *low primary coverage* deriving from a disastrous combination of *low spending, high unit costs driven by extremely high teacher salaries,* and *relatively poor efficiency.*

We conducted two different batteries of statistical tests to assess the validity of these results. First, we tested whether the differences in variables across our three reference groups were statistically significant (at the 5 percent level).[3] Since the samples were small, we used non-parametric tests to compare the distribution of

---

3. We are grateful to Luis Crouch for assistance in this analysis.

Table 3.2
·····································
Regression Analysis of Key Parameters

	Coefficients	t Stat
Intercept	47.86	5.08
1990 PCR	0.40	4.14
Recurrent spending on primary education as % of GDP	12.28	3.90
Average Teacher Salary (as multiple of per capita GDP)	(4.49)	(4.02)
Pupil-teacher ratio	(0.01)	(0.04)
Average repetition rate (%)	(0.72)	(3.46)
R Square 0.81		
Observations 44		

Note: 1990 PCR values were taken from tables 2.4–2.9. All other regression variables were taken from Annex table A.2.

values for each parameter across the three groups. This analysis confirmed that the difference in primary completion rates between Groups 1, 2, and 3 was statistically significant. The difference in primary GER between Group 3 and the other groups was also statistically significant. As expected, the difference in GER between Groups 1 and 2 was not statistically significant.

This analysis also confirmed our hypothesis that key explanatory variables were differentially distributed across the three groups to a statistically significant degree. Between Groups 1 and 2, the difference in the repetition rate was significant. Between Groups 1 and 3, there were statistically significant differences in the teacher salary, the pupil-teacher ratio, and the repetition rate. And between Groups 2 and 3, there were statistically significant differences in the teacher salary and unit costs. In sum, this analysis confirmed that the three stylized groups did in fact reflect statistically significant differences in primary completion rates and in four key underlying variables: the teacher salary, the pupil-teacher ratio, the repetition rate, and unit costs.

We then used regression analysis to evaluate the explanatory power of these variables in relation to the sample as a whole. We used the baseline PCR in 1990 as a way of controlling for the independent effects that national cultural and historical factors have on the evolution of the education system.[4] As a result, the model focuses on the variables that have driven PCR progress over the decade. The regression results are summarized in table 3.2. They show three variables (in addition to the baseline PCR) as statistically significant correlates of differences in primary completion rates. One variable—primary education recurrent spending as a share of GDP—had a strong positive effect. The other two variables—the average teacher salary and the average repetition rate—had a strong negative effect.

These results suggest that indeed the notably high average teacher salaries in some countries in the sample has been a constraint to school system expansion and completion rate progress. They also confirm the more intuitively obvious fact that high repetition constrains primary completion progress. When the pupil-teacher ratio appears

4. Five countries for which we had no 1990 PCR value were omitted from the analysis.

FIGURE 3.2 : Class Size in Relation to Teacher Salary

Average class size

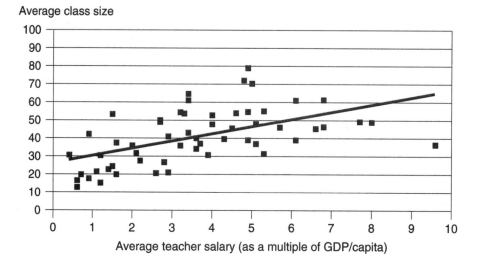

Source: Mingat 2001.

in the regression along with the average teacher salary, its additional explanatory impact is insignificant. But these two variables are correlated, and in alternative regressions without the teacher salary variable, the pupil-teacher ratio became statistically significant, similarly with a negative effect. The regression variables explained about 80 percent of the variance in primary completion rates across the sample.

When compared with the earlier analysis of the three clusters, the regression results point to spending on primary education as an important factor in completion rate outcomes in general, but not an important differentiator of the three stylized groups we analyzed (high GER: high PCR; high GER: low PCR; low GER: low PCR). Those outcome patterns appear to be more clearly linked to *how* resources are used than to the level of resources available.

In sum, these statistical tests confirmed, first, that the three groups we identified on the basis of differential GER and PCR outcomes indeed had statistically significant differences in the distribution of key underlying variables. Second, regression analysis established that three of these key variables are statistically significant factors—both positive and negative—in explaining variance in primary completion rates.

IMPLICATIONS FOR ACCELERATING EFA PROGRESS

The above analysis suggests several things. First, the pattern exhibited by the countries with the highest primary completion rates—relatively healthy spending on primary education as a share of GDP, moderate unit costs, and low repetition—may represent a broadly balanced and sustainable pattern of resource allocation that is a necessary condition for EFA progress. While it is far too strong to label the Group 1 average values for some of these parameters—such as 39 students per teacher or teacher salaries of about 3.3 times per capita GDP—as "norms" for a healthy education system, it appears that deviating very far from these values forces education systems into unhealthy adjustments, if financing is constrained.

Box 3.1 Accounting Framework for Spending on Primary Education

$$\frac{\text{Total public spending on primary education}}{\text{GDP}} = \frac{\text{Average teacher salary as a multiple of GDP/capita}}{\text{pupil-teacher ratio}}$$

$\times \ (1 - \text{share of pupils in privately financed schools}) \times (1 + \text{spending on inputs other than teachers as a multiple of spending on teacher salaries})$

$\times \ \dfrac{\text{total enrollments}}{\text{school-age population}} \times \dfrac{\text{school-age population}}{\text{total population}}$

A relatively simple accounting framework, outlined above, helps to show why increases in some of the parameters we examined must necessarily be balanced by decreases in others. This accounting identity has at least four important implications for our analysis.

First, and most fundamentally, the accounting identity establishes that the total amount of resources spent on primary education in a given country must equal the per-student spending on teachers and inputs other than teachers times the size of the school-age population enrolled. If a country wishes to increase the share of the school-age population enrolled, it must either increase its spending on primary education or find economies in the average teacher salary, the efficiency with which teachers are deployed (the pupil-teacher ratio), and/or the spending on inputs other than teacher salaries. The empirical experience in low-income countries shows that it is often impossible to increase overall spending on primary education as more children are enrolled, and that compression of spending on other inputs and increases in the pupil-teacher ratio are very commonly the balancing items.

Second, the accounting identity shows that the fiscal cost of enrollment expansion is linked to the size of the privately financed schooling sector. Note that the issue is not the extent of privately *delivered* schooling, which in many countries is a positive force for schooling expansion since government resources channeled through NGO, community, or religious schools can often help improve the efficiency of education spending. The privately *financed* schooling sector in this framework refers to the school sector that receives no government funding, typically a for-profit sector that serves only an elite segment of the population. Although the relative size of this sector is not usually an explicit policy variable for countries, it is not uncommon for constraints on public financing of primary education to lead to eroding quality in the public system and to produce a spontaneous shift in enrollments to privately financed schools. Leaving aside the question of whether or not this is good for education policy, the accounting identity shows that this can ease the fiscal costs of achieving universal primary enrollment.

Third, the accounting identity indicates that the fiscal pressure a country faces in achieving universal primary enrollment is also a function of the relative size of the school-age (7- to 12-year-old) population in the overall total—or the "schooling dependency ratio." This ratio varies widely across countries. For example, in the year 2000 in our sample, while the dependency ratio for the sample as a whole was 16 percent, it ranged from 9 percent in Georgia to 18 percent in a number of African countries (see annex table A.5). The average for the African countries was 17 percent. The projected evolution of this variable also differs across regions. Whereas for the African countries in our sample, population projections show little decline in the size of the school-age population before 2020, for many of the countries outside Africa it is expected to decline substantially—creating a "demographic bonus" that will make it relatively easier to achieve universal primary enrollment without

Box 3.1 continued

increasing the share of national resources devoted to education. The accounting identity shows that, other things being equal, Benin and Kenya will have to spend twice as much on education as a share of GDP in 2015 as will Georgia in order to achieve the same degree of primary education coverage and quality.

Finally, and importantly for the present study, while the above accounting identity explains primary education unit costs, it does not explain costs per graduate. If the target of analysis is the primary completion rate (rather than primary enrollments), the above framework must be complemented with one additional variable: the average repetition rate in primary education, which is the key driver of student flow efficiency, completion rates, and costs per graduate.

The expenditure accounting framework shown in box 3.1 explains how these variables are linked. The implications of the accounting framework are clearly borne out by our results. In a resource-constrained setting, if average teacher salaries are very much higher than 3.3 times per capita GDP, there is upward pressure on the pupil-teacher ratio (PTR)—as the data from our sample, graphed in figure 3.2, show. Although from an accounting standpoint, the same ratio of average teacher salary to PTR may be satisfied with many different values for the two variables, from a service delivery standpoint they are not all equally efficient. Research especially points to the adverse impact on student learning when average class size exceeds the range of 40–45 (Lockheed and Verspoor 1991). Thus, very high average teacher salaries balanced by large class size is not an efficient resource mix.

On the other hand, empirical evidence does not suggest that lowering class size below the range of 40–45 is an efficient investment, either. Lowering class size is costly, and research indicates that within the range of 40–45 to as low as 20 pupils per teacher, declines in class size are not correlated with appreciable gains in student learning (Lockheed and Verspoor 1991). If the pupil-teacher ratio is very much below 40, the system needs to employ many more teachers, and as the accounting framework indicates, if financing is constrained this will cause average salaries to be compressed. This is also evident from figure 3.2. This pattern is also suboptimal, as low teacher salaries are linked to other systemic problems: inability to attract the best and brightest into teaching; inability to attract teachers to work in remote or hardship areas; inability to reward high performance; chronic absenteeism caused by low teacher motivation or the need to work multiple jobs; and, in many countries, overwhelming pressures for teachers to demand fees for private tutoring or other direct payments from parents, to supplement their unsustainably low salaries.

The "right" level of teacher salary in a given country is one that is sufficient to attract qualified individuals into teaching and motivate continued good performance, given that the schools are in competition with other sectors for educated workers. The appropriate level will depend on the supply of educated individuals, the demand from all sectors of the economy (and foreign countries), and the combined attractiveness of salary and non-salary compensation (such as the shorter work hours, long vacations, and job stability that are common in the teaching profession). Only labor market data for the individual country can determine the appropriate wage for teachers in a given country context.

FIGURE 3.3 **Evolution of Average Teacher Salary in Primary Education, by Region and Subregion, 1975–2000**

Average teacher salary as a multiple of GDP/capita

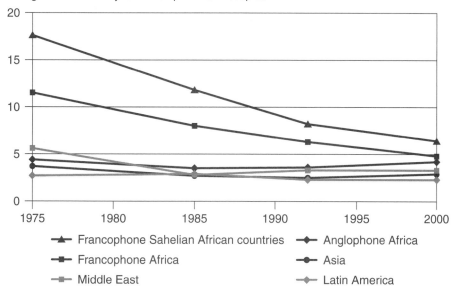

Source: Mingat 2001.

However, there are some broad global patterns. For example, the average wage paid to teachers, as a multiple of country per capita income, tends to decline as countries develop economically. The average annual wage in the sample of very low income countries we studied was in the range of 3 to 4 times per capita GDP (although with substantial variance, as we have noted). In middle-income countries in Latin America it is in the range of 2 to 2.5 times per capita GDP, and in the OECD it is currently about 1.8 times per capita GDP.

Another global pattern is the historical trend recently examined by Mingat (2001), which shows a steady decline in the average teacher wage in developing countries over the last 25 years, from 6.6 to about 3.7 times the per capita GDP (figure 3.3). While disparities across regions still exist, there has been a strong downward movement of wages in the highest wage subregions (francophone Africa and within francophone Africa, the Sahelian countries), moving toward convergence with the other regional averages over time.

The data presented in table 3.1 make clear that the incremental EFA progress from an additional unit of education spending in both the Group 2 and Group 3 countries is much lower than in Group 1. At Group 2's low internal efficiency, in fact, the challenge of reaching 100 percent primary completion (more than a doubling of current completion rates) would be staggering and the costs exorbitant. It would imply construction of nearly 80 percent more schools, with commensurate teacher hiring and other inputs, than will be needed in the Group 1 school systems to achieve the same goal. The ratio is far higher than the average repetition rate (28 percent) in these countries alone, because of the high correlation between repetition and dropout. Research shows that children who have repeated at least one grade are much more likely than non-repeaters to drop out before completing primary school, a probability that is even higher for girls. Countries such as those in Group 2 simply cannot reach the goal of universal primary completion without substantially reducing repetition.

In Group 3 countries, very high unit costs limit the impact of additional spending. The equivalent amount of additional financing in a Group 1 country and a Group 3 country (with equal GDP) could bring 160 children into school in the former for every 100 in the latter. The high cost structure of educational provision in Group 3 countries, driven by very high average teacher salaries, has clearly limited the expansion of coverage in the past and unless addressed will continue to constrain the pace of EFA progress in the future. Extremely high pupil-teacher ratios in these countries and relatively high repetition rates only make things worse, as they contribute to relatively low primary completion rates. Although the internal efficiency of Group 3 countries is not quite as low as for Group 2, it still means that of every 100 children who enter school, only a little more than half complete. For countries in Group 3 to make faster EFA progress, not just one but many parameters of their education systems need to change sharply.

A final implication of table 3.1 is that countries in our sample currently exhibit very different levels of domestic commitment to reaching the goal of universal primary completion. Underlying the average values reported in the table is considerable variance in the share of GDP being spent on primary education, from more than 3 percent in Lesotho and Zimbabwe to less than 1 percent in countries such as Pakistan, Lao PDR, and Georgia. Needless to say, an additional 1-2 percent of GDP for primary education could make a huge difference in any country. Any global strategy for accelerating EFA progress must encourage more domestic effort where it is low, and take care not to penalize the countries currently showing the strongest domestic commitment.

Ultimately, this analysis shows that the road to universal primary completion will be quite different for countries in groups 1, 2, and 3, and for the remaining countries, which essentially present milder versions of the same issues. Although none of the education systems in this low-income sample is without problems, on average the balanced education system parameters of Group 1 countries suggest they are better positioned to reach the MDG without major system change.[5]

But for the other countries in the sample, that is clearly not the case. As the Group 2 countries demonstrate, if the EFA goal were framed as universal primary enrollment, these systems would be close to achieving it. Group 3 countries are much further behind, but even they could eventually get to universal enrollment with adequate financing. But universal primary completion is another story. It is simply unachievable in education systems functioning with internal efficiency this low, no matter how much money is poured in. The inescapable conclusion reconfirms what Colclough and Lewin (1993) asserted a decade ago: the attainment of universal primary education, for most low-income countries, depends even more crucially on education system reform than on incremental financing.

---

5. It should always be recalled, however, that underlying these average values there may be considerable variance in these parameters both across countries in the group and within individual countries that would, in fact, constrain EFA progress.

Costing the MDG of Universal Primary Completion 4

A central implication of chapter 3 is, in essence, the following: *If* the MDG of universal primary completion *is* in fact achieved by 2015, it will be because at-risk countries have succeeded in transforming their education systems to function more like the systems of Group 1 countries. A concerted set of reforms would have improved those countries' resource mix and improved the learning environment for children, resulting in lower repetition and higher retention in school and culminating in a higher rate of primary completion. In countries where domestic financing for education was low (compared to other countries) it would have been increased, either by allocating more budgetary resources to education or by increasing the share of education spending devoted to primary education. And, in countries where domestic resources alone were insufficient, notwithstanding a maximum fiscal effort and strong commitment to financing primary education, external aid would have been available to fill the gap.

In this framework, it is clear that the mix of policy actions required for accelerated MDG progress differs considerably from one country to another. It follows that the domestic and external financing requirements for achieving the MDG will be highly sensitive to the extent to which, and pace at which, appropriate reforms are implemented. Therefore, the soundest basis for estimating global financing requirements is to aggregate these from country-level analysis.

We used a relatively simple simulation model to do this for the 47 low-income countries that have not yet achieved 90 percent completion or higher through grade six and for which adequate data could be compiled.[1] Our sample includes virtually all of the countries that are "seriously off track," many of the countries that are "off track," and nine countries that are currently "on track" but whose progress might be accelerated with appropriate reforms. The model was developed to test the proposition that accelerated MDG progress could be achieved by bringing core financing and service delivery parameters of education systems in at-risk countries into line with the parameters observed in countries that have higher primary completion.

A more detailed discussion of the model is presented in annex box A.1. Key distinguishing features of the model and our approach may be summarized as follows:

1. The simulations are country-specific and the cost of achieving UPC by 2015 is the aggregate of the estimates for the 47 countries analyzed.

---

1. Since the data demands are significant, we focused the analysis on countries relatively far from the goal. Afghanistan also has primary completion below this level, but since we could not obtain adequate data to run the model, we used an alternative methodology to estimate Afghanistan's financing needs (see table 4.11).

2. The target variable is primary completion—that is, the share of each school-age cohort that completes five or six years of schooling.[2]
3. The model tests a dynamic path of policy reform to improve education service delivery.
4. The model specifically responds to concerns about student learning through variables to improve quality.
5. The model responds to concerns about demand-side constraints through explicit provision for targeted subsidies to the most vulnerable populations.
6. The model specifically acknowledges the broader resource needs of the education sector by limiting spending on primary education to a sustainable share of the overall education budget.
7. The model distinguishes between recurrent and capital costs, and generates a separate estimate for each component.
8. It is assumed that universal primary completion will be achieved in all countries using public resources, with no user fees or other costs imposed on students.
9. The 2002 United Nations/World Bank projections of the school-age population through 2015 are used.
10. The baseline year for the projections is 1999 or 2000 for all countries.
11. Because of the prevalence of AIDS in many Sub-Saharan African countries, a separate effort was made to estimate the additional costs that AIDS will impose on the attainment of universal primary completion in Africa (box 4.1).

Because, as argued earlier, it is inherently impossible for many countries to achieve universal primary completion without improving the efficiency of education system functioning, our simulations expressly test how reforming key parameters of the education system in low-completion countries would affect the costs of achieving the MDG. Targets drawn from the observation of higher-performing countries are set as the goal for all countries in the sample.

The model is constructed around four sets of component variables, estimated in sequence:

- *Enrollment:* the number of pupils in publicly funded schools over the period
- *Service delivery:* the recurrent costs of services in publicly funded schools
- *System expansion:* the capital costs of needed classroom construction
- *System financing:* the volume of domestic resources mobilized for primary education.

---

2. In order to avoid biasing the financing gap estimates toward countries with longer primary cycles and away from countries with shorter ones, we modeled student flows through the equivalent of six grades in all countries where the primary cycle is longer than six or shorter than five years. In countries where the primary cycle is five years, we retained that, but adjusted budget shares accordingly.

Annex box A.1 provides more details on the stylized dynamics of the model and the full set of variables used, especially in the calculation of student enrollments over the projection period. The key observation is that, in order to achieve universal primary completion by 2015, each country must achieve 100 percent entry of school-age children into grade 1 by 2010 (for a five-grade system) or 2009 (for a six-grade system). For many countries in this sample, this implies a greatly accelerated pace of primary enrollment expansion over the coming years. The following sections focus on the model's key policy variables, which relate to service delivery, system expansion, and system financing (table 4.1).

Table 4.1

Benchmarks for Primary Education Efficiency and Quality

Variable	Sample Range in 1999/2000[a]	SAMPLE MEAN IN 1999/2000		2015 Benchmarks
		Adjusted Sample[b]	Highest-Completion Countries	
Service delivery				
Average annual teacher salary (as multiple of per capita GDP)	0.6–9.6	4.0	3.3	3.5
Pupil-teacher ratio	13:1–79:1	44:1	39:1	40:1
Spending on inputs other than teachers (as percentage of primary education recurrent spending)	0.1–45.0	24.4	26.0	33
Average repetition rate (percent)	0–36.1	15.8	9.5	10 or lower
System expansion				
Unit construction cost	$6,500–$24,000	—	—	$6,500–$12,600[c]
System financing				
Government revenues (as percentage of GDP)[d]	8.0–55.7	19.7	20.7	14/16/18[e]
Education recurrent spending (as percentage of government revenues)	3.2–32.6	17.3	18.2	20
Primary education recurrent spending (as percentage of total education recurrent spending)	26.0–66.3	48.6	47.6	50/42[f]
Private enrollments (as percentage of total)	0–77.0	9.4	7.3	10

a. The range includes data from the full sample of 55 countries.
b. The adjusted sample excludes European and Central Asian countries.
c. Construction costs in constant dollars based on "good practice" average values observed in each region.
d. Government current revenues, excluding grants.
e. Staggered targets proportional to per capita GDP.
f. Benchmark is 50 percent for a six-year primary cycle; 42 percent for a five-year cycle.

The model highlights the four most important determinants of primary education quality and unit costs per primary graduate: the average teacher salary; the pupil-teacher ratio; the share of spending on inputs other than teacher salaries; and the repetition rate. The dynamics of these four variables in the simulations depend on whether their initial values in a country are above or below the indicative framework targets. Depending on the direction of movement, adjustments to the same parameters in different country contexts are considered either "quality enhancing" or "efficiency enhancing," as discussed below.

TEACHER SALARIES

The single largest cost item in any education system is the salary bill for teachers—accounting for more than 70 percent of recurrent spending in virtually all countries in our sample and as high as 95 percent in some of them. Across these countries there is wide variation in average annual salaries, ranging from 0.6 to 9.6 times per capita GDP. Historical and institutional factors clearly influence this variable, evident in our sample from the distinct regional patterns. In the Sahelian African countries, for example, the average is more than six times per capita GDP; in the Eastern European and Central Asian countries, the average teacher salary is lower than GDP per capita. For the simulations, the 2015 target for this parameter is set at 3.5 times per capita GDP, a round figure that is close to the observed average in the highest-completion countries in our sample (3.3). However, because the average level of teacher salaries is the most politically sensitive of all the parameters, we made special assumptions about the pace at which it could be adjusted.

For countries below the target, where average salaries need to be raised in the simulation, the political dynamics are easier. Although we programmed all other parameters to reach the target values only by 2015 through gradual movement, in the case of upward adjustment of teacher salaries, we assumed that the reform could be implemented more quickly. Given the positive impact on system quality such a change could have, it would be desirable to implement it as quickly as possible. Unlike other parameters (such as lowering the pupil-teacher ratio, which requires additional classroom construction), it is also technically possible to implement an upward salary adjustment almost immediately. And, given the political popularity of such a move, implementing it sooner rather than later could help consolidate support for the reform program as a whole. More than half of the countries in the sample (28 of the 47) were cases of upward adjustment in teacher salaries.

The major constraint to this particular reform is fiscal sustainability, not political opposition. But our financing framework explicitly assumes that countries' adoption of needed reforms (that is, those consistent with this indicative framework) would constitute a "credible plan" for EFA attainment and that any resulting financing gaps would be supported by international donors. So, in order to gain the maximum quality benefits from this reform early in the projection period, and to demonstrate how much this adjustment could maximally add to the costs of EFA, we assumed that upward adjustments of average teacher salaries—where justified, in relation to the reference parameters—are implemented immediately.

Very importantly, we also implicitly assume that such a reform is implemented in an intelligent manner that would maximize the positive impact on schooling quality—for example, by establishing new and higher standards, weeding out the weakest performers, introducing a structure of incentives to reward performance, and putting in place stringent processes for new teacher selection.

The size of the upward adjustment, which is very significant in some cases (particularly in the Europe and Central Asia region), raises obvious questions about the realism of assuming that such a change could be implemented for one segment of the civil service in isolation. In these cases the simulation should be taken as simply laying out the potential cost (and international financing) implications of moving toward the benchmark value in this area.

Because raising average salaries can be expected to improve the quality of the teaching force as well as reduce absenteeism, stimulate greater accountability for teaching effectiveness, and create incentives for high performance or deployment to remote areas, it is considered a quality improvement in countries with salaries currently below the target.

For countries with teacher salaries above the target level, the adjustment downward is considered an efficiency improvement. Since it is legally and politically impossible in most contexts to reduce the salaries of civil servants, the simulations assume that this reform must be implemented in an especially gradual way. It is assumed that a new cadre of teachers is recruited at the pace of new classroom construction and paid at the target level of 3.5 times the per capita GDP, and that all recruitment of higher-paid civil service teachers is suspended. A number of countries in francophone Africa and elsewhere have in fact implemented such a reform in teacher contracting and have generally found no shortage of well-qualified candidates willing to work at the lower salary level, suggesting that the higher salary is not (or is no longer) an efficiency wage in these economies. However, the longer-term impact of this reform on teacher motivation and performance and student learning, as well as its political sustainability, are still open questions and merit further research.

In the simulations we assume that incumbent teachers continue to be paid on their current salary scale, but that over time their weight in the overall salary bill diminishes through retirement. Thus, the average salary approaches the target level. In many countries in the sample, however, it still remains above the 3.5 target by 2015.

PUPIL-TEACHER RATIO

The range in pupil-teacher ratios across the sample is similarly wide, from 13:1 to 79:1. Although the pupil-teacher ratio is not perfectly correlated with average class size in most countries, we take it as a reasonable proxy. The target value for this parameter is 40:1, based on the observed average in the high-completion countries, and also supported by a body of research on class size, as discussed in chapter 3. For countries currently above this level, the downward movement is considered a quality improvement. For countries currently below, the adjustment upward is considered an efficiency improvement. In all countries, the simulations gradually adjust the average pupil-teacher ratio to reach 40:1 by 2015. Although careful teacher deployment to achieve a 40:1 pupil-teacher ratio across all schools is one of the most powerful strategies an education system can pursue to promote efficiency and equity, geographic conditions and extremely low population density in some countries, such as Mongolia and the Republic of Yemen in this sample, can make it difficult to achieve in reality.

RECURRENT SPENDING ON INPUTS OTHER THAN TEACHERS

The amount of resources available for non-teacher-salary items is a crucial factor in education quality. Relatively abundant research indicates that books and other learning materials are highly cost-effective complementary inputs in the learning process. Although less extensively researched, teacher development and supervision, system management, student learning assessment, school maintenance, and other items clearly are also important elements in quality education systems. Yet most countries find that the pressure of teacher salaries means the budget for these other items is constantly squeezed.

The recurrent budget share for spending on items other than teacher salaries is the only variable in the study for which we set the target level (33 percent) significantly higher than the observed average for the high-completion countries (26 percent). We did so for three reasons: (a) to signal the crucial importance of increasing the quality of the learning environment in many countries, especially through the provision of more abundant and better-quality books and materials, if universal primary completion is to be reached; (b) to signal that school supervision, student assessment, teacher development, and many other system management functions are in urgent need of upgrading, and this will require considerable professionalization of these functions and imply additional cost; and (c) to signal that universal primary completion cannot be achieved in most settings without provision of special assistance to "the last 10 percent of children"—those at greatest risk of not enrolling in school or dropping out, be they girls, very poor children, children from ethnic minorities or remote rural communities, children with disabilities, or simply children falling behind in their learning because of illness or their families' needs for intermittent labor. All of these imply additional costs that school systems must be prepared to absorb. Given the projected growth of one particular set of children at risk—HIV/AIDS orphans—an additional specific provision is made for targeted subsidies to these children in the African countries (box 4.1).

The simulation model we used does not go to the level of identifying which specific inputs among the above should be prioritized in a given country; it simply creates budgetary space for a healthy level and appropriate mix of expenditures on schooling quality, efficient system management, and appropriate demand-side interventions. For virtually all of the countries in the sample, the increase in this variable to the target level is considered a quality improvement. Eight countries in the sample are currently above this level. In some cases, this is because the average teacher salary is very low. In other cases, the downward adjustment is considered an efficiency improvement, on the grounds that these budgetary resources—since they are not currently producing the desired outcomes—need to be better spent.

It should be noted that our target variable (the share of recurrent spending on inputs and items other than teacher salaries) is not equivalent to "non-salary

Box 4.1 The Incremental Costs of HIV/AIDS for Universal Primary Completion

The severity differs across countries, but today virtually all of Sub-Saharan Africa is battling HIV/AIDS. The epidemic is already affecting education systems in the region and its impact can be expected only to worsen in most countries between now and 2015. Given HIV/AIDS prevalence in Sub-Saharan Africa and what we know about its implications for teacher supply and student attendance, it is an important element to consider in efforts to cost the achievement of UPC. There are three main ways in which HIV/AIDS affects primary education systems.

First, future growth of the school-age population will be smaller in countries with AIDS prevalence than it would have been otherwise.

Second, the stock of teachers will be greatly affected. Teachers who are sick are likely to be absent and substitutes will be needed to avoid disruptions to school functioning. More teachers are likely to die while they are still in service, implying higher personnel turnover, increased need for new recruitment, and greater need for teacher training than would have been the case in the absence of AIDS.

Third, the proportion of orphans in the school-age population will be larger in an AIDS-affected country than it would have otherwise been. It has been shown that maternal and double orphans are more likely than non-orphans to drop out of school (Subbarao, Mattimore, and Plangemann 2001). Since the MDG goal is to ensure that all children complete at least five or six years of primary education, orphans are likely to need special support if that goal is to be achieved. Demand-side financing such as stipends or other support, tailored locally to best fit the needs of these children, will have to be developed.

Our costing exercise made special provisions in order to estimate these incremental impacts of AIDS. The United Nations/World Bank population projections used have been updated by demographers to reflect the impact of HIV seroprevalence on future population growth. To model the impact on teachers, we used new estimates produced by a team at the Imperial College, U.K., of AIDS incidence among teachers. This research shows that (a) teachers are affected in the same proportion as adults in general (the figures used are UNAIDS estimates between 2000 and 2015), and (b) the sickness evolves over 10 years and during that period, on average, teachers are absent 260 days.

To estimate the costs of keeping orphans in school, we used UNAIDS-provided estimates of the population of maternal and double orphans in 1999 and projected these to 2015 for 10 countries, using a simulation model developed by the Imperial College. We then extrapolated the pattern of evolution in these 10 countries to other countries in Africa by subregion (West Africa, East Africa, and southern Africa). Finally, we estimated that $50 per year would be required to maintain each maternal and double orphan in school, a cost estimate that is consistent with some of the recent programs in the region channeling financial support to such children.

Overall, these projections showed that the impacts of HIV/AIDS will add at least $287 million per year to the estimated costs of achieving the MDG in the 33 Sub-Saharan African countries in our sample.

spending." Our target variable includes all non-salary spending plus all salaries of personnel other than teachers—administrators, watchmen, cooks, and others employed by the education ministry who are not assigned to classroom teaching. In some countries where total spending on inputs other than teacher salaries is relatively high yet system outcomes are still poor, an excess of administrative staff on the payroll is a factor.

AVERAGE REPETITION RATE

Reported grade repetition in the countries studied ranges from 0 to 36 percent. High repetition is incompatible with the goal of universal primary completion, and the observed average in the higher-completion countries (9.5 percent, which is well below the sample mean) corroborates this. Accordingly, we assume that countries with average repetition rates above 10 percent would adopt policies to bring repetition gradually down to 10 percent by 2015.

The repetition rate is often viewed as an education outcome rather than a policy variable, but there is accumulating country experience with tailored strategies that are effective in reducing repetition. These strategies include introducing local language instruction in the critical early grades of primary school; designing the first two grades as a single curriculum block with strong emphasis on basic literacy and numeracy, to provide children more time to master key concepts; assigning the most experienced teachers to the first few grades; and providing cross-peer tutoring for children falling behind. It should be stressed that effective strategies such as these positively affect the repetition rate by increasing students' learning achievement. In contrast, a mandatory policy of universal promotion, which does not produce real effects on student learning, is not considered an effective strategy for reducing repetition.

The repetition rate is a key driver of the costs of primary completion, so in high-repetition countries effective policies to reduce it are crucial. For countries with repetition rates already below 10 percent, no change was made. Consistent with this, when universal primary completion is achieved in 2015, the gross enrollment ratio for the sample is 107 percent.

SYSTEM EXPANSION

Unit construction costs, expressed in 2000 constant U.S. dollars per classroom, were based on values recently reported in World Bank project appraisals and other sources for the countries in the sample. In all cases the cost estimate was for a fully furnished and equipped classroom built to adequate standards. Wherever possible, regional average "good practice" cost estimates were used. For the African countries and the European and Central Asian countries, an average figure of $8,000 was used. For South Asian and East Asian countries, an average cost of $6,500 was used. For Haiti, Honduras, and Nicaragua, values of $11,000–$12,000 were used. The highest estimate in the sample—$12,600 for the Republic of Yemen—is considered by regional experts a good practice target for the country and is considerably below past unit construction costs.

For the countries outside Africa in the sample, system expansion was projected from actual data on the baseline number of classrooms. However, it was not possible to obtain these data for all of the African countries, and an assumption had to be made that the number of teachers was a rough proxy for the number of functioning classrooms. This assumption is somewhat problematic, as virtually all school systems in this sample have some degree of double-shift or even triple-shift utilization of classrooms, which means that the simulations underestimate the true incremental capital costs of reaching the UPC goal.

For all of the countries, we projected the number of additional classrooms needed to ensure universal primary completion by 2015 on the assumption of 40 students per classroom and one classroom per teacher. The projections, therefore, implicitly assume that the existing stock of classrooms is adequate, even though the baseline number of classrooms in some countries in our sample includes those as rudimentary as "classrooms" under a tree. Thus, it is important to note that the very real needs for upgrading current school facilities to the standards we assume for the future are not captured in our simulations. However, we attempt to make an adjustment for this in the final section of this chapter.

Similarly implicit in the simulations is the assumption that other system infrastructure (district and central administrative offices, teacher resource centers, teacher training institutes, and so forth) exists at the beginning of the projection period in sufficient quantity and adequate quality to support system functioning. Although our simulation target for *recurrent* spending on inputs other than teacher salaries is designed to cover operating and maintenance costs for *all* school system infrastructure—and not only classrooms—our capital cost estimates are limited to the need for incremental classroom construction, and do not capture the need for incremental expansion of other system facilities. This also clearly underestimates what may be significant needs in the countries analyzed. It was impossible within our time frame to obtain the country-specific baseline data on the quantity and quality of existing school system infrastructure, other than classrooms, that would be required to project the incremental needs in these other areas. However, in the final section of this chapter, we also make a rough estimate of these needs for the sample.

Thus, the classroom construction requirements projected in these simulations must be understood as a *minimum* estimate of the total capital costs these countries will likely need to incur in order to achieve fully functional school systems capable of realizing universal primary completion. More detailed, country-specific work is needed to estimate infrastructure and rehabilitation needs more precisely. It can be assumed that in this set of countries these additional needs are significant.

SYSTEM FINANCING

DOMESTIC RESOURCE MOBILIZATION

The financing block of the model estimates the domestic resource flows for primary education over the projection period. In 1999/2000, public spending on primary education ranged from 0.2 to 3.3 percent of GDP in the countries studied, a huge range. In this costing exercise, it is assumed that external financing will only be available to those countries that show evidence of a strong domestic commitment to achieving universal primary completion by allocating a fair share of national resources to the goal.

But what constitutes a "fair share"? In order to ensure that our target parameters for domestic resource mobilization did not penalize the poorest countries with the most fragile tax bases, we decomposed the share of GDP spent on primary education into three underlying variables and set separate targets for each:

- The revenue-GDP ratio, reflecting differences in the overall size of the public sector and the national resource base
- The share of domestic revenues allocated to education, an indication of public priority given to education
- The share of the education budget allocated to primary education, an indication of specific commitment to universal primary completion.

Since the lowest-income countries typically have more difficulty mobilizing tax revenues than do wealthier countries, we staggered the target values for the revenue-GDP ratio in 2015—either 14 percent, 16 percent, or 18 percent of GDP, depending on the level of per capita GDP.

For the second variable—the share of government revenues devoted to education—we set a target of 20 percent, a round number reasonably close to the 18.2 percent average for the high-completion countries in our sample.

For the third variable—the primary education share of total education spending—we set a target of 50 percent for countries with a six-year primary cycle, again a round number slightly above but consistent with the reference countries. For countries with a five-year primary cycle, a pro-rated share of 42 percent was used.

Where countries' current values were lower than these targets, they were adjusted upward—in essence, asking the country to increase the domestic resources it is mobilizing for EFA. But there were several country cases where spending on one or more of these subcomponents currently exceeds the targets. While from the standpoint of an EFA costing exercise it is tempting to maintain these levels—which would unquestionably aid in reaching the goal—we were concerned that some of the spending patterns may not be sustainable over the medium term. And, if the higher levels of resource mobilization were retained, the external financing requirements estimated for these countries in the simulation would be correspondingly lower. This seemed a perverse outcome, effectively penalizing the countries with the highest domestic commitment to EFA attainment and rewarding those doing less.

Thus, we opted for a scenario (C2) that put all countries on an equal financial footing by instituting the target values, even when this forced an artificial decline in spending on primary education from current levels. However, because the overall financing estimates are so sensitive to these variables, and because one of these—the tax-GDP relationship—is exogenous to the education sector, we also ran two sensitivity analyses, in which countries' higher spending levels were assumed to persist. Under scenario C1, we allowed higher-than-target spending on education and primary education to be maintained. Under scenario C3, we retained higher-than-target tax-GDP ratios. The assumptions in each scenario are summarized in table 4.2. As expected, scenarios C1 and C3 did change the results for particular countries and lowered the size of the overall financing gap.

Table 4.2
....
Alternative Scenarios for Domestic Resource Mobilization

Simulation Variable	TARGETS FOR 2015 UNDER THREE ALTERNATIVE SCENARIOS		
	C1	C2	C3
Government revenues as percentage of GDP	14/16/18[a]	14/16/18	14/16/18, but if current share exceeds 18% it stays unchanged
Public spending on education as percentage of government recurrent revenues, excluding grants	20–26[b]	20	20
Primary education spending as percentage of total public recurrent education spending[c]	If current share is higher than 50/42 it stays unchanged	50/42	50/42

a. Staggered targets proportional to per capita GDP.
b. Values below 20 percent are increased to a target of 20 percent by 2015. Values above 26 percent are reduced to a target of 26 percent by 2015. Values in the range of 20–26 percent remain unchanged.
c. The target is 50 percent for six-year primary systems and 42 percent for five-year systems.

PRIVATE ENROLLMENTS AS A SHARE OF TOTAL

The share of enrollments in privately financed schools has an important impact on public sector financing requirements. A target for the share of private enrollments was set at 10 percent in these simulations. This share is relatively close to the observed average for the high-completion group (7.3 percent) and for the sample (9.4 percent), but the rationale for this target was more conceptual than empirical.

The conceptual framework of this report is that attainment of universal primary completion is a responsibility of national governments and that the children in any country that are currently out of school are those least able to contribute to the costs of education. As countries progress toward universal primary completion, the target populations are increasingly poor, remote, and marginalized. Cost recovery and cost sharing are less appropriate financing strategies for these populations than for any other segment. Therefore, we assume that no user fees or other costs are imposed on public school students, and on top of this we make explicit provision for targeted subsidies to the most vulnerable groups.

Government responsibility to *finance* universal primary completion, however, does not imply that all schooling must or should be publicly *provided*. To the contrary, the target parameters we use are very consistent with service delivery arrangements that channel government financing to private providers, especially to NGO or community-run schools. For simplicity, enrollments in these alternative schools are classified as "public" in our simulations, since they are publicly funded.

However, we assume that in every country the uppermost income decile *does* have the capacity to contribute to the financing of primary education. In virtually all countries an elite private school sector exists, serving from 5 to 15 percent of primary students. To avoid having scarce public resources subsidize elite groups in a setting where EFA has not been achieved, we assume that 10 percent of primary enrollments in all countries modeled will be privately financed. In countries where the current share of enrollments in private schools is below this level, the increase to 10 percent in the simulation is a resource gain.

In many countries in the sample, the private share of primary enrollments is currently above 10 percent, usually reflecting the limited supply or poor quality of public schooling. Since our simulation exercise explicitly models a scenario of quality improvement and expansion in public primary education, it may be expected that some shift in enrollments back to public schooling would occur. However, an alternative scenario in which a significant number of students are served by private providers that are publicly subsidized is also consistent with the simulations. In the latter case, enrollments in for-profit private schools are assumed to be no more than 10 percent of all enrollments, but an unspecified number of children could be enrolled in nonprofit private schools, financed with public education resources.

COUNTRY-LEVEL SIMULATION RESULTS

For each country in the exercise, the adjustment from initial parameters to the full set of target parameters effectively generates a threefold strategy of:
- Quality improvement
- Efficiency improvement
- Increased domestic resource mobilization.

The specific elements of the strategy in each of these three broad areas depend upon the country's initial conditions, the number of parameters that would require adjustment toward the benchmarks, and the direction of the adjustment required. It should be noted that the combined effect of the above strategies is the achievement of an equitable primary education system, implicit in the goal of universal primary completion.

In order to demonstrate in each country case the relative need for either quality improvement, efficiency improvement, or increased domestic resource mobilization, the model generates separate results in each area. For each country, these are summarized in an analytical table that shows the hypothetical financing gap under each of the three sets of policy measures. These disaggregated financing gaps are hypothetical because in reality it would be ill-advised as well as unrealistic to try to implement one or another of the scenarios in isolation. First, there are clear interaction effects among these different reforms which demand that, from a technical standpoint, actions be taken concurrently. For example, it would be very difficult to achieve reductions in the repetition rate (an efficiency reform) in the absence of actions to improve quality (lowering class size, increasing spending on textbooks and teacher training, and so forth). Second, from a financial standpoint it would be completely unsustainable to implement quality reforms that generate high incremental costs (such as an increase in average teacher salaries) without the key counterbalancing efficiency reform of an increase in the pupil-teacher ratio, where that is below the target. Nonetheless, presenting the results in this format helps to clarify the impact of the various reforms needed in a specific country context. For each country, the "status quo" parameters are contrasted with:

Scenario A (quality reform): the change in parameters and resulting annual financing gap when *only quality* measures are implemented

Scenario A+B (quality plus efficiency reforms): the change in parameters and resulting annual financing gap when *both quality and efficiency* measures are implemented

Scenario A+B+C (quality, efficiency, and financing reforms): the change in parameters and resulting annual financing gap when *quality and efficiency and system financing* parameters are adjusted.

The model also generates a second analytical table for each country that compares the total cost estimates for reaching the MDG target for that country with the potential financing sources. Recurrent and capital costs are presented separately. Potential financing sources are also disaggregated, as follows:

• *Domestic resources:* recurrent, capital, and total
• *Gap for external financing:* recurrent, capital, and total.

The simulations assume that *all* of the recurrent costs in each country case will be covered as much as possible by domestic resources. Only if they exceed domestic financing are the remaining recurrent costs presented as part of the gap for external financing. This is in recognition of the fact that donor assistance is more often channeled to capital costs than to recurrent budget support. Finally, for the African countries, the special incremental costs that can be attributed to the impact of AIDS in these countries are presented as a separate line item. We were not able to obtain sufficient data to extend the AIDS analysis to all countries in the sample, but this could certainly be done in the future.

The full set of analytical tables for the 47 low-income countries modeled is presented in annex C. The results for four sample countries are discussed below in order to demonstrate how the financing estimates are generated, to show how the indicative framework can serve as a diagnostic tool for countries seeking to accelerate MDG progress, and to highlight some of the important limitations of this exercise.

INDIA

The largest country in the sample is India, with approximately 100 million children of primary school age. Although the officially reported gross enrollment ratio in 1999 was 100 percent, it is commonly estimated that 20–30 million primary-age children in India are not in school. By these estimates, India alone accounts for as much as one-quarter of the estimated 113 million children worldwide not attending primary school—or one-quarter of the global challenge of achieving Education for All. The proxy primary completion rate we estimated for India (76 percent in 1999) confirms that about 25 percent of children do not complete the five-year primary cycle. Current data on the schooling profile are not available, but a reasonable estimate is that roughly 5–10 percent of children never enter primary school (mainly rural children, scheduled tribes, scheduled castes, and girls), and of those who enter school, about 20 percent drop out before completing, producing a primary completion rate on the order of 76 percent. This is broadly consistent with national survey data showing that about 20 percent of children aged 6–10 are not attending school (World Bank 2002e).

Survey data also suggest that either the official 100 percent GER estimate is overstated, or that primary school repetition is higher than officially reported and there are a significant number of overage children in the primary schools. For the purposes of our India simulation, we assumed the latter. There are clearly areas of classroom overcrowding in India and small population areas where schools are not available. However, overall it appears that the Indian government's policy commitment to site a school within one kilometer of every community with more than 300 people has achieved a very high degree of access to primary schooling. The greater issue is the high dropout rate before completion due to low schooling quality and high household demand for child labor.

Although a 76 percent completion rate was sufficient to place India among the Group 1 countries we used to estimate the target parameters (see chapter 3), it is clear that India, at the low end of that group, still has a substantial way to go to meet the MDG target of universal primary completion. The primary completion rate increased over the 1990s from an estimated 70 percent[3] to 76 percent, which is undeniable progress, but this trend rate (about 0.9 percentage point per year) would put India's PCR at only 90 percent in 2015. More encouraging are household survey data that indicate strong progress on gender equity, with the share of rural girls aged 6–10 enrolled in primary school increasing from 55 to 75 percent between 1993 and 1999, a truly remarkable achievement.

The continuing challenge for a very large, ethnically diverse, and federal country such as India is both to accelerate overall primary education progress and to ensure that gains are evenly distributed across a highly decentralized and, as of today, unequal education system. The service delivery and financing parameters we focus on vary considerably across different states and districts in India. Teacher salaries, for example, are negotiated at the state level in India, but are pegged to national benchmarks and vary widely in relation to state-level per capita GDP, a phenomenon that has led states such as Rajasthan and Bihar to introduce para-teachers at lower wages. Our simulation, which relies on a single target ratio of salary to per capita GDP, cannot capture the differing degrees of salary adjustment (either upward or downward) that may in fact be needed in many parts of India. Similarly, while the pupil-teacher ratio averaged nationally is 52:1, it ranges from below 30:1 in some states to 59:1 in others. This in effect results in an underestimate by the model of the true number of teachers that

---

3. Because of discrepancies in official enrollment data, we estimated the 1990 completion rate for India on the basis of data from the National Family Health Survey, rather than official enrollment statistics, as the latter produced a value that India experts considered artificially high. The 1999 completion rate is calculated according to our standard methodology.

would be required to achieve the target ratio of 40:1 in all parts of the country by 2015 if, in reality, teachers cannot be redeployed or students reassigned across states.

Tables 4.3 and 4.4 summarize the simulation results. Under the quality enhancement simulation generated for India (scenario A), the key actions would be the hiring of additional teachers to reduce the number of pupils per teacher from 52 to 40 by 2015; a slight increase in average teacher salaries, from 3.4 to 3.5 times per capita GDP; and a substantial increase in spending on inputs other than teacher salaries, which would increase from 23 to 33 percent of the recurrent primary budget (table 4.3). The combined effect of the three quality adjustments and the impact of growth on factor costs is that per-pupil spending almost triples over the period to 2015 in constant dollars (from $35 in 2000 to $101 in 2015), with a particularly large increase in spending on complementary inputs to improve school quality, such as books, materials and system management, and possibly demand-side subsidies to target populations.

Under the quality plus efficiency enhancement scenario (A+B), the major change would be policy actions to reduce repetition gradually over the period from the starting level, estimated at 20 percent based on data from states and districts, to the target of 10 percent. This improvement in system internal efficiency would "finance" some of the costs of quality improvement, reducing the estimated financing gap.

However, financing gap estimates generated by this model for India should be interpreted carefully and taken as an indicative exercise only. While it may give an overall sense of the broad policy priorities and the direction of change required, a modeling exercise based on national average indicators may significantly underestimate the true costs of attaining the indicative framework parameters, since in a decentralized education system, quality "surpluses" in some parts of the country that push up the national averages are not transferable to lower-quality states and districts. An excess of classrooms in Kerala in reality will not reduce the need to build more schools in Bihar, but in a simple simulation model such as the one we used, this is effectively what happens.

Virtually every country in the sample faces similar equity issues in service delivery and financing across different subregions, but in federal education systems these issues are harder to resolve both in principle and in practice. Although it may not be easy politically, in a unitary system disparities across regions in the pupil-teacher ratio or spending allocations can be managed with teacher redeployment and adjusted allocation rules. In federal systems, the scope for such administrative redeployment and/or fiscal redistribution typically does not exist, at least in the short term. Reforms of the "rules of the game" in these areas at the federal and state levels may take years to negotiate and enact.

Thus, the India simulation underestimates the true magnitude of reforms and new investments needed in some subnational entities in order to bring service delivery quality and efficiency in all parts of the country to our benchmarks. More precise estimates for India should be developed through modeling exercises at the subnational level and aggregation of these resource gaps.

Table 4.3

India: MDG-2015 Financing Gap under Alternative Policy Measures

Policy Scenario[a]		A: Quality Measures			B: Efficiency Measures	C: Financing Measures				
		Pupils per Teacher	Spending on Inputs Other than Teachers[b]	Average Annual Teacher Salary (as Multiple of Per Capita GDP)	Average Repetition Rate	Government Revenues[c] As % of GDP	% for Education	Primary Education Recurrent Spending[d]	Private Enrollments (As % of Total)	Annual Financing Gap[e]
Status quo		52	23.2%	3.4	20.0%	21.2%	12.4%	32.1%	12.5%	146
A only		40	33.3%	3.5						2,470
A + B		40	33.3%	3.5	10.0%					1,782
"Best practice":	C1	40	33.3%	3.5	10.0%	16.0%	20.0%	42.0%	10.0%	67
	C2					16.0%	20.0%			67
A + B +	C3					21.2%	20.0%			28

Note: Shaded cells denote no change from values directly above.

a. Policy scenarios are: A for quality improvement, B for efficiency improvement, and three alternative resource mobilization scenarios (C1, C2, and C3). The combination of scenarios A+B+C is considered "best practice"

b. As a share of primary education recurrent spending.

c. Current revenues, excluding grants.

d. As a share of total education recurrent spending.

e. In millions of 2000 U.S. dollars. Calculated as the difference between the total cost of service delivery under the specific policy scenario and the total resources for primary education mobilized domestically.

A simulation exercise at the national level is, however, important on the resource mobilization side, given the crucial role of federal authorities in assuring fiscal equity across decentralized entities. In this case, it shows that India's fiscal parameters are quite far from the targets. While government revenues as a share of GDP (21.2 percent) exceed the 16 percent target we set for countries with its level of per capita GDP, spending on education is very low compared with the indicative benchmarks. The share of the consolidated state and federal recurrent budget spent on education in 1999, at 12.4 percent, is substantially below our target value of 20 percent. The share of education spending allocated to the primary level, 32.1 percent, is also low, compared to the target of 42 percent for a five-year primary system.[4] Thus, even though the tax-GDP ratio in India is quite high, the combined effect of low allocations for education in general and for primary education in particular is that public spending on primary education in India amounts to only 1.0 percent of GDP, compared to 1.7 percent of GDP for high-completion countries.

Thus, the indicative framework points to insufficient allocation of public resources as a root cause of India's incomplete primary education coverage and the quality problems that lead a relatively high share of children to drop out before completing primary school.

The United Nations/World Bank population projections for India show fertility declines after 2010 resulting in a stable primary school-age population between 2000 and 2015. This helps to ease the financing requirements for meeting the MDG substantially. But to lower the pupil:classroom ratio and improve school quality, the simulations indicate that India will need to spend at least $435 million per year on classroom construction. There may also be significant short-term needs for upgrading and rehabilitation of existing schools and core system infrastructure that are not captured in our simulations, for India or for any other country.

The simulation exercise also points to a need for increased recurrent expenditures to achieve universal primary completion—with considerably higher per-student spending on additional teachers, books, better system management, demand-side stipends, and other inputs. Under the quality and efficiency scenarios we model, these improvements in school quality and policy actions to reduce repetition effectively produce a steady improvement in the efficiency of student flows. The private share of enrollments also declines slightly, from 12.7 percent currently to 10 percent by 2015. Although the total financing needed over the period is close to $8 billion per year, the simulation indicates that if India's resource allocation for education and for primary education were to increase to the target values by 2015, domestic resources could cover the great bulk of these needs (table 4.4). However, a financing gap of between $200 and $500 million per year would remain, concentrated in the early years of the period (see annex table A.8). Annualized over the entire projection period, India's external gap would be $67 million per year.

---

4. In some states, the official primary cycle is still only four years, so this share could legitimately be slightly lower. However, since the government has established eight years as the official duration of compulsory schooling, it is reasonable to analyze system completion rates and costs through grade 5.

Table 4.4

India: MDG-2015 Cost Estimates and Sources of Financing under "Best Practice" Policies and Alternative Resource Mobilization Scenarios

(millions of 2000 constant U.S. dollars)

Cost Item	Period	Scenario	Domestic Resources Mobilized	Cost of MDG-2015			Financing Sources					
							Domestic Resources			Gap for External Financing		
				Recurrent	Capital	Total	Recurrent	Capital	Total	Recurrent	Capital	Total
Education service delivery	Cumulative, 2001–2015	C1	115,278	109,754	6,525	116,279	109,754	5,524	115,278	0	1,001	1,001
		C2	115,278	109,754	6,525	116,279	109,754	5,524	115,278	0	1,001	1,001
		C3	115,858	109,754	6,525	116,279	109,754	6,104	115,858	0	422	422
	Annual	C1	7,685	7,317	435	7,752	7,317	368	7,685	0	67	67
		C2	7,685	7,317	435	7,752	7,317	368	7,685	0	67	67
		C3	7,724	7,317	435	7,752	7,317	407	7,724	0	28	28
AIDS-related costs	Annual	C1		0		0	0		0	0		0
		C2		0	0	0	0	0	0	0	0	0
		C3		0	0	0	0	0	0	0	0	0
Both items	Annual	C1	7,685	7,317	435	7,752	7,317	368	7,685	0	67	67
		C2	7,685	7,317	435	7,752	7,317	368	7,685	0	67	67
		C3	7,724	7,317	435	7,752	7,317	407	7,724	0	28	28

Note: "Best practice" policies refer to the combination of scenarios A + B + C. Shaded cells denote no change from values directly above.

The model generates a single target for domestic revenue mobilization for primary education, but the financing of primary education in India is a concurrent central government and state responsibility, with only about 12 percent of total spending at the central government level. In a decentralized fiscal context such as this, the indicative framework financing targets can in effect only be achieved if: (a) states currently spending below the indicative targets are able to increase their spending; (b) the central government increases its spending on education and transfers the increment to the neediest states; or (c) states with higher fiscal capacity mobilize increased resources and the central government develops the fiscal intermediation capacity to equalize education resources across states.

Analyzing the fiscal and political feasibility of these or other options in the Indian context is beyond the scope of this study. But the case of Brazil may be instructive. After decades of severe disparities in education spending and quality in a context of decentralized education financing, Brazil made major national strides after a 1997 constitutional reform set an equal per-student funding floor for primary education across the country (box 2.2) and redistributed resources across states and municipalities accordingly. Our simulation for India points to reform of primary education finance as a key issue for the country in order to achieve the MDG by 2015.

Finally, it should be noted that our simulation results for India are significantly different from the estimates for India in an earlier World Bank financing gap calculation for the education MDG (Devarajan, Miller, and Swanson 2002). In that estimate, India accounts for more than $2 billion of an estimated global financing gap of $10 million to $15 million per year. But that estimate assumed no change in unit costs or system efficiency, and made no assumptions about the capacity for domestic resource mobilization The three hallmarks of our approach—adjusting for population trends, examining the potential for efficiency improvements, and, most importantly, establishing an expectation that scarce donor assistance will not substitute for an appropriate commitment of domestic resources to EFA—greatly affect the size of our estimated financing gap for India and a number of other countries in our sample.

PAKISTAN

As with India, official education statistics for Pakistan are limited and present internal inconsistencies. In Pakistan's case, though, it is clear that a significant share of children do not today have access to primary school: of the estimated 19.2 million children in the school-age population in 2000, only 12.5 million are enrolled, for a GER of 65 percent. Although data are sketchy, we estimate a completion rate in 2000 of around 59 percent. Pakistan also has a school-age population that is projected to continue to grow, and would be about 15 percent higher in 2015 than in 2000.

As table 4.5 shows, service delivery in the public system in Pakistan is currently far from our benchmarks. Although average teacher salaries, at 3.6 times per capita GDP, are relatively close to the target, spending on inputs other than teacher salaries, at 19 percent of recurrent spending, is well short of the 33.3 percent target. Teacher salaries would decline slightly and spending on other inputs would rise substantially under the quality improvement scenario for Pakistan.

Table 4.5

Pakistan: MDG-2015 Financing Gap under Alternative Policy Measures

Policy Scenario[a]		A: Quality Measures			B: Efficiency Measures	C: Financing Measures				
		Pupils per Teacher	Spending on Inputs Other than Teachers[b]	Average Annual Teacher Salary (as Multiple of Per Capita GDP)	Average Repetition Rate	Government Revenues[c]		Primary Education Recurrent Spending[d]	Private Enrollments (As % of Total)	Annual Financing Gap[e]
						As % of GDP	% for Education			
Status quo		32	19.3%	3.6	6.2%	16.7%	10.2%	51.8%	29.4%	285
A only		32	33.3%	3.5						450
A + B		40	33.3%	3.5	6.2%					261
"Best practice":	C1	40	33.3%	3.5	6.2%	16.0%	20.0%	42.0%	10.0%	204
A + B +	C2					16.0%	20.0%			204
	C3					16.7%	20.0%			173

Note: Shaded cells denote no change from values directly above.

a. Policy scenarios are: A for quality improvement, B for efficiency improvement, and three alternative resource mobilization scenarios (C1, C2, and C3). The combination of scenarios A + B + C is considered "best practice".

b. As a share of primary education recurrent spending.

c. Current revenues, excluding grants.

d. As a share of total education recurrent spending.

e. In millions of 2000 U.S. dollars. Calculated as the difference between the total cost of service delivery under the specific policy scenario and the total resources for primary education mobilized domestically.

The reported pupil-teacher ratio, at 32:1, is quite low compared to the benchmark of 40:1. It is unusual to see such a low pupil-teacher ratio in a country that has not reached universal primary coverage, but there has been a significant shift of enrollments to private schools in Pakistan in recent years, driven by the erosion of quality in the public system. While about 29 percent of total primary enrollments are now in fully private—that is, privately financed—schools, it appears that employment in the public schooling sector has not experienced any corresponding retrenchment. The share of privately financed primary enrollments in Pakistan today is quite extraordinary for a low-income country and means that the subsector is serving far more than the elite in Pakistan.

Under the quality plus efficiency (A + B) scenario, Pakistan would steadily increase the pupil-teacher ratio in the public system to 40:1 by 2015. This could in effect be accomplished in two very different ways. One route would be a substantial improvement in the management and quality of the public schools that would provoke a spontaneous shift of students back to the public system. But a second possible route would be a greater reliance on privately managed schools for service delivery, given evidence of these schools' higher efficiency.

Under the latter route, the government would transfer capitation grants to nonprofit private schools that serve low-income populations. Even though the services would remain privately managed, by our definition the enrollments in these schools would be "public." The rationale for public subsidization is that as Pakistan, like other countries in our sample, moves to increase its primary completion rate, it must reach increasingly poor, rural, and disenfranchised populations. Expecting these groups to finance the full cost of their primary education is not only inequitable, it would also, we know from research, impede the attainment of the goal. It is important to note that this assumes no subsidies for private schools serving the highest-income students, so there would still remain a fully private (that is, privately financed) sector accounting for 10 percent of total primary enrollments in 2015.

As table 4.5 shows, even under the status quo case, Pakistan would have a resource gap of $285 million annually, because of the projected increase in the school-age population and the fact that not all children are enrolled today. The table also shows that if Pakistan were to implement the quality measures only, this financing gap would swell to $450 million per year. However, if the complementary efficiency measure of an increase in the pupil-teacher ratio were also achieved, the gap would be lowered to $261 million per year.

On the resource mobilization side, Pakistan's ratio of government revenues to GDP is currently at the target value of 16 percent. However, the share of the budget going to education, about 10 percent, is far below the 20 percent target. And, even though spending on primary education—52 percent of the education budget in Pakistan—is above the target of 42 percent for a five-year primary system, the net effect of these patterns is a low ratio of education spending to GDP, at 0.9 percent currently.

Thus, when the indicative targets for domestic resource mobilization are introduced in the simulations, Pakistan's spending on primary education increases as a share of GDP. But an estimated financing gap of $204 million per year would

Table 4.6

Pakistan: MDG-2015 Cost Estimates and Sources of Financing under "Best Practice" Policies and Alternative Resource Mobilization Scenarios

(millions of 2000 constant U.S. dollars)

Cost Item	Period	Scenario	Domestic Resources Mobilized	Cost of MDG-2015			Financing Sources					
							Domestic Resources			Gap for External Financing		
				Recurrent	Capital	Total	Recurrent	Capital	Total	Recurrent	Capital	Total
Education service delivery	Cumulative, 2001–2015	C1	15,919	16,748	2,224	18,972	15,919	0	15,919	829	2,224	3,053
		C2	15,919	16,748	2,224	18,972	15,919	0	15,919	829	2,224	3,053
		C3	16,373	16,748	2,224	18,972	16,373	0	16,373	375	2,224	2,599
	Annual	C1	1,061	1,117	148	1,265	1,061	0	1,061	55	148	204
		C2	1,061	1,117	148	1,265	1,061	0	1,061	55	148	204
		C3	1,092	1,117	148	1,265	1,092	0	1,092	25	148	173
AIDS-related costs	Annual	C1		0		0	0		0	0		0
		C2		0	0	0	0	0	0	0	0	0
		C3		0	0	0	0	0	0	0	0	0
Both items	Annual	C1	1,061	1,117	148	1,265	1,061	0	1,061	55	148	204
		C2	1,061	1,117	148	1,265	1,061	0	1,061	55	148	204
		C3	1,092	1,117	148	1,265	1,092	0	1,092	25	148	173

Note: "Best practice" policies refer to the combination of scenarios A + B + C. Shaded cells denote no change from values directly above.

remain, with about three-quarters of this total needed for new classroom construction (table 4.6).

ARMENIA

Of the low-income countries in Europe and Central Asia in our starting sample, only three appear not to have achieved universal primary completion (through sixth grade)—Armenia, Georgia, and Moldova—although data for all countries in this region are considered problematic. According to official statistics, Armenia's gross enrollment ratio in the year 2000 was over 100 percent, but the completion rate through sixth grade was below 70 percent.[5]

The core service delivery parameters in Armenia, Georgia, and Moldova all deviate sharply from the benchmarks in a pattern that is common to ECA countries: the number of teachers employed (relative to the student population) is far higher than in other countries and the average teacher salary is far lower. In Armenia, the average teacher salary would increase dramatically, from 0.6 to 3.5 times per capita GDP, as a quality measure in the simulation. But as a corresponding efficiency measure, the current 13:1 pupil-teacher ratio would rise to 40:1, also a tremendous adjustment—even if phased in gradually over a 15-year period. Given no projected growth of the school-age population, the clear implication is that the number of teachers employed would decline gradually but significantly over the period.

Although this could probably be handled through attrition and selective retrenchment linked to the introduction of new certification or performance standards, the management challenge would be significant. The realism of such a dramatic increase in teacher salaries must be considered questionable as well, in a broader civil service context, and in light of current fiscal pressures in Armenia (recall, however, that our approach assumes that incremental external resources will finance any resulting gaps). But the simulation serves to illuminate the root causes of Armenia's key educational issues: excess staffing; inadequate salaries leading to low teacher motivation, absenteeism, and informal shifting of costs to families; and high operating and maintenance costs for an inefficient number of schools and classrooms, which divert resources from other needed areas such as modernization of curriculum and learning materials, teacher retraining, and system management.

On the resource mobilization side, the simulations show that in addition to an inefficient pattern of spending, Armenia's level of spending on primary education as a share of GDP is inadequate. Armenia's revenue-GDP ratio is close to the target, but the budget share for education, at 15 percent, is below the 20 percent benchmark. This is the principal financing variable that would adjust in the simulation, as the share of education spending going to the primary level is already at the target.

The upward adjustment in the budget share for education by 2015 generates significant additional resources. Nonetheless, given the magnitude of the spending increases required for increased teacher salaries, the model projects a financing gap

---

5. Armenia's primary cycle is officially three years, but for the purposes of this simulation, we adjusted values for all countries to the equivalent of a six-year primary system.

Table 4.7

Armenia: MDG-2015 Financing Gap under Alternative Policy Measures

Policy Scenario[a]		A: Quality Measures			B: Efficiency Measures	C: Financing Measures				
		Pupils per Teacher	Spending on Inputs Other than Teachers[b]	Average Annual Teacher Salary (as Multiple of Per Capita GDP)	Average Repetition Rate	Government Revenues[c]		Primary Education Recurrent Spending[d]	Private Enrollments (As % of Total)	Annual Financing Gap[e]
						As % of GDP	% for Education			
Status quo		13	52.9%	0.6	0.1%	15.8%	15.1%	51.3%	0.0%	0
A only		13	33.3%	3.5						61
A + B		40	33.3%	3.5	0.1%					12
"Best practice":	C1	40	33.3%	3.5	0.1%	16.0%	20.0%	50.0%	10.0%	15
A + B +	C2					16.0%	20.0%			15
	C3					16.0%	20.0%			15

Note: Shaded cells denote no change from values directly above.

a. Policy scenarios are: A for quality improvement, B for efficiency improvement, and three alternative resource mobilization scenarios (C1, C2, and C3). The combination of scenarios A + B + C is considered "best practice".

b. As a share of primary education recurrent spending.

c. Current revenues, excluding grants.

d. As a share of total education recurrent spending.

e. In millions of 2000 U.S. dollars. Calculated as the difference between the total cost of service delivery under the specific policy scenario and the total resources for primary education mobilized domestically.

of about $15 million per year over the period, notwithstanding efficiency gains from the huge increase in the pupil-teacher ratio that is assumed. All of the gap would be for recurrent financing, given the projected slow growth of the primary school-age population and—in relation to the simulation benchmarks—the tremendous scope for absorbing increased enrollments into the existing physical plant. Obviously, even where the numbers of students and classrooms appear theoretically in balance, there will still be infrastructure needs—for school consolidation, rehabilitation, and even additional classroom construction in response to migration. It is impossible to factor these into the relatively simple model we used. Nonetheless, a result such as this signals that the bulk of the incremental costs of reaching the MDG in Armenia will be of a recurrent nature, rather than costs for expansion. As in other countries, however, capital costs for system rehabilitation, which we could not capture, may be significant.

The year-by-year financing projections show that Armenia's needs for external financing would be heaviest in the first years of the simulation period and would decline to zero by about 2008, as the reforms to improve efficiency and to increase domestic financing take hold. Thus, although Armenia's financing gap does not appear large when averaged over the entire 2000–2015 period, for the initial five years the need for external financing would be significant, averaging about $40 million per year. This is because our simulation assumes that actions to improve the level and structure of teacher remuneration are introduced as early as possible, in order to maximize the potential impact on school quality and also to reduce teachers' informal demands on households for support, which may constrain student attendance. While the teacher compensation reform is assumed to be implemented quickly, however, achieving school consolidation and increases in average class size and mobilizing increased domestic financing for primary education would take longer.

As annex table A.8 shows, the simulations produce a similar pattern of relatively high needs for external financing in the initial years for the other two ECA countries in our sample, Georgia and Moldova. Georgia's gap averages about $35 million per year and Moldova's about $15 million per year up to 2005. In all cases, the gap begins to decline thereafter and is eliminated by 2009.

The simulations for the ECA countries in our sample provide a framework for identifying the key reform directions and tradeoffs facing these countries. They also indicate that the needs for external financing in this region are likely to be larger at the outset of the period than later. But the simulation benchmarks are so far from the institutional and political reality of these countries that the financing gap estimates for these countries should be interpreted as illustrative only. It should also be recalled that we modeled the costs of achieving universal primary completion through six grades of schooling, rather than the shorter cycle these countries actually have. More detailed modeling is needed to cost reform trajectories toward targets that are more realistic for these countries—such as average class size in the range of 25–30 and average teacher salaries in the range of 2–2.5 times per capita GDP, and three- or four-grade primary completion. And while, recalling box 3.1, these alternative parameters would have a neutral effect on the overall financing gap, they would lower the size of the gap in the initial years of the simulation.

Table 4.8

Armenia: MDG-2015 Cost Estimates and Sources of Financing under "Best Practice" Policies and Alternative Resource Mobilization Scenarios

(millions of 2000 constant U.S. dollars)

Cost Item	Period	Scenario	Domestic Resources Mobilized	COST OF MDG-2015			FINANCING SOURCES						
							DOMESTIC RESOURCES			GAP FOR EXTERNAL FINANCING		
				Recurrent	Capital	Total	Recurrent	Capital	Total	Recurrent	Capital	Total
Education service delivery	Cumulative, 2001–2015	C1	491	712	0	712	491	0	491	221	0	221
		C2	491	712	0	712	491	0	491	221	0	221
		C3	491	712	0	712	491	0	491	221	0	221
	Annual	C1	33	47	0	47	33	0	33	15	0	15
		C2	33	47	0	47	33	0	33	15	0	15
		C3	33	47	0	47	33	0	33	15	0	15
AIDS-related costs	Annual	C1		0	0	0	0	0	0	0		0
		C2		0		0	0		0	0		0
		C3		0	0	0	0	0	0	0	0	0
Both items	Annual	C1		47	0	47	33	0	33	15	0	15
		C2		47	0	47	33	0	33	15	0	15
		C3		47	0	47	33	0	33	15	0	15

Note: "Best practice" policies refer to the combination of scenarios A + B + C. Shaded cells denote no change from values directly above.

NIGER

The primary completion rate in Niger, at 20 percent in 2000, is one of the lowest in the world. Only one child in three in Niger is enrolled in primary school (GER 33 percent), and only one child in five completes it—and among girls the completion rate is one in 10. Niger, Mali, Chad, Ethiopia, and a handful of other Sub-Saharan African countries are unquestionably the setting for EFA's greatest challenges. For these countries to meet the MDG, education system expansion and simultaneous quality improvement will need to occur at a pace no country has ever seen. In the case of these very low completion countries, in fact, there is a clear question of the realism of our simulations, which model the resource requirements of a trajectory of system expansion leading by definition to 100 percent completion in 2015. Even if financing were unconstrained, this trajectory may simply be physically and institutionally impossible. But the simulation exercise serves to illuminate the issues that Niger, and several other African countries in our sample, must confront.

Niger's incipient education system is relatively close to the normative targets in a few areas: the pupil-teacher ratio is 37:1 instead of 40:1, and repetition averages 13 percent instead of 10 percent. Under the quality scenario, the share of recurrent spending on items other than teacher salaries would increase from 26 percent currently to the target of 33.3 percent (table 4.9).

The underlying driver of Niger's inability, in the 40 years since independence, to offer all children a primary education is found in the very high unit cost of public primary education, due to extraordinarily high average teacher salaries—9.6 times the per capita GDP, compared with the benchmark of 3.5 times per capita GDP. Recognizing this, the Ministry of Education launched a bold reform in 2000 to suspend the recruitment of civil service teachers and to establish a new cadre of contract teachers at a more sustainable salary rate. Since 2000, the pace of teacher recruitment and enrollment expansion has accelerated tremendously. Like Senegal and other countries that have adopted this approach, Niger has been able to recruit new teachers with the same level of formal qualification as the existing force, and in fact has had an excess supply of candidates. In the simulation, we model the expansion of the new teacher cadre at the target salary of 3.5 times per capita GDP, while providing for gradual attrition of the higher-paid teaching force. Reflecting this mix, by 2015 the average teacher salary in Niger declines to a value of 4.3.

The other issue for Niger can be seen from the resource mobilization targets. Unlike many countries in the sample, Niger is currently making a huge fiscal effort in support of primary education: the government allocates 31.5 percent of domestic resources to education and 62 percent of the education budget to primary education, both values well above the benchmarks. But Niger's slight resource base and undeveloped economy are clear in the very limited ability of the country to mobilize tax revenues—only 9.1 percent of GDP—compared with the target of 14 percent for Niger's level of GDP. Our simulations require that Niger gradually increase government revenues to reach 14 percent of GDP by 2015, which may be difficult to achieve. At the same time, though the country's strong fiscal commitment to EFA is laudable, the 31.5 percent budget share for education cannot be considered sustainable, and the 62 percent allocation to primary education will also need to

Table 4.9
Niger: MDG–2015 Financing Gap under Alternative Policy Measures

Policy Scenario[a]		A: Quality Measures			B: Efficiency Measures	C: Financing Measures				
		Pupils per Teacher	Spending on Inputs Other than Teachers[b]	Average Annual Teacher Salary (as Multiple of Per Capita GDP)	Average Repetition Rate	Government Revenues[c] As % of GDP	Government Revenues[c] % for Education	Primary Education Recurrent Spending[d]	Private Enrollments (As % of Total)	Annual Financing Gap[e]
Status quo		37	25.9%	9.6	13.0%	9.1%	31.5%	62.0%	4.0%	135
A only		37	33.3%	9.6						146
A + B		40	33.3%	4.3	10.0%					48
"Best practice":	C1	40	33.3%	4.3	10.0%	14.0%	26.0%	50.0%	10.0%	46
	C2					14.0%	20.0%			53
	C3					14.0%	20.0%			53

Note: Shaded cells denote no change from values directly above.
a. Policy scenarios are: A for quality improvement, B for efficiency improvement, and three alternative resource mobilization scenarios (C1, C2, and C3). The combination of scenarios A + B + C is considered "best practice".
b. As a share of primary education recurrent spending.
c. Current revenues, excluding grants.
d. As a share of total education recurrent spending.
e. In millions of 2000 U.S. dollars. Calculated as the difference between the total cost of service delivery under the specific policy scenario and the total resources for primary education mobilized domestically.

Table 4.10

Niger: MDG-2015 Cost Estimates and Sources of Financing under "Best Practice" Policies and Alternative Resource Mobilization Scenarios

(millions of 2000 constant U.S. dollars)

Cost Item	Period	Scenario	Domestic Resources Mobilized	Cost of MDG-2015			Financing Sources					
							Domestic Resources			Gap for External Financing		
				Recurrent	Capital	Total	Recurrent	Capital	Total	Recurrent	Capital	Total
Education service delivery	Cumulative, 2001–2015	C1	796	1,078	403	1,481	796	0	796	282	403	685
		C2	684	1,078	403	1,481	684	0	684	394	403	797
		C3	684	1,078	403	1,481	684	0	684	394	403	797
	Annual	C1	53	72	27	99	53	0	53	19	27	46
		C2	46	72	27	99	46	0	46	26	27	53
		C3	46	72	27	99	46	0	46	26	27	53
AIDS-related costs	Annual	C1		1	27	1	0	0	0	1	27	1
		C2		1		1	0	0	0	1		1
		C3		1		1	0	0	0	1		1
Both items	Annual	C1	53	73	27	100	53	0	53	20	27	47
		C2	46	73	27	100	46	0	46	28	27	54
		C3	46	73	27	100	46	0	46	28	27	54

Note: "Best practice" policies refer to the combination of scenarios A + B + C. Shaded cells denote no change from values directly above.

decline, as primary completion increases and a larger share of children reach secondary and tertiary levels.

Thus, about 50 percent of the $99 million annually that Niger would need to spend on the trajectory of accelerated progress we model would need to come from external financing sources. About $27 million of the total would be for school construction, which we assume could be completely financed by donors. But Niger would need an equal amount from the outside world in recurrent budget support (table 4.10).

Given Niger's relatively low HIV seroprevalence, the impacts on the system from HIV/AIDS (to replace sick teachers and provide support to maternal or double orphans) would add only an estimated $1 million per year to recurrent costs. But this amount would also need to be externally supported. In sum, Niger is a clear case of a country where, even with maximum domestic resource commitment and reform progress on the key issue of teacher salaries, a significant financing gap remains. The absence of external support would place a binding constraint on Niger's progress toward universal primary completion. The fact that the country has already started on the path of reform toward the indicative framework benchmarks suggests that Niger is a case of a country with a "credible plan" for EFA.

AFGHANISTAN

The reconstruction of primary education in Afghanistan will be a massive challenge for the country and international partners over the coming decade. It was impossible to obtain sufficient public finance data to carry out a full simulation for Afghanistan. Population, education enrollment, and service delivery data are also scarce, outdated, and inconsistent. Nonetheless, because Afghanistan's needs will clearly contribute to the global costs and external financing requirements of achieving EFA, we used the target parameters for service delivery to try to estimate what the order of magnitude of resource requirements for Afghanistan would be in the same framework.

The last population census for Afghanistan was conducted in 1978 and all published population statistics since then are extrapolations of these census data. However, these are based on a wide variety of assumptions and lead to population estimates between 20.6 and 26.9 million. We used an estimate at the midpoint of this range.

We estimated the total resource cost of achieving 100 percent completion in Afghanistan by 2015 based on the following assumptions:
- Repetition rate over the planning horizon is 10 percent (no baseline data available)
- In the absence of salary data, figures for average teacher salaries in Pakistan were used
- Construction costs for a fully equipped classroom are $6,500 (constant 2000 dollars), the average we used for other countries in South Asia
- Non-teacher-salary expenditures are 33 percent of recurrent expenditure on primary education
- The pupil-teacher ratio is 40:1.

Table 4.11
....
Possible Costs of Achieving UPC in Afghanistan, 2000–2015

(millions of 2000 constant U.S. dollars)

Period	Recurrent Costs	Capital Costs	Total
Cumulative	613	827	1,440
Annual	41	55	96

Under these assumptions, estimated resource requirements to rebuild and improve education service delivery in Afghanistan during 2000–2015 would be as shown in table 4.11.

In the absence of fiscal data, we made no assumptions about the scope for domestic resource mobilization and instead present these as the total requirements, which for the next several years at least may well need to be financed almost entirely from donor sources. Even with the need to reconstruct a largely defunct school system, however, it should be noted that about 40 percent of the requirements will be for recurrent budget support.

AGGREGATE RESULTS

The simulation results were aggregated into an estimate of the average annual financing gap for this set of 47 low-income countries (table 4.12). Scenario C2 (the base case) shows the highest financing requirements, reflecting the reduction of higher spending levels we imposed for some countries on grounds of sustainability. Under this scenario, a total of $2.4 billion per year in external financing would be required to meet the MDG target by 2015 in only the 47 countries studied. If the resource requirements for Afghanistan, estimated using a different methodology, are included, the total for these 48 countries would be about $100 million per year higher. A discussion of how the aggregate results were constructed from the different policy scenarios follows.

Table 4.12 shows that under Scenario A, which introduces only quality improvement measures, a financing gap of about $7.5 billion per year is generated for the sample as a whole, close to $2 billion of which is for India. The reduction of this gap to $4.3 billion per year under Scenario A + B shows the impact of introducing efficiency measures, such as increasing class size where it is currently below 40 and reducing repetition where it is above 10 percent. When the target parameters for domestic financing are also introduced, the gap is cut roughly in half, to about $2.1 billion per year under scenario C2. Under scenario C1, which maintains higher spending shares for primary education in those countries currently spending more, the financing gap is slightly lower, about $2 billion per year.

The financing gap shrinks significantly under scenario C3 to less than $1.6 billion per year. Scenario C3 maintains higher overall government spending in those countries whose tax-GDP ratio currently exceeds our targets. Maintaining this level of domestic resource mobilization would clearly aid in reaching the

Table 4.12

All 47 Countries: MDG-2015 Financing Gap under Alternative Policy Measures

Policy Scenario[a]		A: Quality Measures			B: Efficiency Measures	C: Financing Measures				
		Pupils per Teacher	Spending on Inputs Other than Teachers[b]	Average Annual Teacher Salary (as Multiple of Per Capita GDP)	Average Repetition Rate	Government Revenues[c]		Primary Education Recurrent Spending[d]	Private Enrollments (As % of Total)	Annual Financing Gap[e]
						As % of GDP	% for Education			
Status quo		13–79	0.1–45	0.6–9.6	0–36%	8–56	1.4–32.6	26–66	0–77	
A only		36	33.7%	4.5						7,489
A + B		40	33.3%	3.8	8.2%					4,348
"Best practice":	C1	40	33.3%	3.7	8.2%	15.2%	21.1%	48.6%	10.0%	2,033
	C2					15.2%	20.0%			2,151
A + B +	C3					20.3%	20.0%			1,563

Note: Shaded cells denote no change from values directly above.
a. Policy scenarios are: A for quality improvement, B for efficiency improvement, and three alternative resource mobilization scenarios (C1, C2, and C3). The combination of scenarios A + B + C is considered "best practice".
b. As a share of primary education recurrent spending.
c. Current revenues, excluding grants.
d. As a share of total education recurrent spending.
e. In millions of 2000 U.S. dollars. Calculated as the difference between the total cost of service delivery under the specific policy scenario and the total resources for primary education mobilized domestically.

MDG, and in countries such as Angola, Nigeria, and the Republic of Yemen, where domestic revenue mobilization is currently in the range of 35–50 percent of GDP and greatly exceeds our 18 percent maximum target, scenario C3—or something closer to it—may be a more appropriate fiscal scenario than the C2 scenario. However, since even in these countries it is not clear that current levels of public revenue mobilization can be sustained over the long period we analyzed, we focus our discussion on the results under scenario C2.

Table 4.13 compares these cost estimates to potential sources of financing. As can be seen, under scenario C2 the total cost of achieving universal primary completion in these 47 countries would average about $16 billion per year over the period. About 90 percent of this cost ($14.8 billion per year) would be recurrent. Incremental school construction requirements for the sample would be about $1.5 billion per year.

Under the indicative parameters, these countries would increase their domestic resource mobilization for EFA from about $8 billion–$9 billion in 2000 to $23 billion per year by 2015. Averaged over the period, domestically mobilized primary education funding would total about $13.8 billion per year (under scenario C2). We assume that all of the domestic resources are applied first to the recurrent budget requirements. But approximately $1.1 billion per year in recurrent needs would remain uncovered. Since the countries' domestic resources are not adequate to cover their recurrent budget needs, virtually all of the incremental capital costs would need external financing, about another $1.1 billion. (About $0.4 billion of capital costs could be financed in part by a few countries in the sample.)

The special exercise we undertook to estimate the impact of HIV/AIDS on MDG attainment in Africa indicated that the additional costs for these education systems could be on the order of $286 million per year. These costs are all of a recurrent nature—for providing subsistence support to maternal and double orphans and for recruiting and training additional teachers. The Sub-Saharan African countries in our sample clearly will be ill prepared to bear these additional costs, so they are added to the gap for external financing. Thus, the total external financing gap for these 47 countries is estimated to average about $2.4 billion per year over the period. Including Afghanistan, it would average $2.5 billion per year.

An important finding is that about 55 percent of the external financing needed would be for recurrent budget support, and only about 45 percent for capital support (new classroom construction). Since construction investments are generally easiest for donors to mobilize, we assume that *all* of the new construction needed in these countries would be financed externally. But the simulations make clear that an even larger volume of external support would be needed for recurrent budget requirements. Under our target parameters, virtually all countries in the sample would increase their domestic financing for primary education, and would finance 85 percent of the total cost of achieving the MDG themselves. But the biggest constraint to achieving the goal will be the availability of external financing for recurrent expenses, not capital.

Figure 4.1 provides a graphic picture of these financing requirements to 2015 and their likely evolution thereafter. It should be remembered that underlying this evolution are substantial shifts in education system coverage and quality over the

Table 4.13

All 47 Countries: MDG-2015 Cost Estimates and Sources of Financing under "Best Practice" Policies and Alternative Resource Mobilization Scenarios

Cost Item	Period	Scenario	Domestic Resources Mobilized	Cost of MDG-2015			Financing Sources					
				Recurrent	Capital	Total	Domestic Resources			Gap for External Financing		
							Recurrent	Capital	Total	Recurrent	Capital	Total
Education service delivery	Cumulative, 2001–2015	C1	214,897	222,665	22,728	245,393	208,811	6,085	214,896	13,853	16,643	30,496
		C2	213,124	222,665	22,728	245,393	207,109	6,014	213,123	15,556	16,714	32,270
		C3	234,632	222,665	22,728	245,393	212,430	9,521	221,951	10,234	13,208	23,442
	Annual	C1	14,326	14,844	1,515	16,360	13,921	406	14,326	924	1,110	2,033
		C2	14,208	14,844	1,515	16,360	13,807	401	14,208	1,037	1,114	2,151
		C3	15,642	14,844	1,515	16,360	14,162	635	14,797	682	881	1,563
AIDS-related costs	Annual	C1		286		286	0		0	286		286
		C2		286		286	0		0	285		286
		C3		286		286	63		63	223		286
Both items	Annual	C1	14,326	15,130	1,515	16,646	13,921	406	14,326	1,210	1,110	2,319
		C2	14,208	15,130	1,515	16,646	13,807	401	13,208	1,323	1,114	2,437
		C3	14,860	15,130	1,515	16,646	13,226	635	14,860	905	881	1,785

Note: "Best practice" policies refer to the combination of scenarios A + B + C. Shaded cells denote no change from values directly above.

FIGURE 4.1

Domestic and External Financing Required to Achieve the Education MDG in 47 Countries, 2001–2030

Millions of 2000 constant U.S. dollars

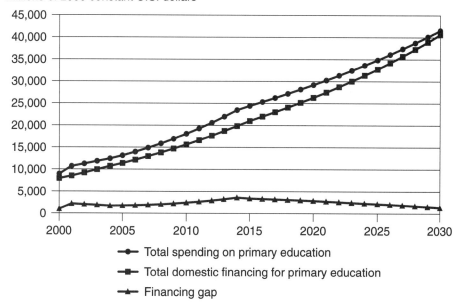

- ● Total spending on primary education
- ■ Total domestic financing for primary education
- ▲ Financing gap

period. Under our scenario of MDG attainment, these 47 countries increase primary enrollments from 229 million children in 2000 to 301 million children in 2015. The increase is almost entirely driven by progress in Africa, where primary enrollments would almost double, from 71 million to 136 million children. This will be a huge management challenge for education systems that are perceived to be weakly managed today. In the other regions, where starting coverage is higher and the population of school-age children is projected to stabilize or decline, total primary enrollments will barely change, increasing from 159 million to 164 million by 2015.

Total expenditure on primary education in all 47 countries increases in our simulations to about $25 billion per year in 2015, or about $76 per child (in constant 2000 dollars). This compares to a starting level of about $32 per student. This increase in unit costs in real terms reflects both the impact of economic growth on factor costs, notably teacher salaries, and the increase in schooling quality required to achieve universal primary completion. Underpinning the increase in quality is an important shift in the composition of spending toward non-salary inputs. Per-student spending on inputs other than teacher salaries triples in real terms over the period.

Figure 4.1 shows very clearly that as primary education *costs* increase, due to expanding enrollments and improvements in quality, the indicative framework targets also require countries to increase their domestic *spending* on primary education. These 47 countries' own financing for primary education increases from a base of about $8.5 billion in 2000 to about $21 billion in 2015. Notwithstanding this significant domestic effort, there is a financing gap over the period to 2015, and it reaches a peak in 2014, when total financing requirements approach $25 billion and the financing gap rises to $4 billion.

Figure 4.1 also shows that after 2014 the external financing gap will decline, for four main reasons: (a) construction needs will decline sharply from $1.5 billion per year to the lower pace of expansion required by natural growth of the school-age population; (b) the demographic transition expected in most of the countries will cause the share of children aged 7–12 in the population to drop, which, other things equal, will reduce the share of national resources needed to finance primary education; (c) continued GDP growth will boost the tax-GDP ratio for these countries to levels higher than the targets we assumed; and (d) the secular decline in the level of teacher salaries relative to per capita GDP observed with economic development and expansion of the formal labor market (recall figure 3.3) will set in. Indeed, these dynamic effects would in reality probably affect our target parameters before 2015.

On the other hand, the figure shows that the financing gap for these very low income countries will not disappear entirely. By 2015, these countries—most of which are currently very far from the goal of universal primary education—will have achieved a transformation of their primary education systems in terms of quantity, quality, and efficiency. They will also have increased their own financing for primary education and will be on the road to sustainable and self-financing systems. After 2015, the dependence on foreign financing will gradually decline, from 15 percent of total expenditures to about 3–5 percent. However, it is sobering to realize that the primary education systems in these very low income countries will require some degree of external assistance for a long time to come.

The size of that assistance relative to domestic financing varies substantially across the countries in our sample—with the greatest needs, not surprisingly, in the poorest of the Sub-Saharan African countries. External financing needs as a share of total primary education expenditure for the African countries rise from 28 percent at the outset to a peak of 36 percent in 2014, before declining to 6 percent by 2030. This higher dependency reflects both the African countries' weaker economies and their greater distance from universal primary education coverage.

While the very high dependence of these 33 countries on external support for education over the period to 2015 is troubling, the projections clearly indicate a path toward self-sustaining education systems thereafter (figure 4.2). It should also be recalled that some of these countries may have the capacity to contribute more domestic resources to the financing of primary education than we assumed under the C2 resource mobilization scenario profiled here. Under our alternative fiscal scenario C3, in which higher tax-GDP ratios are retained for countries that are in fact currently above our targets, the financing gap for the African countries is about 25 percent lower over the period, averaging $1.3 billion, rather than $1.8 billion per year. Under this scenario, in the peak year of 2014 the financing gap represents 26 percent of total primary education expenditure, rather than 36 percent under scenario C2.

The time profile of external financing requirements to attain the MDG merits further analysis. We modeled only one basic scenario, setting 2015 as the date for

FIGURE 4.2 | Domestic and External Financing Required to Achieve the Education MDG in Sub-Saharan Africa, 2001–2030

Millions of 2000 constant U.S. dollars

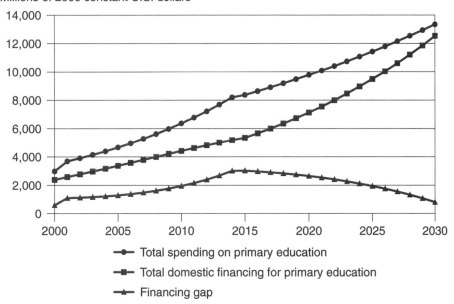

achievement of universal primary completion in all countries in the sample, irrespective of their actual trends. For many countries, particularly in Africa, this was an ambitious target. But for some others, it actually forced a slowing of their trend rate of progress. An alternative scenario might set all countries on at least the trajectory of "maximum feasible" progress to the goal that has been observed empirically (about 3 percentage points per year increase in the primary completion rate). This would effectively shift forward some of the external financing gap to the years before 2015 and flatten the curve.

REQUIREMENTS BY REGION

The regional breakdown of the financing gap in table 4.14 shows that, including costs for the impact of AIDS, about 75 percent ($1.9 billion) of the external support would be needed for 33 countries in Sub-Saharan Africa. In South Asia, four countries (India, Pakistan, Bangladesh, and Nepal) would need $397 million per year in external funding. In Latin America and the Caribbean, three countries (Nicaragua, Honduras, and Haiti) would need $48 million per year. In East Asia and the Pacific, two countries (Lao PDR and Cambodia) would need $36 million per year. In the Middle East, one country (the Republic of Yemen) would need $70 million per year, and in Europe and Central Asia, three countries (Armenia, Georgia, and Moldova) would require about $34 million per year. Only one country in our sample (Mongolia) showed no financing gap in these simulations, largely

Table 4.14

Estimated Annual Financing Gap to Achieve the Education MDG, by Region (Scenario C2)

(millions of 2000 constant U.S. dollars)

Type of Financing	Africa	South Asia	Latin America and the Caribbean	East Asia and the Pacific	Middle East and North Africa	Europe and Central Asia	Total	Percentage of Total Financing Gap
Recurrent	1,127	97	14	30	21	34	1,323	55
Operation	841	97	14	30	21	34	1,037	43
AIDS	286	0	0	0	0	0	286	12
Capital	725	300	34	6	49	0	1,114	45
Total	1,852	397	48	36	70	34	2,437	100

Note: Numbers may not sum to totals because of rounding.

because the school-age population is not projected to increase and the baseline pupil-teacher ratio is far below the benchmark we used. All results for individual countries may be found in annex C, and the simulation model and baseline data for all countries may be found in the CD-ROM accompanying this book.

The financing gap estimated in this study must be understood as a lower-bound estimate of the global costs of attaining the education MDG, for several reasons. First and most crucially, these simulations estimated the incremental costs of *expanding* primary education systems from the baseline numbers of classrooms and teachers in each of the 47 countries in 2000 to the numbers that would be needed in order to reach the goal by 2015. But they did not capture the important needs—particularly in these very low income countries—for rehabilitation and upgrading of existing classrooms; expansion or upgrading of other system infrastructure such as teacher support centers, district offices, and teacher training institutes; key "software" investments such as curriculum design, management information systems, student assessment systems, textbooks, and so forth; and training and capacity building for teachers, school directors, and system administrators to bring all of them up to an adequate level of functioning. Our data set did not permit the detailed appraisal of existing school-level and system-level infrastructure or the adequacy of current system functioning that would be required to estimate the costs of needed upgrading, rehabilitation, and capacity building in each of these 47 countries, in order to complement the expansion costs we estimated. Given the precarious functioning of the education system in very many of the countries in our sample, it can be assumed that these needs are substantial. Because these investments are needed immediately, moreover, our simulation results for the first few years of the projection period particularly underestimate the true needs for external financing in these countries.

Second, although our 47-country sample includes all of the most populous low-income countries and accounts for 94 percent of all children without access to primary education in the low-income world, there are about 20 small low-income countries and several conflict-affected countries that we could not analyze, for lack of data. Moreover, we also only estimated financing requirements through six grades of primary schooling for some countries whose official cycle is longer. A full costing of the external needs in low-income countries would have to include all of the countries and reflect the full length of the primary cycle in each.

Third, this costing exercise simulated a path to the MDG for each country that assumed that system reforms would be initiated immediately, and pursued steadily to 2015. In reality, there will be many cases where it is politically impossible to launch all needed reforms at the same time, where the pace of implementation will not always be linear, and where there is a need for the education system to deliver better service immediately, while key reforms—particularly on the resource mobilization side—may necessarily take longer to legislate and implement. To the extent that external assistance may facilitate such processes, transitional external financing requirements may be higher than the simulation estimates. However, the record on aid effectiveness also clearly points to the pitfalls of external assistance as a substitute for country commitment to needed reforms.

Finally, this costing exercise focused on the millennium education goal of universal primary completion by 2015, and not on the full set of Education for All goals established at the Dakar conference. Developing countries are committed to pursuing all six of the Dakar education goals, and the incremental costs to attain some of them—especially the elimination of gender disparities in secondary education, the achievement of a 50 percent improvement in adult literacy by 2015, and the expansion of early childhood care and education targeted to the most vulnerable children—will be significant. The financing framework introduced in this study provides for increased spending on *all* levels of education, not only primary education, and would provide some fiscal space for education systems to pursue the full set of Dakar goals. But parallel efforts to the current study, to research the "best practice" policies, service delivery parameters, and external financing needed for attainment of the other Dakar goals, are needed for a full costing of the Education for All agenda.

ESTIMATING THE GLOBAL COSTS OF REACHING THE EDUCATION MDG

Despite these limitations, the current study does represent one of the most careful efforts to date to analyze and cost a strategy for attaining the education MDG. In a world where both developing and developed countries face competing priorities and budget constraints, we insist on the importance of a global strategy—such as the one outlined here—that seeks to achieve the goal at minimum adequate cost, rather than "at any cost." Current patterns of education spending, where they clearly are not producing results today, should not be the basis for MDG costing. "External financing gaps" should reflect a true residual need after sound national policies and resource commitments are in place, and should not substitute for these. Even the conservative estimate put forward here is many times higher than aid flows currently available for primary education; it will take strong effort and commitment from development partners to mobilize this incremental funding, and equal effort from developing countries to use it well.

Is it possible, then, to generate a plausible estimate of the likely costs of achieving the education MDG—through five or six years of schooling—in *all* developing and transition countries, building on the detailed analysis done here for 47 low-income countries?[6] We try in this section to do so. Since our cost estimates are for only 47 countries, and cover only expansion costs at the classroom level, "scaling up" our analysis to a truly global estimate requires four steps. (See table 4.15.)

First, we need to estimate the system rehabilitation needs for which we were unable to get country-by-country data, at both the classroom level and the system infrastructure level. We obtained more detailed data for a small subset of countries in our sample and found that, on average, about 30 percent of existing infrastructure was estimated in need of replacement or upgrading. The estimated annual cost of this rehabilitation—assumed to be carried out over a three year period—equaled roughly 50 percent of the total primary education recurrent budget over that period. On this basis, the total additional requirement for our 47 countries over the first three years would be slightly over $3.9 billion per year, or $11.6 billion in total. These are one-time expenditures, however. Averaged over our 15 year projection period, they add $0.8 billion per year, or 10 percent, to the estimated annual incremental cost to reach the MDG of $8 billion, and add 33 percent to our estimated annual financing gap.

The second step is to estimate infrastructure expansion needs at the system level, since our analysis focused on classroom expansion. We roughly estimate that system infrastructure (teacher resource centers, district offices, central ministry facilities, and so forth) should expand at an equal pace with classroom construction and in general should not exceed 20 percent of the costs of classroom expansion. This would add another $4.6 billion to the $23 billion in capital requirements we estimated for the period to 2015, or $0.3 billion per year. This represents an additional 12 percent increase in the estimated financing gap.

The third step is to extend this comprehensive estimate to countries we did not analyze. Our 47 countries account for about 94 percent of the out-of-school population in low-income countries. Scaling up our estimated incremental costs to cover the total needs for all low-income countries is relatively straightforward, as unit costs and appropriate system parameters are similar. Scaling up from the 47 countries we analyzed to the full group of 79 IDA countries would increase the incremental costs by an estimated $0.6 billion per year, or 7 percent. If we assume the same capacity for domestic resource mobilization in the low income countries as in our sample countries, our estimated financing gap would increase by a further $0.2 billion per year.

In sum, we estimate that the incremental cost of achieving the education MDG in all low-income countries, including all needs, would total about $9.7 billion per year over the period to 2015, of which about $3.7 billion per year would need to be financed externally. This is about 50 percent higher than the gap we estimated for the 47 countries in our sample.

---

6. We obtained detailed data on costs and parameters for five or six years of primary schooling in all countries in the sample, regardless of the official length of the primary cycle. The scaled-up costs estimated in this section similarly correspond to the equivalent of getting all children through five or six years of primary education in all countries. To the extent that countries actually have longer primary education cycles, these costs underestimate the true costs of reaching the education MDG.

The fourth and final step—projecting the likely costs and financing gaps for the 47 middle-income countries that have not yet reached the MDG—is more difficult. On the one hand, the middle-income countries are much closer to the goal, with an average primary completion rate of 87 percent (on a country-weighted basis), compared with 62 percent for the low-income countries. These more diversified economies also have more scope for domestic resource mobilization. With appropriate domestic commitment, the upper-middle-income countries in particular—with a tax-GDP ratio averaging 23 percent compared to 19 percent for our sample—should be able to finance a substantial part of the costs of universal primary education. Demographic factors are also more favorable: the school-age population is a lower, and typically declining, share of the overall population, which makes it easier for a fixed share of national income to cover education system needs.

On the other hand, there are several offsetting factors. The share of the overall education budget typically available for primary education is lower in middle-income countries, given higher enrollment ratios in secondary and tertiary education and funding pressures from these levels. Most importantly, the unit costs of primary education in middle-income countries are much higher in dollar terms, because of lower pupil-teacher ratios and the higher (dollar) costs of teacher salaries, construction, and other inputs.

Pupil-teacher ratios in middle-income countries tend to be lower than 30:1 and are often under pressure from teachers' unions to decline further. It would be difficult in most middle-income countries to establish 40:1 as an appropriate target, although high-performing education systems in Singapore and South Korea provide a clear example of how cost-effective such a policy can be. An even bigger factor is the average teacher salary: while teacher salaries in middle-income countries are lower in per capita GDP terms than in our sample countries, they are much higher in dollar terms. The dollar value of non-salary inputs and construction costs is also higher, reflecting the average level of incomes and prices in these more developed economies. Overall, primary education unit costs in middle-income countries are in the range of $180–220 per student, or 5–6 times the unit cost in our sample.

Table 4.15

A Global Estimate of the Annual Incremental Costs to Achieve the Education MDG and Likely Financing Gap

	ESTIMATED INCREMENTAL COST (ANNUAL AVERAGE)	ESTIMATED EXTERNAL GAP (ANNUAL AVERAGE)
Estimate for 47 countries	$8 billion	$2.4 billion
Rehabilitation	$0.8 billion	$0.8 billion
System expansion	$0.3 billion	$0.3 billion
Other low-income countries	$0.2 billion	$0.2 billion
All low-income countries	$9.7 billion	$3.7 billion
Middle-income countries	$23–28 billion	$1–$3 billion
All developing countries	$33–38 billion	$5–$7 billion

Based on current unit costs and enrollment data, but applying population and economic growth projections, we estimate that the incremental costs of reaching the education MDG in the middle income countries would be in the range of $23–28 billion, compared to spending on primary education estimated at about $80 billion in 2000.

However, this estimate is not strictly parallel to our estimate for the lower income countries, because it assumes no changes in service delivery efficiency or domestic financing. Without country-by-country analysis, it is impossible to say what the possible impact of appropriate policy reforms on these costs might be, nor to estimate the potential for increased domestic resource mobilization to contribute to their financing. The one study so far that has applied our methodology (with regionally appropriate benchmark parameters) to 10 middle-income countries in Latin America and the Caribbean found that the countries should be able to finance the limited amount of school-level expansion needed to reach the MDG, without an external gap, if they also adopt policies to improve the efficiency of student flows and devote reasonable domestic budget allocations to primary education (di Gropello, Dubey, and Winkler 2002). (The study did not evaluate rehabilitation needs or infrastructure expansion needs at the system level.)

Against this, one can set an earlier World Bank analysis of MDG attainment that assumed no change in unit costs, student flows, or domestic financing. In this analysis, the estimated financing gap for middle-income countries was in the range of $4 billion per year (Devarajan, Miller, and Swanson 2002). However, we believe that this overstates the likely financing gap because, just as in the countries we analyzed, there is clear scope in middle-income countries to increase resource mobilization and improve efficiency in service delivery.

The most that can be said without country-by-country analysis of the type we have done is that the incremental costs of reaching the education MDG in middle-income and transition countries are likely to be in the range of $23–28 billion per year. Of this, the need for external financing may be in the range of $1 billion per year, with appropriate policy reforms, to $3 billion per year.

Summing these estimates with our scaled up estimate of the incremental costs and financing gap for low-income countries results in a global estimate that roughly $33–38 billion per year in additional spending on primary education will be needed to reach the goal. It should be kept in mind that this is the annual average of a spending increase that would take place gradually over the period to 2015, from the roughly $90 billion that developing countries are spending today on primary education to a projected $160 billion in 2015. We estimate that between $5 and $7 billion per year of this total amount needed will not be able to be generated domestically by these countries and would need to come through external aid.

This range is fairly wide, but it is anchored in the most careful country-by-country analysis available. Our belief is that an extension of our methodology to the middle-income developing countries, with an explicit focus on achieving the MDG at minimum and sustainable global cost, would result in a global financing gap at the lower end of this range. It would also prompt a refocusing of external assistance for education on the lowest-income countries currently furthest from the goal of universal primary completion.

Implications for Countries and Donors

At the World Education Forum in Dakar in 2000, the international community pledged that no developing country with a "credible plan" for achieving EFA would fall short of the 2015 goal for lack of external support. At the Monterrey conference on development finance in 2002, the donor community pledged increased development support channeled in a new and more selective framework to countries with both sound policies and a willingness to be held accountable for clear results. This study was written in the spirit of those commitments, to try to understand which policies are essential drivers of universal primary completion and what would constitute a credible plan for achieving the education MDG.

Our analysis of primary completion rates across a sample of 55 low-income countries showed that a relatively small set of key parameters are important determinants of primary education outcomes: overall spending on primary education; average class size; average teacher salaries; spending on inputs other than teacher salaries; and the rate of repetition. When the overall level of resources is adequate and the distribution is balanced, education systems have the basic ingredients they need to perform well. If resource allocation skews any of the core parameters too much in one direction or the other (for example, average class size of 10 or average class size of 70), other areas are forced into compensating adjustments that are almost always unhealthy. Many chronic problems of low quality, inefficiency, and inequity—for low-performing systems are always inequitable—can be traced to imbalances in these key elements, and the unhealthy adjustments that primary education systems make.

IMPORTANCE OF A FLEXIBLE APPROACH

As important as these core elements are, however, there are at least three reasons why this framework is not *sufficient* for a credible EFA plan, and must not be applied rigidly:
- System-wide averages do not guarantee an efficient underlying distribution.
- Target parameters may not be optimal in different country contexts.
- The overall level and mix of resources do not guarantee the transformation of those resources into quality schools and higher student learning.

AVERAGE VALUES

The analysis in this report hinges on system-wide average values for the core parameters. Yet a reasonable average value does not guarantee an efficient or equitable underlying distribution—particularly in large federalized education systems such as those of India or Nigeria. A system-wide average of 40 students per teacher could reflect a very efficient underlying pattern in which teachers in urban areas working in double-shift schools teach more than 40 students each while teachers in sparsely populated rural areas working in multigrade schools teach fewer. Or it could reflect the exact opposite—an excess of teachers stationed in the desirable urban areas and a serious shortage of teachers and schools in rural zones, which is very commonly seen in developing countries. The two patterns will produce very different student learning outcomes and completion rate progress. Our analysis implicitly assumes the efficient and intelligent underlying allocations that would cause these core parameters to be associated with primary completion progress. But a credible EFA plan would have to make this explicit.

TARGET PARAMETERS

The target parameters used in this exercise can provide useful points of reference or benchmarks for all countries. But there will be many cases where they are culturally, institutionally, or financially inappropriate, and rigid adherence to any particular target values must be avoided. The ultimate value of this framework is as a guide to the direction of reform, not as a dictate regarding where it should end. In the case of Armenia, for example, the current pupil-teacher ratio of 13:1 and average teacher salary of 0.6 times per capita GDP are not conducive to a quality primary education system. Comparison with the reference parameters of 40:1 and 3.5 times per capita GDP points clearly to the directions in which the system needs to move. But it may be just as adequate and more feasible politically for Armenia to aim for a pupil-teacher ratio of 30:1 and an average salary of 2.5 times per capita GDP. From the standpoint of resource allocation, this balance is equivalent to our target parameters. The key is to recognize when the starting imbalance is untenable and then to move in the right direction.

TRANSFORMATION OF RESOURCES INTO LEARNING OUTCOMES

The "indicative framework" presented in this study can ensure that education systems have adequate overall resources and a healthy mix of core inputs. But it cannot guarantee the next—and crucial—step: the management of those resources to transform them into student learning. Paying teachers on average an adequate wage does not automatically produce the high standards, careful recruitment, quality in-service training, and performance management needed to turn those teachers into an effective force in the classroom. The 33 percent of total recurrent spending we target for spending on inputs other than teacher salaries is ample enough for an education system to cover many important needs—from design of a relevant curriculum to national student learning assessments to proper building maintenance—but there are also many ways such resources can be spent badly, with little impact on MDG progress.

Even more important than mobilizing more resources for primary education is improving the management of resources: at the national level, at the school level, and in the classroom. At the national level, ministries of education must achieve greater equity and efficiency in resource allocation and personnel deployment between administrative support services and schooling delivery, across different regions and across schools. The share of resources absorbed into central administration in many systems is very high, with little value added for system functioning or student learning. Across different regions, schools with similar enrollments often differ widely in the number of teachers deployed to them, with no formal rationale but with clear implications for system quality and equity. Similarly, expenditure tracking studies frequently find that only a fraction of the overall education resources allocated to schools actually reaches them, and often too late in the school year to be used productively. Finally, crucial central support functions are often handled poorly or are nonexistent. National systems to assess student learning and monitor progress at the classroom and school level are essential for holding education actors accountable and stimulating system-wide improvement, yet they exist in very few of the countries in our sample. Education statistics are rarely audited and often years out of date, and thus cannot serve as a tool for management decisions on an ongoing basis.

Management capacity at the school level is also crucial. The quality of school leadership makes the difference between an orderly environment where teachers perform and children can learn, and a chaotic environment marked by rampant absenteeism, poor school maintenance, disappearance of books and materials, and poor relations with parents and the community, as seen in all too many education systems. Simple and often costless actions such as assigning the best teachers to the early grades, adapting the school calendar to the needs of the community, or making sure that teachers show up on time and work a full week, can greatly boost student attendance and learning. Effective school-level management makes these happen.

Ultimately, it is management in the classroom that transforms education resources into student learning outcomes. Research shows that after controlling for student characteristics, learning outcomes can differ greatly even across equally endowed classrooms in the same school. What teachers do matters more for learning outcomes than any other single factor. Teachers must use class time effectively; they must make good use of learning materials; they must have the capacity to adapt their teaching practice to individual students' learning needs; and, above all, they must be motivated to devote time and hard work to proving that "every child can learn." In most of the countries in our sample, teachers' incentives, capacity, and practice are greatly in need of strengthening.

In short, good policies, innovative programs, and effective management in a great many areas must accompany a good core distribution of resources in a high-performing education system. Box 5.1 gives an idea of the wide range of management challenges a primary education system must address and outlines good-practice policies from across the developing world. These are aimed at ensuring that adequate resources translate into cost-effective expansion of schooling coverage, effective teaching and learning, and the flexibility in service delivery and other support needed to keep girls, the poorest, disabled, and other vulnerable children in school. A new World Bank paper (2002c), drawing lessons from a number of country case studies, provides more insights into what has worked and offers a set of principles to guide effective program and policy interventions. These are a crucial complement to the resource allocation framework we analyzed as elements of a credible EFA plan.

Box 5.1 Key Education Policy Options

GOAL	POLICY CHOICES	MEANS
EXPAND SUPPLY	Low-cost and carefully targeted expansion	• Lower-cost designs and construction material • Community-based construction • Streamlined preservice training (that is, shorter formal training, more hands-on training in classrooms, distance delivery) • Locally recruited teachers • Incentives for teacher deployment to remote and rural areas
	More cost-effective use of existing school infrastructure	• Double-shift schools • Multigrade schools • Teacher redeployment and efficient class size
	Greater private provision and financing of education	• Simple regulatory framework for private providers (that is, accreditation system and collection of basic statistics) • Grants to cost-effective nonpublic providers
	Tighter system management	• Planning for HIV/AIDS impact • School mapping (and later, more sophisticated education management information systems) • Review of role, selection, and training of school heads • Control of teacher absenteeism • Equitable funding across schools (per-student allocations)
IMPROVE QUALITY	Quality teaching	• Emphasis on literacy and numeracy skills and clear learning goals for students • Student-centered interactive teaching methods • Ongoing professional development in content areas and pedagogical skills • Teacher networks and resource centers • Quality teacher manuals • Mother-tongue instruction in initial years • Increased hours and/or days of instruction • Salary structure that rewards teaching performance and rural or difficult postings
	Quality instructional materials	• Local teaching materials • Timely and equitable distribution of low-cost learning materials (textbooks) to schools and students • Curriculum revision to improve relevance • Distance education (for example, radio education)
	Tighter accountability mechanisms	• Simple school monitoring and reporting system (including private schools) • Periodic assessment of student learning outcomes • Stakeholders empowered in school affairs
	Institutional strengthening	• Reinforced management functions (planning, budgeting, staffing) • Greater school autonomy
STIMULATE DEMAND: RELIEVE HOUSEHOLD CONSTRAINTS	Promote education of girls	• Targeted stipends for girls • Labor-saving technologies, water points, and school-based childcare facilities to ease girls' household work • Schools located closer to communities • Separate latrines for girls • Recruitment of more female teachers and administrators • More mothers involved in school committees
	Ensure school affordability	• Elimination of school fees • Textbooks and school supplies provided free • Additional stipends for poor households and AIDS orphans
	Make schooling attractive to parents and communities	• Parents involved in school councils with decisionmaking power • School calendar compatible with local economic activity • School environment improved with latrines, water, electricity • School health and nutrition programs • Early childhood development programs • Nonformal education programs for youths and adults • Community libraries (eventually Internet centers)

The above are very important caveats. But they do not negate the fact that the first step toward a quality school system is to ensure adequate resources, allocated in a healthy balance across core system parameters. Without this, few other policy objectives and programs can be implemented or sustained.

Placing the EFA planning process within this type of policy and financing framework—with internationally agreed values or ranges for target parameters—would mean that countries would compare their performance on a set of key domestic resource mobilization and service delivery parameters to the benchmarks observed in better-performing education systems.

When a country's initial parameters deviate significantly from the benchmarks, a clear criterion for a "credible EFA plan" would be commitment to a gradual yet well-defined process of reform, to bring those areas of system performance into line. Progress would be evaluated annually, and in a very transparent manner, as the initial parameters, benchmark values, and appropriate annual targets for progress would be clear.

This kind of technical rigor, transparency, and financial discipline has been missing from EFA planning to date—which has in many cases consisted of "wish lists" of actions that are neither prioritized, realistically costed, nor, in many cases, physically feasible. The analytical framework proposed here would help ensure that policy actions, new investments in school expansion, domestic financing, and external assistance are sustainable and lead to progressive improvements in system functioning, measured against clear benchmarks. Key outcomes, such as the primary completion rate and learning outcomes (when standardized assessment systems in these countries become more widespread), would also be tracked. Sustained and predictable external financing would be the quid pro quo for steady progress in improving these core indicators of system functioning and progressive improvement in outcomes.

Some key implications of this approach for developing countries are as follows:

- The criteria for a "credible plan" would be less ambiguous and more technically rigorous.
- Countries' own commitments to achieving the MDG could be evaluated more transparently, as the allocation of a "fair share" of domestic fiscal resources to primary education.
- Steady improvement in service delivery would be a quid pro quo for continued external support.
- The EFA process would be focused more sharply on key outcomes, especially the primary completion rate, student learning progress, and gender parity, and more accurate and timely measurement of these would be required.
- Countries and their partners would both be accountable for ensuring that external funding catalyzes tangible progress toward universal primary completion and is not wasted in ineffective delivery systems.

- Countries' overall domestic resource mobilization and spending, not only education ministry spending, would become subject to transparent monitoring.

CONSIDERATIONS FOR THE DONOR COMMUNITY

The implications of this study for international development partners are equally strong. Our results clearly show that even with a maximum domestic effort, these 47 countries plus Afghanistan will not be able to achieve the education MDG by 2015 without:
- A significant increase in donor funding for primary education
- Better targeting of donor assistance to "EFA priority" countries
- A change in the mix of assistance
- Greatly increased efficiency of aid transfers
- Transfer of funds via new mechanisms; and
- More effective monitoring of progress, increased research, and faster diffusion of knowledge about what works.

INCREASED AID FOR PRIMARY EDUCATION

The average external financing needed for the 48 low-income countries we studied, including Afghanistan, at $2.5 billion per year over the next 12 years (constant 2000 dollars) represents a significant increase over current aid for primary education to these countries. Although it is difficult to compile solid country-level data, we estimate that this is almost triple the level of external support for primary education these countries currently receive.

If the numbers are disaggregated regionally, the even greater disparity between current levels of assistance and estimated needs for Sub-Saharan Africa becomes clear. For the 33 African countries that account for $1.9 billion of the overall $2.4 billion per year gap (excluding Afghanistan), estimated disbursements of official development aid for primary education over the last three years have averaged only about $500 million per year. New commitments have averaged little more than $600 million per year (table 5.1). In other words, the annual external disbursements to these countries would have to almost quadruple. For the 13 countries outside Africa with projected financing gaps, the estimated needs would average $586 million per year over the period, almost 50 percent higher than the estimated current level of disbursements of about $400 million per year.

BETTER TARGETING TO "EFA PRIORITY" COUNTRIES

The preceding analysis shows that, although our financing gap estimate is lower than some previous global estimates, it would nonetheless require a substantial increase in donor funding for primary education in these countries to fill it—and a fourfold increase for Africa. This will not be easy to achieve. On the country side, although the scenario for accelerated MDG progress we model explicitly assumes that institutions and policies in the education sector (and fiscal management more generally) gradually become stronger through implementation of reforms and shifts in resource allocation, there is no question that institutional "capacity gaps" currently constrain the level of assistance to many of these countries.

Table 5.1

....

Official Development Assistance to Basic Education in Sub-Saharan Africa, by Donor, 1998–2000

(commitment basis, millions of current U.S. dollars)

Donor	1998	1999	2000
International Development Association			
Total education	1,201.5	534.8	468.7
Africa education	372.3	194.1	159.7
Africa basic education	218.3	131.0	58.8
Other multilateral development banks			
Total education	1,274.7	773.7	1,335.5
Africa education	868.9	309.5	1,041.3
Africa basic education	28.2	110.6	116.2
Development Assistance Committee countries			
Total education	4,459.2	5,014.3	3,541.6
Africa education	2,328.4	1,259.2	1,405.6
Africa basic education	422.2	418.4	378.8
All donors			
Total education	6,935.4	6,322.8	5,345.8
Africa education	3,569.6	1,762.8	2,606.6
Africa basic education	668.7	660.0	553.8

Note: The World Bank (IBRD and IDA) reports flows to "primary education," whereas the Development Assistance Committee (DAC) of the OECD reports flows to "basic education." DAC countries and African Development Bank regional classifications cover continental Africa and not Sub-Saharan Africa, as reported by the World Bank. Therefore the regional totals are approximate.

Sources: World Bank Business Warehouse; OECD DAC Database.

But the current low level of external support for primary education may also reflect relatively unfocused commitment to the MDG on the donor side. When our estimated gap of $2.4 billion per year is compared against *total* assistance for education reported by international donors and multilateral banks, which averages about $7 billion per year, it looks relatively small (annex table D.1). That assistance—for all levels of educational development and all developing (low- and middle-income) countries—serves many different, and potentially important, purposes. But, very clearly, it is not today giving priority to the countries where achievement of the MDG is at greatest risk without external support. Only about 20 percent of donor assistance for education is currently channeled to basic education (annex table D.2).

At Dakar, the international community pledged that no developing country's EFA progress would be constrained for lack of external support. If that commitment is to be upheld, the development partners will need to either:

• Mobilize a significant real increase in funding for primary education, channeled largely to Sub-Saharan Africa, or

- Achieve an equally dramatic reallocation of existing assistance, from other levels of education to primary education, and from middle-income countries to low-income, especially African, countries.

A CHANGING MIX OF ASSISTANCE

According to our analysis, close to 60 percent of the external financing requirements for these countries over the next 13 years will be of a recurrent nature. Although recent data show that World Bank/IDA disbursements to these countries for primary education have begun to approach this mix, it is not clear that this is true for other donors. Assistance from all external partners has traditionally given heavy priority to capital investments, such as school construction or equipment. A clear message of the simulation results is that if donors want to see the MDG of universal primary completion attained, a relatively high share of external assistance will have to be channeled to recurrent budget support. And for greater gender parity and supporting HIV/AIDS orphans, in particular, recurrent budget support for stipend programs will be critical.

Of course, donors will be reluctant to go this route without clear acceptance by countries that their entire budget—and domestic resource mobilization effort—will be on the table for discussion and monitoring. This is already happening in the PRSP and PRSC processes that most of the countries in our sample are engaged in. Uganda is a good example of a country whose receptivity to greater budgetary transparency—and outcome monitoring—has been directly associated with a large increase in the share of development assistance channeled to the country as budgetary support.

GREATER EFFICIENCY OF EXTERNAL SUPPORT

There is a related and overarching need for more efficient transfers of development assistance. The average annual gap we estimate can be considered as the minimum cost of achieving EFA under the most optimistic (although gradual and achievable) scenarios of policy reform and efficient aid flows. Another way of conceiving of the $2.4 billion is as the net or "core resource transfer" that would be needed. But it is clear that $2.4 billion in reported donor assistance does not today equal $2.4 billion of core resource transfer to recipient countries.

For example, we estimate that roughly $286 million per year (2000 constant dollars) would be needed on average over the period by the 33 African countries in our sample to address the impact of AIDS on their education systems. A significant part of this derives from the projected need to provide subsistence support (food, cash, clothing) to AIDS orphans to prevent them from dropping out of school, a cost we estimated at $50 per orphan per year based on data from some existing programs. This represents the actual transfer to the child, without any specific provision for the overhead and administrative costs required to channel support. But it may be noted that various donor/NGO programs of this nature operating today generally cost $100–$150 per child in order to achieve the equivalent of a $50 net transfer to the beneficiary. Although these programs usually include counseling and other services that cannot be classed simply as overhead, it does give a sense of the margins that can exist between the "core resource transfers" we costed and the total costs of assistance.

Similarly, the unit construction costs we assumed are lower than those many donors report. If the aid-financed construction of a fully equipped classroom in Africa costs close to $24,000, as reported by some donors, it should be realized that only $8,000 of that amount (the unit cost we used for African countries in the sample) would count against our estimated capital financing gap. On the other hand, involving communities in school construction has been shown in many countries to lower unit costs, and this could result in lower capital costs than we estimated and effectively narrow the gap. However, as we assumed that virtually all school construction over the period would be financed externally, shifting more systematically to community-based approaches would require flexibility on the part of donors.

Finally, a significant share of donor assistance typically supports technical assistance contracts, consultancies, study tours, seminars, and other activities. No matter how laudable or even crucial these may be for inspiring education reforms or building capacity, they cannot be counted directly against the "net" resource needs we estimate. The costs that enter into our financing gap, outside of construction needs, are very largely the core, local cost requirements for running a primary education system.

It is impossible to say with any precision what equivalent "gross" level of development assistance would be needed to fill our estimated $2.4 billion net gap. It could conceivably be 50–100 percent higher. But the efficiency of transfers varies considerably across donors. And the readiness of international partners to move in coming years toward greater use of pooled assistance and direct budgetary transfers in the context of SWAPs, PRSCs, or other program lending could greatly improve the efficiency with which each dollar of future external assistance offsets the estimated financing gap in these countries.

NEW TRANSFER MECHANISMS

A renewed push for EFA by 2015 will require major changes from business as usual for both at-risk countries and their development partners. The policy and financing framework laid out in this report could afford a basis for gauging countries' commitments to EFA and guiding service delivery reforms. The quid pro quo for monitorable improvements in service delivery quality and efficiency and for key results such as increasing primary completion rates and student learning would be adequate, sustained, and predictable levels of financing from international partners.

The stability and predictability of external assistance is crucial if countries are to take on recurrent expenditures (such as hiring of additional teachers) that are not easily compressed when external support fluctuates. On the other hand, it is not easy for bilateral donors, subject to their own political processes and budget constraints, to make long-term funding commitments. Greater used of pooled donor assistance and direct budget transfers in the context of SWAPs and other programmatic support could help match donor assistance more effectively to countries' core financing needs and ensure a more stable and predictable flow of funding.

Both parts of this compact would require client countries and international partners to collaborate in new ways. Countries would need to accept benchmarks for system performance and a non-bureaucratic yet participatory way of involving development partners in monitoring budgets and progress. Donors would need to forego many of the trappings of the way aid is channeled today in favor of resource transfers that would permit them to monitor only overall outcomes, and not their national share of procured inputs. Whether this flow of assistance could be coordinated across agencies as they currently operate or would merit a specific new mechanism for pooling EFA support in new ways cannot be said. It is clear, however, that whether existing or new arrangements are used, they must be made to function better, with lighter and more effective coordination and with an increase in the efficiency with which resource transfers effectively meet countries' financing needs.

GLOBAL RESEARCH AND KNOWLEDGE DIFFUSION

A potentially important byproduct of a more technically rigorous (and data-intensive) EFA planning process could be a deeper and wider base for global research on how primary education systems improve. An internationally accessible database of key expenditure and service delivery variables for a large number of countries would clearly result from any mainstream adoption of the policy and financing framework proposed in this report. Verified and internationally comparable data on these parameters and education outcomes could be a major boon to education researchers. Under the most optimistic scenario, this could produce a deeper understanding of how to accelerate primary completion rate progress that would benefit those countries currently furthest from the MDG. Although the costs of EFA monitoring, data collection, international research, and global and local activities to diffuse new knowledge are not included in the estimated financing gap, these investments in the global public good should be considered core responsibilities of the international community.

THE EFA FAST-TRACK INITIATIVE

Building on the above framework, a new compact for primary education designed to accelerate global progress toward the education MDG was endorsed by the Development Committee of the World Bank and the International Monetary Fund in April 2002 and by the G-8 in its action plan for education at the June 2002 summit in Kananaskis, Alberta, Canada. The new compact, called the EFA Fast-Track Initiative, is the first global proposal to emerge since the Monterrey conference that aims at accelerating MDG progress using the Monterrey framework of increased development support in exchange for increased accountability for results. The new initiative is supported by all major bilateral donors for education and by UNESCO, UNICEF, the World Bank, and the regional development banks, all of which have jointly formed the EFA Fast-Track Partnership. At the heart of the Fast-Track Initiative are:

- A commitment by developing countries to accelerate efforts to achieve universal primary education cost-effectively, within a transparent global accountability framework (the EFA indicative framework outlined in this study); and
- A commitment by donors to provide sustained incremental financing (as much as possible on a grant basis), where credible plans to accelerate progress in primary education exist.

In June 2002, a first set of 18 low-income countries was invited to join the initiative and to submit their EFA plans, including baseline "indicative framework" indicators and annual targets for 2003, for donor financing. The 18 countries (box 5.2) are diverse regionally and in terms of their proximity to universal primary completion; together, they account for an estimated 18 million children without access to education. This first set of countries was invited to consider committing to the Fast-Track Initiative on the basis of two simple and transparent criteria: (a) they have formally adopted national poverty reduction strategies (PRSPs) that integrate their education plans into overall national development priorities; and (b) they have education sector plans in place. The rationale for these two criteria is that having these elements in place should allow the Fast-Track Initiative to catalyze measurable progress more quickly. It should be noted that the initiative is aimed at accelerating MDG progress in, and learning lessons from, countries that are currently on track to reach the goal as well as countries that are off track. The first group of countries includes one— Vietnam—that has virtually achieved the goal and others such as The Gambia and Uganda that are considered on track. In countries such as these, the aim of the Fast-Track Initiative is to help countries reach the goal more quickly and in the process generate lessons and demonstration effects for other countries.

A second set of five high-priority countries was also invited to join the initiative, but with a different status initially, as they did not yet have sector plans and/or national poverty reduction strategies in place. These "Big Five" countries are deemed high priority because they account for the largest numbers of children without access to primary education globally—about 50 million of the 113 million children in total estimated to be out of school. The spirit of the Fast-Track Initiative is that country commitment to sound sector programs integrated into a broader poverty reduction strategy as well as commitment to appropriate policy actions in line with the EFA indicative framework are important for effective use of development resources.

Box 5.2

First EFA Fast-Track Group, 2002

Albania
Bolivia
Burkina Faso
Ethiopia
The Gambia
Ghana
Guinea
Guyana
Honduras
Mauritania
Mozambique
Nicaragua
Niger
Tanzania
Uganda
Vietnam
Republic of Yemen
Zambia

Analytical Fast-Track Countries

Bangladesh
Democratic Republic of Congo
India
Nigeria
Pakistan

"Analytical Fast-Track" support aims to help these countries reach that status. India is the first of the "Big Five" countries to meet the two criteria, and the government is considering participation in the Fast Track.

In countries that have plans in place, the Fast-Track process involves a complementary in-country analysis to benchmark the education system's performance relative to the EFA indicative framework; to appropriate annual targets for their country context; and to refine estimates of the external financing needs for accelerated progress in primary education, consistent with the implementation of appropriate reforms and the country's medium-term expenditure framework. Although for the first set of countries these adjustments and targets have been set out in "Fast-Track proposals," it is expected that the process of identifying priority policy actions to align system functioning with the indicative framework benchmarks will increasingly become a natural part of the development of a PRSP and a credible education sector plan and separate FTI proposals will not be needed. The first FTI proposals have represented a more comprehensive assessment of financing needs than we costed, as they include rehabilitation requirements. The estimated expansion needs, however, may be compared with the financing needs estimated in this study.

An important part of the process is also careful assessment of the physical and institutional capacity to execute increased primary education investment and expenditure. The Fast-Track Initiative in all cases implies a major expansion of the management challenge for systems that are generally perceived to be weakly managed today. But this cannot be an argument against such expansion; it simply means that attention to capacity building and institutional support must be an equal part of the partnership effort.

Finally, the estimated needs are compared with the pipeline of existing donor commitments for primary education in each country, including general budget support under PRSCs or other multisector programs. It should be recalled that the financing gaps estimated in the present study are gross financing gaps, with no adjustment for the current level of external assistance to the primary sector.

As of March 2003, ten of the first 18 countries invited to join the Fast-Track Initiative submitted proposals for consideration. The Fast-Track partners committed, upon verification of the estimated financing gaps, to ensure that these gaps are filled for the next three years, contingent on the countries' continued progress in executing the accelerated program and improving sector functioning in line with their indicative framework targets. The partners also agreed to meet every six months to consider additional country proposals, review implementation, and harmonize their education assistance to Fast-Track countries. Intensified collaboration among donor representatives at the client country level is a key part of this process.

For their part, Fast-Track recipient countries are committed to annual monitoring of their progress against indicative framework targets. Key outcomes such as the net intake rate into first grade for girls and boys, the primary completion rate for girls and boys, and student learning achievement will also be monitored, although it is understood that these outcome indicators can be slow to reflect progress.

CONCLUSION

Without a substantial acceleration of progress in as many as 86 developing countries, the Millennium Development Goal of universal primary education by the year 2015 will not be met. The good news is that many of these countries *could* meet the goal, if they could achieve and sustain the same rate of primary completion progress averaged by the best-performing developing countries over the 1990s. We know from country experience that it can be done.

We also know, from country experience, the key building blocks for a healthy system of primary education. We know what constitutes a broadly adequate level of resources, and how to balance two key elements of the resource mix: (a) spending on teachers and (b) the equally crucial spending on complementary inputs, supervision, and support needed to make teachers effective in the classroom.

Domestic commitment to universalizing primary education is the first key. As countries from the Republic of Korea in the 1960s to Zimbabwe in the 1980s to Brazil in the 1990s have demonstrated, when political will is mustered, primary completion progress can accelerate quickly.

But for the 48 low-income countries with the world's lowest completion rates, even maximum commitments of domestic resources for primary education plus steady progress in reforming service delivery will not be enough to ensure achievement of the education MDG by 2015. A resource gap of at least $2.5 billion per year in these countries will threaten their achievement of the goal in the absence of external assistance.

Mobilizing this amount of increased aid should not be an insurmountable challenge for the international community, but it will require very significant changes in donor priorities and the mechanisms through which aid is channeled. Accompanying increased financing with support for capacity building and implementation is also important to ensure that donor and national resources effectively produce the desired results.

The new compact for accelerating progress embodied in the EFA Fast-Track Initiative—if launched successfully and expanded steadily to include all of the at-risk developing countries—could provide a framework in which countries' steady progress in improving core indicators of education system functioning and progressive improvement in outcomes would be the quid pro quo for sustained and predictable budgetary support from international partners, channeled in new and more flexible ways. Few global goals have been as consistently and deeply supported as the notion that every child in the world should have the chance to complete primary school. With global effort, it could become a reality.

BIBLIOGRAPHY

Azariadis, Costas, and Allan Drazen. 1990. "Threshold Externalities in Economic Development." *Quarterly Journal of Economics* 105 (2): 501-26.

Barro, Robert J. 1999a. "Determinants of Democracy." *Journal of Political Economy* 107 (6): 158-83.

_____. 1999b. "Human Capital and Growth in Cross-Country Regressions." *Swedish Economic Policy Review* 6 (2): 237-77.

Barro, Robert J., and Jong-Wha Lee. 2000. "International Data on Educational Attainment Updates and Implications." Working Paper 7911. National Bureau of Economic Research, Cambridge, Mass.

Birdsall, Nancy, and Juan Luis Londoño. 1998. "No Tradeoff: Efficient Growth Via More Equal Human Capital Accumulation in Latin America." In Nancy Birdsall, Carol Graham, and Richard Sabot, eds., *Beyond Trade-Offs: Market Reform and Equitable Growth in Latin America* . Washington, D.C.: Brookings Institution and Inter-American Development Bank.

Brossard, Mathieu, and Luc-Charles Gacougnolle. 2001. "Financing Primary Education for All: Yesterday, Today and Tomorrow." United Nations Educational, Scientific, and Cultural Organization, Paris. Processed.

Colclough, Christopher, and Samer Al-Samarrai. 2000. "Achieving Schooling for All: Budgetary Expenditures on Education in Sub-Saharan Africa and South Asia." *World Development* 28 (11): 1927-44.

Colclough, Christopher, and Keith Lewin. 1993. *Educating All the Children: Strategies for Primary Schooling in the South.* New York: Oxford University Press.

De, Anuradha, and Jean Dreze. 1999. *Public Report on Basic Education in India (PROBE).* New Delhi: Oxford University Press.

de la Fuente, Angel, and Rafael Domenech. 2000. "Human Capital in Growth Regressions: How Much Difference Does Data Quality Make?" Paper 2466. Centre for Economic Policy Research Discussion, London.

Delamonica, Enrique, Santosh Mehrotra, and Jan Vandemoortele. 2001. "Is EFA Affordable? Estimating the Global Minimum Cost of Education for All." Innocenti Working Paper 87. United Nations Children's Fund, New York.

Devarajan, Shantayanan, Margaret J. Miller, and Eric V. Swanson. 2002. "Goals for Development: History, Prospects and Costs." Policy Research Working Paper 2819. World Bank, Washington, D.C.

di Gropello, Emanuela, Ashutosh Dubey, and Donald Winkler. 2002. "Reaching Millennium Development and Regional Goals for Education in Latin America and the Caribbean—Second Draft." World Bank, Latin America and Caribbean Region, Human Development Department, Washington, D.C. Processed.

Filmer, Deon. 2000. "The Structure of Social Disparities in Education: Gender and Wealth." Policy Research Working Paper 2268. World Bank, Development Research Group, Washington, D.C. Underlying data available at http://www.worldbank.org/research/projects/edattain/edattain.htm

Filmer, Deon, and Lant Pritchett. 1999. "The Effect of Household Wealth on Educational Attainment: Evidence from 35 Countries." *Population and Development Review* 25 (1): 85-120. Underlying data available at http://www.worldbank.org/research/projects/edattain/edattain.htm

Godoy, Ricardo, and Manuel Contreras. 2001. "A Comparative Study of Education and Tropical Deforestation among Lowland Bolivian Amerindians: Forest Values, Environmental Externality, and School Subsidies." *Economic Development and Cultural Change* 49 (3): 555-74.

Gregson, S., H. Waddell, and S. Chandiwana. 2001. "School Education and HIV Control in Sub-Saharan Africa: From Discord to Harmony?" *Journal of International Development* 13: 467-85.

Hanushek, Eric A., and Dennis D. Kimko. 2000. "Schooling, Labor Force Quality, and the Growth of Nations." *American Economic Review* 90 (5): 1184-1208.

Kelly, M. J. 2000. "Planning for Education in the Context of HIV/AIDS." UNESCO, International Institute for Educational Planning, Paris.

Kitaev, Igor. 1999. "Private Education in Sub-Saharan Africa: A Re-examination of Theories and Concepts Related to Its Development and Finance." UNESCO, International Institute for Educational Planning, Paris.

Lockheed, Marlaine E., Adriaan M. Verspoor, and associates. 1991. *Improving Primary Education in Developing Countries.* New York: Oxford University Press for the World Bank.

Mehrotra, Santosh. 1998. "Education for All: Policy Lessons from High-Achieving Countries." Staff Working Paper, Evaluation, Policy and Planning Series, No. EPP-EVL-98-005. United Nations Children's Fund, New York.

Mehrotra, Santosh, and Peter Buckland. 1998. "Managing Teacher Costs for Access and Quality." Staff Working Paper, Evaluation, Policy and Planning Series, No. EPP-EVL-98-004. United Nations Children's Fund, New York.

Mingat, Alain. 2001. "Teacher Salary Issues in African Countries." World Bank, Africa Region, Human Development Analysis and Policy Development Support Team. Washington, D.C. Processed.

Mingat, Alain, Ramahatra Rakotomalala, and Jee-Peng Tan. 2002. "Financing Education for All by 2015 in Africa: Simulation Results for 33 Countries." Human Development Working Paper. World Bank, Africa Region, Washington, D.C.

O'Connell, Lesley, and Nancy Birdsall. 2001. "Race, Human Capital Inequality, and Income Distribution in South Africa, Brazil and the United States." Discussion Paper 4. Carnegie Endowment for International Peace, Washington, D.C.

OECD (Organisation for Economic Co-operation and Development). 2000. *Investing in Education: Analysis of the 1999 World Education Indicators.* Paris.

OECD and Statistics Canada. 2000. *Literacy in the Information Age: Final Report of the International Adult Literacy Survey* . Paris: OECD.

Oxfam International Global Campaign for Education. 2002. "Broken Promises? Why Donors Must Deliver on the EFA Action Plan." Global Campaign for Education Briefing Paper. Oxfam International, Oxford, U.K.

Porter, Michael. 1998. "Microeconomic Foundations of Competitiveness: The Role of Education." In *The Global Competitiveness Report 1998.* Cambridge, Mass.: Harvard University, Center for International Development, World Economic Forum.

Psacharopoulos, George. 1995. "The Profitability of Investment in Education: Concept and Methods." Human Capital Development and Operations Policy Working Paper. World Bank, Washington, D.C.

Psacharopoulos, George, and Harry Anthony Patrinos. 2002. "Returns to Investment in Education: A Further Update." Policy Research Paper 2881. World Bank, Education Department, Latin America and Caribbean Region, Washington, D.C.

Sen, Amartya. 1999. *Development as Freedom.* New York: Knopf.

Smith, Lisa C., and Lawrence Haddad. 2000. "Explaining Child Malnutrition in Developing Countries: A Cross-Country Analysis." Food Consumption and Nutrition Division Discussion Paper 60. International Food Policy Research Institute, Washington, D.C.

Subbarao, K., Angel Mattimore, and Kathrin Plangemann. 2001. "Social Protection of Africa's Orphans and Other Vulnerable Children." Human Development Working Paper. World Bank, Africa Region, Washington, D.C.

Vandemoortele, J., and E. Delamonica. 2000. "Education 'Vaccine' Against HIV/AIDS." *Current Issues in Comparative Education* 3 (1).

Voluntary Services Organization. 2002. "What Makes Teachers Tick? A Policy Research Report on Teachers' Motivation in Developing Countries." London. Processed.

Watkins, Kevin. 1999. *Education Now: Break the Cycle of Poverty.* Oxford, U.K.: Oxfam International.

World Bank. 2001. *Engendering Development: Through Gender Equality in Rights, Resources, and Voice.* World Bank Policy Research Report 21776. New York: Oxford University Press.

_____. 2002a. "Development Effectiveness and Scaling Up: Lessons and Challenges from Case Studies." Synthesis paper DC2002-0018, prepared for the September 28, 2002 Development Committee meeting. Washington, D.C.

_____. 2002b. *Education and HIV/AIDS: A Window of Hope.* Washington, D.C.

_____. 2002c. "EFA: The Lessons of Experience: The Impact of Policy in 20 Case Studies." World Bank, Education Department, Human Development Network, Washington, D.C. Processed.

_____. 2002d. "India; Karnataka: Financing Education in the Context of Economic Restructuring." Report 24207-IN. South Asia Region, Human Development Department, Washington, D.C.

_____. 2002e. "School Enrollment and Attainment in India: Progress during the 1990s." South Asia Region, Washington, D.C. Processed.

TECHNICAL ANNEXES

Background Data and Aggregate Simulation Results

ABOUT THE SIMULATION MODEL

A discussion of the key assumptions underlying the target variables used for the 2000-2015 simulations may be found in chapter 4. This section describes the mechanics and key building blocks of the relatively simple simulation model we used.

The stylized dynamics of some key variables. Achieving the MDG by 2015 implies that all children in an age cohort enter the system and remain in it until they have completed the primary cycle (or six years of the cycle if it lasts longer than that). Figure A.1 shows how the student flow profile in a hypothetical country would shift over time as it attains the MDG. In panel A, the profiles at four points in time are shown. In the initial year (2000), 75 percent of the school-age population enters first grade, and 40 percent of that population completes sixth grade. By 2005, the dotted line profile shows these rates rising to 90 percent and 65 percent, respectively. By 2010 the entry rate reaches 100 percent, while the completion rate climbs to 85 percent. By 2015, both the entry and completion rates reach 100 percent, signifying attainment of universal primary completion.

In panel B of the figure, the same information is presented differently to emphasize that in order to attain the MDG by 2015, countries must necessarily have achieved universal entry to first grade by 2010, in the case of a five-year primary system, or 2009, for a six-year cycle. Panel B also shows that the repetition rate would need to decline over the period (if it is high in the initial year), given that extensive grade repetition is correlated with dropout and is therefore incompatible with the MDG goal.

The student flow profiles in figure A.1 are applied to projections of the school-age population in order to obtain estimates of total primary school enrollments over the course of the simulation period. Figure A.2 shows in panel A typical patterns in the size of the school-age population, as well as the corresponding number of primary school pupils and non-repeaters among them. Notice that as the year approaches 2015, the gap between total enrollments and the number of non-repeaters narrows, reflecting the assumed decline in repetition rates. Panel B of the figure shows the distribution of enrollments between publicly and privately financed schools. The share of pupils in the public sector is expected to grow because as schooling extends to the whole population of school-age children, the new entrants would increasingly be children from poorer families or otherwise deprived circumstances (rural children, girls, orphans). Our thesis is that the families of these children are neither willing nor able to afford fee-charging schools in the private sector. Hence, the simulation model assumes that the share of enrollments in the privately financed sector would fall as countries approach the

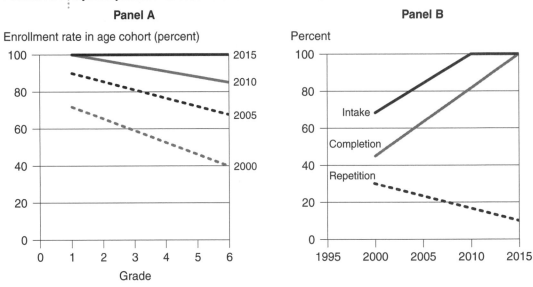

FIGURE A.1 : Stylized Dynamics of Selected Indicators of Student Flow, 2000–2015

Panel A

Panel B

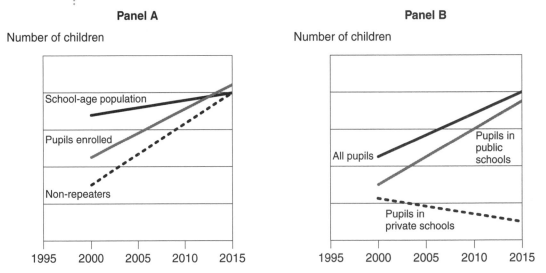

FIGURE A.2 : Stylized Dynamics of Primary School Enrollments, 2000–2015

Panel A

Panel B

MDG by 2015. As noted in chapter 4, however, this assumption does not preclude growing enrollments in schools that are publicly funded but privately managed.

Overview of the simulation model. The model has a simple and parsimonious structure that seeks to incorporate key policy variables relevant to projecting the EFA external financing gap while minimizing data requirements. For each country, estimation of the external financing gap involves four steps.

The first step is to estimate the recurrent cost of achieving the MDG by 2015. Two sets of variables are relevant to the calculation. The first set pertains to the projected number of children served by publicly funded schools. As indicated earlier, this number depends on: (a) the projected size of the school-age population over the simulation period; (b) the intake rate to first grade; (c) the share of first graders who complete the primary cycle; (d) the prevalence of grade repetition (which affects the efficiency of student flows through the system); and (e) the proportion of pupils enrolled in publicly funded schools. The second set of variables relates to the cost of service delivery in the publicly funded sector. The estimate depends on the following factors: (a) the ratio of pupils to teachers in publicly funded schools (which allows the number of teachers in such schools to be estimated); (b) the average salaries of public sector teachers (which is combined with the estimate of teacher numbers to obtain the aggregate salary bill); and (c) the cost of complementary school inputs to promote student learning as well as to finance targeted subsidies to the most disadvantaged children who might otherwise not attend school (such as those from the poorest families or hard-to-reach communities).

Because of the high prevalence of HIV/AIDS in many African countries, a separate calculation is made to estimate the epidemic's impact on the cost of delivering primary education services. The epidemic's impact on the size of the school-age cohort is already incorporated into the population projections referred to in the preceding paragraph. Beyond this effect, the simulation model allows for two additional effects: (a) the costs associated with increased teacher absenteeism, which effectively translates into an increase in the number of teachers needed to ensure service delivery beyond the number determined solely by the average pupil-teacher ratio; and (b) the cost to support the growing cohorts of orphans created by the epidemic (see box 4.1 in chapter 4 for more details on the AIDS-related part of the simulation model).

The second step in the simulation involves estimation of the capital costs of building and furnishing classrooms to accommodate the growing number of children enrolled in the publicly funded sector. The calculation involves determining the number of new classrooms implied by the growth in enrollments, assuming that the pupil-classroom ratio is the same as the pupil-teacher ratio (which is equivalent to assuming that teachers are assigned to teach all subjects to the same group of pupils). The unit cost to construct and furnish classrooms ranges widely across countries. In these simulations, we set it at what regional experts consider to be a "good practice" level for each country.

The third step in the simulation involves estimating the volume of resources that the country itself will be able to mobilize to reach the MDG. The amount mobilized depends on the behavior of the following factors over the course of 2001–2015: (a) the projected growth rate of the country's GDP; (b) the size of government revenues relative to the GDP; (c) the share of government revenues devoted to education; and (d) the share of public spending on education that is set aside specifically for primary education. We used a GDP growth projection of 5 percent per year for all countries across the period.

The fourth and final step in the calculation is to determine the resource gap for external financing in order to achieve the MDG by 2015. The calculation simply involves subtracting the results of steps 1 and 2 from those of step 3. The algorithm is arranged to reflect the assumption that domestic resources would first be used to finance the recurrent costs of service delivery, and any surplus would be applied toward the capital costs. In countries where domestic resources are insufficient to cover the recurrent costs, the assumption is that external resources would be available to help finance the shortfall in financing for both the recurrent and capital costs.

Table A.1
....
Countries Included in Financing Simulation

   I. Countries eligible for IDA lending in 2001 (GDP per capita less than $885)

  II. Countries with populations less than 1 million

 III. Countries for which adequate data could not be obtained

 IV. Full sample of 55 countries

  V. Countries omitted from adjusted sample (see chapter 3, footnote 1, for rationale for omitting these)

 VI. Countries not modeled (estimated to have achieved or to be close to achieving UPC, defined as 90 percent completion through grade 6)

VII. Countries for which simulations were run (47)

I. IDA countries: 79

Afghanistan	Chad	Haiti	Mongolia	Solomon Islands
Albania	Comoros	Honduras	Mozambique	Somalia
Angola	Congo, Dem. Rep. of	India	Myanmar	Sri Lanka
Armenia	Congo, Rep. of	Indonesia	Nepal	Sudan
Azerbaijan	Côte d'Ivoire	Kenya	Nicaragua	Tajikistan
Bangladesh	Djibouti	Kiribati	Niger	Tanzania
Benin	Dominica	Kyrgyz Republic	Nigeria	Togo
Bhutan	Eritrea	Lao PDR	Pakistan	Tonga
Bolivia	Ethiopia	Lesotho	Rwanda	Uganda
Bosnia and Herzegovina	Gambia, The	Liberia	St. Lucia	Uzbekistan
Burkina Faso	Georgia	Madagascar	St. Vincent	Vanuatu
Burundi	Ghana	Malawi	São Tomé and Principe	Vietnam
Cambodia	Grenada	Maldives	Samoa	Yemen, Rep. of
Cameroon	Guinea	Mali	Senegal	Zambia
Cape Verde	Guinea-Bissau	Mauritania	Serbia and Montenegro	Zimbabwe
Central African Republic	Guyana	Moldova	Sierra Leone	

II. Countries with populations less than 1 million: 16

Bhutan	Dominica	Maldives	St. Lucia
Cape Verde	Grenada	Samoa	St. Vincent
Comoros	Guyana	São Tomé and Principe	Tongo
Djibouti	Kiribati	Solomon Islands	Vanuatu

III. Countries with inadequate data: 8

Afghanistan[a] Bosnia and Herzegovina	Liberia Myanmar	Serbia and Montenegro Somalia	Sri Lanka Tajikistan

a. Included in alternative simulation.

IV. Full sample: 55

Albania	Central African Republic	Guinea-Bissau	Mali	Senegal
Angola	Chad	Haiti	Mauritania	Sierra Leone
Armenia	Congo, Dem. Rep. of	Honduras	Moldova	Sudan
Azerbaijan	Congo, Rep. of	India	Mongolia	Tanzania
Bangladesh	Côte d'Ivoire	Indonesia	Mozambique	Togo
Benin	Eritrea	Kenya	Nepal	Uganda
Bolivia	Ethiopia	Kyrgyz Republic	Nicaragua	Uzbekistan
Burkina Faso	Gambia, The	Lao PDR	Niger	Vietnam
Burundi	Georgia	Lesotho	Nigeria	Yemen, Rep. of
Cambodia	Ghana	Madagascar	Pakistan	Zambia
Cameroon	Guinea	Malawi	Rwanda	Zimbabwe

V. Countries omitted from adjusted sample: 6

Albania	Armenia	Azerbaijan	Georgia	Kyrgyz Republic	Uzbekistan

VI. Countries not modeled (PCR through grade 5 or 6 over 90 percent): 8

Albania Azerbaijan	Bolivia Indonesia	Kyrgyz Republic Uzbekistan	Vietnam Zimbabwe

VII. Final adjusted sample for which simulations were run: 47

Angola	Congo, Rep. of	India	Nepal	Uganda
Armenia	Côte d'Ivoire	Kenya	Nicaragua	Yemen, Rep. of
Bangladesh	Eritrea	Lao PDR	Niger	Zambia
Benin	Ethiopia	Lesotho	Nigeria	
Burkina Faso	Gambia, The	Madagascar	Pakistan	
Burundi	Georgia	Malawi	Rwanda	
Cambodia	Ghana	Mali	Senegal	
Cameroon	Guinea	Mauritania	Sierra Leone	
Central African Republic	Guinea-Bissau	Moldova	Sudan	
Chad	Haiti	Mongolia	Tanzania	
Congo, Dem. Rep. of	Honduras	Mozambique	Togo	

Table A.2

Core Education Parameters for 55 Low-Income Countries

Country	Year of data	Primary GER (%)	Primary completion rate (%)	Government current revenues (excluding grants) as % of GDP	EDUCATION RECURRENT SPENDING — As % of government current revenues, excluding grants	EDUCATION RECURRENT SPENDING — As % of GDP	PRIMARY EDUCATION RECURRENT SPENDING — As % of recurrent education spending	PRIMARY EDUCATION RECURRENT SPENDING — As % of GDP	Unit cost as % of per capita GDP	Average annual teacher salary (as multiple of per capita GDP)	Spending on inputs other than teachers (as % of primary education recurrent spending)	Pupils per teacher	Private enrollments (as % of total)	Average repetition rate (%)
Albania	1998	103	91	19.5	12.6	2.5	41.3	1.0	7.7	1.4	17.5	22.7	0.6	0.0
Angola	2000	80	29	55.7	4.3	2.4	41.6	1.0	7.8	1.5	19.0	24.4	6.0	25.0
Armenia	2000	87	70	15.8	15.1	2.4	51.3	1.2	12.6	0.6	52.9	12.8	0.0	0.1
Azerbaijan	2000	107	99	20.8	18.4	3.8	19.7	0.8	5.9	0.9	15.8	17.6	1.0	0.4
Bangladesh	2000	112	70	12.8	14.7	1.9	49.9	0.9	6.6	2.7	25.0	55.2	12.5	15.0
Benin	1998	86	39	15.3	16.5	2.5	62.6	1.6	11.6	4.6	26.4	54.0	10.8	25.0
Bolivia	2000	113	97	21.2	25.2	5.3	47.5	2.5	15.9	2.2	19.4	20.6	9.4	3.7
Burkina Faso	1998	45	25	14.7	17.1	2.5	64.0	1.6	23.6	8.0	30.7	48.9	10.8	17.7
Burundi	1998	60	43	17.4	20.4	3.6	35.5	1.3	12.4	5.3	22.1	55.1	0.0	27.5
Cambodia	2000	134	60	11.5	15.0	1.7	51.0	0.9	3.6	1.5	20.0	53.3	0.0	16.6
Cameroon	1999	82	43	15.5	10.8	1.7	66.3	1.1	9.5	3.4	32.5	64.6	19.0	25.9
Central African Republic	2000	45	19	9.6	12.5	1.2	52.4	0.6	8.7	4.9	28.5	78.9	3.3	32.8
Chad	2000	71	19	8.0	20.9	1.7	65.5	1.1	10.1	4.8	34.2	72.0	8.8	24.6
Congo, Dem. Rep. of	2000	60	40	10.6	3.2	0.3	65.1	0.2	2.4	0.9	10.3	42.2	10.0	15.0
Congo, Rep. of	2000	84	44	26.7	8.6	2.3	36.6	0.8	7.0	3.4	20.3	61.0	15.2	31.1

Country	Year													
Côte d'Ivoire	1999	77	40	16.5	21.5	3.5	49.0	1.7	16.0	5.7	22.5	46.0	11.6	24.7
Eritrea	1999	53	35	34.6	8.0	2.8	53.6	1.5	22.2	7.7	29.6	49.2	10.1	19.4
Ethiopia	1999	55	24	17.8	15.0	2.7	46.2	1.2	14.0	6.8	20.5	61.3	5.0	8.0
Gambia, The	2000	88	70	18.5	16.6	3.1	51.7	1.6	13.2	3.7	24.9	37.0	8.5	10.6
Georgia	1999	86	79	13.7	9.3	1.3	26.0	0.3	4.2	0.6	16.0	16.5	1.0	0.5
Ghana	1999	79	64	21.8	17.6	3.8	37.2	1.4	12.7	3.6	17.7	34.1	18.0	5.0
Guinea	2000	62	34	11.1	18.1	2.0	37.2	0.8	8.4	2.7	34.7	48.9	16.1	23.3
Guinea-Bissau	2000	70	31	19.6	9.8	1.9	35.0	0.7	6.7	1.6	34.3	37.4	8.5	27.1
Haiti	1997	112	40	9.3	20.6	1.9	38.7	0.7	16.2	6.8	10.0	46.3	76.6	17.0
Honduras	2000	105	67	18.5	30.1	5.6	49.6	2.8	17.8	5.0	12.0	31.7	6.9	8.0
India	1999	101	76	21.2	12.4	2.6	38.5	1.0	8.4	3.4	23.2	51.8	12.5	20.0
Indonesia	2000	106	91	18.4	9.7	1.8	59.3	1.1	10.3	1.6	19.9	19.9	15.7	5.9
Kenya	1999	91	64	24.2	26.2	6.3	44.2	2.8	17.6	5.3	4.2	31.4	2.2	14.2
Kyrgyz Rep.	1999	100	99	18.7	22.0	4.1	36.0	1.5	10.3	1.2	21.8	15.2	0.0	0.0
Lao PDR	1999	121	67	38.1	1.4	0.5	58.6	0.3	1.5	0.4	19.6	30.6	1.9	22.6
Lesotho	2000	103	70	35.9	22.2	8.0	40.2	3.2	20.8	6.6	29.9	45.3	0.0	18.3
Madagascar	1998	90	26	10.6	18.8	2.0	54.7	1.1	10.8	3.3	42.4	53.7	22.0	33.0
Malawi	1999	117	65	18.1	19.8	3.6	49.2	1.8	8.8	4.0	14.0	52.8	2.0	14.7
Mali	1998	49	23	16.8	13.7	2.3	42.1	1.0	14.3	6.1	31.1	61.0	21.2	17.9
Mauritania	1998	88	46	26.5	13.7	3.6	49.0	1.8	13.1	5.1	18.2	48.0	1.8	16.0
Moldova	1999	81	79	29.8	18.5	5.5	25.5	1.4	15.8	1.1	67.8	21.4	0.0	0.9
Mongolia	1999	92	67	29.2	24.6	7.2	33.6	2.4	15.1	3.9	15.0	30.7	0.5	0.9
Mozambique	1998	79	36	11.3	18.1	2.0	46.4	1.0	7.9	3.2	26.1	54.4	0.0	23.7
Nepal	1998	113	56	10.4	18.4	1.9	63.8	1.2	7.1	2.0	20.0	35.9	8.1	29.9
Nicaragua	2000	101	65	25.3	16.8	4.3	48.7	2.1	13.2	3.2	32.7	35.9	6.8	12.0
Niger	1998	31	20	9.1	31.5	2.9	62.0	1.8	35.5	9.6	25.9	36.5	4.0	13.0
Nigeria	2000	85	67	46.1	9.9	4.6	41.0	1.9	13.8	4.9	9.1	39.0	1.0	1.0
Pakistan	2000	65	59	16.7	10.2	1.7	51.8	0.9	14.0	3.6	19.3	32.1	29.4	6.2

(Continued)

147

Table A.2
(Continued)

Country	Year of data	Primary GER (%)	Primary completion rate (%)	Government current revenues (excluding grants) as % of GDP	Education Recurrent Spending — As % of government current revenues, excluding grants	Education Recurrent Spending — As % of GDP	Primary Education Recurrent Spending — As % of recurrent education spending	Primary Education Recurrent Spending — As % of GDP	Unit cost as % of per capita GDP	Average annual teacher salary (as multiple of per capita GDP)	Spending on inputs other than teachers (as % of primary education recurrent spending)	Pupils per teacher	Private enrollments (as % of total)	Average repetition rate (%)
Rwanda	2000	101	28	9.8	32.6	3.2	44.7	1.4	9.1	4.0	8.6	47.7	0.8	36.1
Senegal	2000	70	41	18.1	18.6	3.4	43.9	1.5	14.2	4.9	36.6	54.7	10.7	13.6
Sierra Leone	2000	64	37	11.4	30.4	3.5	51.3	1.8	16.4	4.3	33.1	39.6	0.0	9.3
Sudan	2000	61	35	11.1	16.2	1.8	50.5	0.9	10.3	2.2	22.5	27.5	0.0	1.2
Tanzania	1999	66	59	10.9	16.4	1.8	63.0	1.1	10.0	3.6	11.2	40.0	0.0	3.2
Togo	1999	115	63	14.9	25.6	3.8	48.3	1.8	13.2	4.5	25.2	45.5	35.6	27.0
Uganda	2000	102	82	10.8	30.1	3.2	53.2	1.7	9.8	2.9	26.2	40.9	2.0	9.8
Uzbekistan	1999	100	100	32.4	22.3	7.2	41.2	3.0	18.7	2.9	27.0	21.0	0.0	0.1
Vietnam	1998	110	99	22.3	10.9	2.4	46.5	1.1	7.1	1.2	45.0	30.4	0.0	3.5
Yemen, Rep. of	1998	67	58	35.2	15.8	5.6	48.0	2.7	18.5	3.4	26.7	25.0	1.4	7.0
Zambia	1998	85	72	18.8	12.3	2.3	43.2	1.0	6.9	2.7	21.7	50.0	1.6	6.2
Zimbabwe	1997	112	103	27.4	28.3	7.1	46.1	3.3	19.4	6.1	25.0	39.0	11.0	2.0
Average, all countries		86	57	19.7	17.3	3.2	47.3	1.4	12.2	3.7	24.5	40.9	8.4	14.1
Average, African countries		77	45	19.0	17.8	3.0	49.2	1.4	12.9	4.5	24.1	47.7	8.2	17.7
Average, best performers		103	83	20.7	18.2	3.8	47.6	1.7	11.8	3.3	26.0	39.0	7.3	9.5

Note: Primary GERs and PCRs presented here have been adjusted to an equivalent basis for purposes of comparison. For countries with five-year or six-year systems, the values presented here correspond to the official cycle. But for countries whose primary cycle is shorter or longer than this, we have estimated a six-year equivalent GER and PCR. For this reason, data in this and subsequent tables may differ from completion-rate data in chapter 2.

Table A.3

Key Education System Parameters for Countries, Grouped by Relative EFA Success (Adjusted Sample)

Country	Primary GER (%)	Primary completion rate (%)	Government current revenues (excluding grants) as % of GDP	Education Recurrent Spending: As % of government current revenues, excluding grants	Education Recurrent Spending: As % of GDP	Primary Education Recurrent Spending: As % of recurrent education spending	Primary Education Recurrent Spending: As % of GDP	Unit cost as % of per capita GDP	Average annual teacher salary (as multiple of per capita GDP)	Spending on inputs other than teachers (as % of primary education recurrent spending)	Pupils per teacher	Private enrollments (as % of total)	Average repetition rate (%)
Group 1: High enrollment (GER 85% or above) and high completion (PCR 70% or above)													
Bangladesh	112	70	12.8	14.7	1.9	49.9	0.9	6.6	2.7	25.0	55.2	12.5	15.0
Bolivia	113	97	21.2	25.2	5.3	47.5	2.5	15.9	2.2	19.4	20.6	9.4	3.7
Gambia, The	88	70	18.5	16.6	3.1	51.7	1.6	13.2	3.7	25.0	37.0	8.0	10.6
India	101	76	21.2	12.4	2.6	38.5	1.0	8.4	3.4	23.2	51.8	12.5	20.0
Indonesia	106	91	18.4	9.7	1.8	59.3	1.1	10.3	1.6	19.9	19.9	15.7	5.9
Lesotho	103	70	35.9	22.2	8.0	40.2	3.2	20.8	6.6	30.0	45.3	0.0	18.3
Uganda	102	82	10.8	30.1	3.2	53.2	1.7	9.8	2.9	26.0	40.9	2.0	9.8
Vietnam	110	99	22.3	10.9	2.4	46.5	1.1	7.1	1.2	45.0	30.4	0.0	3.5
Zambia	85	72	18.8	12.3	2.3	43.2	1.0	6.9	2.7	22.0	50.0	2.0	6.2
Zimbabwe	112	103	27.4	28.3	7.1	46.1	3.3	19.4	6.1	25.0	39.0	11.0	2.0
Average	**103**	**83**	**20.7**	**18.2**	**3.8**	**47.6**	**1.7**	**11.8**	**3.3**	**26.1**	**39.0**	**7.3**	**9.5**
Group 2: High enrollment (GER 80% or above) but low completion (PCR 60% or lower)													
Angola	80	29	55.7	4.3	2.4	41.6	1.0	7.8	1.5	19.0	24.4	6.0	25.0
Benin	86	39	15.3	16.5	2.5	62.6	1.6	11.6	4.6	26.0	54.0	11.0	25.0
Cameroon	82	43	15.5	10.8	1.7	66.3	1.1	9.5	3.4	33.0	64.6	19.0	25.9
Congo, Rep. of	84	44	26.7	8.6	2.3	36.6	0.8	7.0	3.4	20.0	61.0	15.0	31.1
Madagascar	90	26	10.6	18.8	2.0	54.7	1.1	10.8	3.3	42.0	53.7	22.0	33.0
Mauritania	88	46	26.5	13.7	3.6	49.0	1.8	13.1	5.1	18.0	48.0	2.0	16.0
Nepal	113	56	10.4	18.4	1.9	63.8	1.2	7.1	2.0	20.0	35.9	8.1	29.9
Rwanda	101	28	9.8	32.6	3.2	44.7	1.4	9.1	4.0	9.0	47.7	1.0	36.1
Average	**91**	**39**	**21.3**	**15.5**	**2.5**	**52.4**	**1.3**	**9.5**	**3.4**	**23.4**	**48.7**	**10.5**	**27.8**

(Continued)

Table A.3
(Continued)

Country	Primary GER (%)	Primary completion rate (%)	Government current revenues (excluding grants) as % of GDP	Education Recurrent Spending: As % of government current revenues, excluding grants	Education Recurrent Spending: As % of GDP	Primary Education Recurrent Spending: As % of recurrent education spending	Primary Education Recurrent Spending: As % of GDP	Unit cost as % of per capita GDP	Average annual teacher salary (as multiple of per capita GDP)	Spending on inputs other than teachers (as % of primary education recurrent spending)	Pupils per teacher	Private enrollments (as % of total)	Average repetition rate (%)
Group 3: Low enrollment and low completion (GER and PCR both 60% or lower)													
Burkina Faso	45	25	14.7	17.1	2.5	64.0	1.6	23.6	8.0	31.0	48.9	11.0	17.7
Burundi	60	43	17.4	20.4	3.6	35.5	1.3	12.4	5.3	22.0	55.1	0.0	27.5
Central African Republic	45	19	9.6	12.5	1.2	52.4	0.6	8.7	4.9	29.0	78.9	3.0	32.8
Eritrea	53	35	34.6	8.0	2.8	53.6	1.5	22.2	7.7	30.0	49.2	10.0	19.4
Ethiopia	55	24	17.8	15.0	2.7	46.2	1.2	14.0	6.8	21.0	61.3	5.0	8.0
Mali	49	23	16.8	13.7	2.3	42.1	1.0	14.3	6.1	31.0	61.0	21.0	17.9
Niger	31	20	9.1	31.5	2.9	62.0	1.8	35.5	9.6	26.0	36.5	4.0	13.0
Average	**48**	**27**	**17.1**	**16.9**	**2.6**	**50.8**	**1.3**	**18.7**	**6.9**	**27.1**	**55.8**	**7.7**	**19.5**
Group 4: Remaining countries													
Cambodia	134	60	11.5	15.0	1.7	51.0	0.9	3.6	1.5	20.0	53.3	0.0	16.6
Chad	71	19	8.0	20.9	1.7	65.5	1.1	10.1	4.8	34.0	72.0	9.0	24.6
Congo, Dem. Rep. of	60	40	10.6	3.2	0.3	65.1	0.2	2.4	0.9	10.0	42.2	10.0	15.0
Côte d'Ivoire	77	40	16.5	21.5	3.5	49.0	1.7	16.0	5.7	22.0	46.0	12.0	24.7
Ghana	79	64	21.8	17.6	3.8	37.2	1.4	12.7	3.6	18.0	34.1	18.0	5.0

Guinea	62	34	11.1	18.1	2.0	37.2	0.8	8.4	2.7	35.0	48.9	16.0	23.3
Guinea-Bissau	70	31	19.6	9.8	1.9	35.0	0.7	6.7	1.6	34.0	37.4	9.0	27.1
Haiti	112	40	9.3	20.6	1.9	38.7	0.7	16.2	6.8	10.0	46.3	76.6	17.0
Honduras	105	67	18.5	30.1	5.6	49.6	2.8	17.8	5.0	12.0	31.7	6.9	8.0
Kenya	91	64	24.2	26.2	6.3	44.2	2.8	17.6	5.3	4.0	31.4	2.0	14.2
Lao PDR	121	67	38.1	1.4	0.5	58.6	0.3	1.5	0.4	19.6	30.6	1.9	22.6
Malawi	117	65	18.1	19.8	3.6	49.2	1.8	8.8	4.0	14.0	52.8	2.0	14.7
Moldova	81	79	29.8	18.5	5.5	25.5	1.4	15.8	1.1	67.8	21.4	0.0	0.9
Mongolia	92	67	29.2	24.6	7.2	33.6	2.4	15.1	3.9	15.0	30.7	0.5	0.9
Mozambique	79	39	11.3	18.1	2.0	46.4	1.0	7.9	3.2	26.0	54.4	0.0	23.7
Nicaragua	101	65	25.3	16.8	4.3	48.7	2.1	13.2	3.2	32.7	35.9	6.8	12.0
Nigeria	85	67	46.1	9.9	4.6	41.0	1.9	13.8	4.9	9.0	39.0	1.0	1.0
Pakistan	65	59	16.7	10.2	1.7	51.8	0.9	14.0	3.6	19.3	32.1	29.4	6.2
Senegal	70	41	18.1	18.6	3.4	43.9	1.5	14.2	4.9	37.0	54.7	11.0	13.6
Sierra Leone	64	37	11.4	30.4	3.5	51.3	1.8	16.4	4.3	33.0	39.6	0.0	9.3
Sudan	61	46	11.1	16.2	1.8	50.5	0.9	10.3	2.2	23.0	27.5	0.0	1.2
Tanzania	66	59	10.9	16.4	1.8	63.0	1.1	10.0	3.6	11.0	40.0	0.0	3.2
Togo	115	63	14.9	25.6	3.8	48.3	1.8	13.2	4.5	25.0	45.5	36.0	27.0
Yemen, Rep. of	67	58	35.2	15.8	5.6	48.0	2.7	18.5	3.4	26.7	25.0	1.4	7.0
Average	**85**	**53**	**19.5**	**17.7**	**3.3**	**47.2**	**1.4**	**11.8**	**3.5**	**23.3**	**40.5**	**10.4**	**13.3**
Average Adjusted Sample	**84**	**53**	**19.7**	**17.3**	**3.1**	**48.6**	**1.5**	**12.4**	**4.0**	**24.4**	**43.7**	**9.4**	**15.8**

Note: Primary GERs and PCRs presented here have been adjusted to an equivalent basis for purposes of comparison. For countries with five-year or six-year systems, the values presented here correspond to the official cycle. But for countries whose primary cycle is shorter or longer than this, we have estimated a six-year equivalent GER and PCR.

Table A.4

Group 1 Parameters with Six Eastern European and Central Asian Countries Included

Country	Primary GER (%)	Primary completion rate (%)	Government current revenues (excluding grants) as % of GDP	EDUCATION RECURRENT SPENDING ON SPENDING		PRIMARY EDUCATION RECURRENT SPENDING		Unit cost as % of per capita gdp	Average annual teacher salary (as multiple of per capita gdp)	Spending on inputs other than teachers (as % of primary education recurrent spending)	Pupils per teacher	Private enrollments (as % of total)	Average repetition rate (%)
				As % of government current revenues, excluding grants	As % of GDP	As % of recurrent education spending	As % of GDP						
Albania	104	91	19.5	12.6	2.5	41.3	1.0	7.7	1.4	17.5	22.7	0.6	0.0
Armenia	87	70	15.8	15.1	2.4	51.3	1.2	12.6	0.6	52.9	12.8	0.0	0.1
Azerbaijan	107	99	20.8	18.4	3.8	19.7	0.8	5.9	0.9	15.8	17.6	1.0	0.4
Bangladesh	112	70	12.8	14.7	1.9	49.9	0.9	6.6	2.7	25.0	55.2	12.5	15.0
Bolivia	113	97	21.2	25.2	5.3	47.5	2.5	15.9	2.2	19.4	20.6	9.4	3.7
Gambia, The	88	70	18.5	16.6	3.1	51.7	1.6	13.2	3.7	25.0	37.0	8.0	10.6
Georgia	86	79	13.7	9.3	1.3	26.0	0.3	4.2	0.6	16.0	16.5	1.0	0.5
India	101	76	21.2	12.4	2.6	38.5	1.0	8.4	3.4	23.2	51.8	12.5	20.0
Indonesia	106	91	18.4	9.7	1.8	59.3	1.1	10.3	1.6	19.9	19.9	15.7	5.9
Kyrgyz Rep.	100	99	18.7	22.0	4.1	36.0	1.5	10.3	1.2	21.8	15.2	0.0	0.0
Lesotho	103	70	35.9	22.2	8.0	40.2	3.2	20.8	6.6	30.0	45.3	0.0	18.3
Uganda	102	82	10.8	30.1	3.2	53.2	1.7	9.8	2.9	26.0	40.9	2.0	9.8
Uzbekistan	100	100	32.4	22.3	7.2	41.2	3.0	18.7	2.9	27.0	21.0	0.0	0.1
Zambia	85	72	18.8	12.3	2.3	43.2	1.0	6.9	2.7	22.0	50.0	2.0	6.2
Zimbabwe	112	103	27.4	28.3	7.1	46.1	3.3	19.4	6.1	25.0	39.0	11.0	2.0
Vietnam	110	99	22.3	10.9	2.4	46.5	1.1	7.1	1.2	45.0	30.4	0.0	3.5
Average	**101**	**86**	**21.0**	**17.6**	**3.7**	**43.2**	**1.6**	**11.1**	**2.5**	**25.7**	**31.0**	**4.7**	**6.0**

Table A.5
Demographic Burden and Resource Mobilization, by Country and Region, 2000 and 2015

Country	Year	School-age population (thousands)	Total population (thousands)	Demographic burden[a]	Number of students enrolled in primary school (5 or 6 years, thousands)	Recurrent public spending on primary education (millions of dollars)	Per-pupil spending on public education (PCGDP unit)	Total available resources for primary education (millions of dollars)	GDP per capita (2000 constant dollars)
Angola	2000	2,182	12,717	0.17	1,728	88	0.08	88	695
	2015	3,180	18,961	0.17	3,498	400	0.13	331	969
Armenia	2000	432	3,827	0.11	375	24	0.11	24	500
	2015	282	4,061	0.07	282	33	0.13	64	980
Bangladesh	2000	15,748	129,754	0.16	17,668	285	0.07	285	281
	2015	14,941	166,142	0.11	16,435	884	0.13	890	456
Benin	2000	1,050	5,948	0.18	907	31	0.12	31	326
	2015	1,411	8,972	0.16	1,552	100	0.14	71	496
Burkina Faso	2000	1,805	10,730	0.18	816	33	0.24	33	192
	2015	2,567	15,340	0.17	2,824	123	0.16	66	309
Burundi	2000	1,123	6,548	0.18	671	7	0.12	7	83
	2015	1,460	8,796	0.17	1,606	30	0.15	18	142
Cambodia	2000	1,803	12,021	0.15	2,408	24	0.04	24	282
	2015	1,807	14,757	0.12	1,988	112	0.13	99	478
Cameroon	2000	2,451	14,691	0.17	2,010	84	0.10	84	518
	2015	3,299	19,264	0.17	3,629	380	0.13	266	863
Central African Republic	2000	590	3,597	0.16	267	6	0.09	6	267
	2015	675	4,461	0.15	743	39	0.13	28	448
Chad	2000	1,283	7,694	0.20	914	15	0.10	15	183
	2015	1,956	11,661	0.17	2,152	71	0.15	43	252
Congo, Dem. Rep. of	2000	8,748	51,390	0.17	5,270	9	0.02	9	75
	2015	12,779	74,952	0.17	14,057	178	0.13	112	107
Congo, Rep. of	2000	497	2,936	0.17	419	27	0.07	27	1,082
	2015	705	4,326	0.16	775	140	0.13	119	1,526
Côte d'Ivoire	2000	2,471	15,545	0.16	1,911	189	0.16	189	700
	2015	2,828	20,250	0.14	3,111	526	0.16	460	1,174

(Continued)

Table A.5
(Continued)

Country	Year	School-age population (thousands)	Total population (thousands)	Demographic burden[a]	Number of students enrolled in primary school (5 or 6 years, thousands)	Recurrent public spending on primary education (millions of dollars)	Per-pupil spending on public education (PCGDP unit)	Total available resources for primary education (millions of dollars)	GDP per capita (2000 constant dollars)
Eritrea	2000	559	3,991	0.17	296	8	0.22	8	140
	2015	744	5,616	0.16	819	26	0.16	14	217
Ethiopia	2000	10,719	62,782	0.18	5,847	74	0.14	74	95
	2015	14,173	87,895	0.16	15,307	364	0.15	212	173
Gambia, The	2000	192	1,286	0.15	168	7	0.13	7	322
	2015	258	1,769	0.15	284	17	0.13	12	487
Georgia	2000	510	5,452	0.09	438	11	0.04	11	612
	2015	371	5,349	0.07	373	60	0.13	117	1,362
Ghana	2000	3,264	18,785	0.17	2,578	54	0.13	54	201
	2015	3,851	24,349	0.16	4,044	163	0.13	148	338
Guinea	2000	1,270	7,415	0.17	790	23	0.08	23	421
	2015	1,516	9,845	0.15	1,668	130	0.13	91	659
Guinea-Bissau	2000	191	1,207	0.16	133	1	0.07	1	179
	2015	235	1,586	0.15	259	9	0.13	6	283
Haiti	2000	1,306	7,492	0.17	1,459	18	0.16	18	325
	2015	1,352	10,039	0.13	1,487	151	0.15	121	751
Honduras	2000	1,064	6,653	0.16	1,109	173	0.18	173	944
	2015	1,154	8,890	0.13	1,246	216	0.13	235	1,469
India	2000	112,970	997,515	0.14	113,610	3,666	0.08	3,666	437
	2015	97,346	1,221,862	0.10	107,081	9,840	0.13	12,775	778
Kenya	2000	5,248	29,410	0.18	4,792	272	0.18	272	330
	2015	5,752	37,185	0.16	6,327	579	0.18	445	570
Lao PDR	2000	710	5,097	0.17	859	3	0.02	3	256
	2015	918	7,214	0.15	1,010	47	0.13	38	395

	Year								
Lesotho	2000	324	2,154	0.15	333	31	0.21	31	454
	2015	371	2,450	0.15	408	59	0.19	41	830
Madagascar	2000	2,114	14,592	0.18	1,893	33	0.11	33	207
	2015	2,838	22,247	0.15	3,122	115	0.13	81	311
Malawi	2000	1,879	10,788	0.18	2,198	24	0.09	24	124
	2015	2,397	14,229	0.17	2,636	68	0.14	41	206
Mali	2000	1,766	10,334	0.18	863	21	0.14	21	209
	2015	2,813	14,876	0.19	3,094	131	0.14	69	332
Mauritania	2000	399	2,529	0.17	353	14	0.13	14	315
	2015	561	3,675	0.15	618	42	0.15	29	497
Moldova	2000	469	4,281	0.11	378	14	0.16	14	229
	2015	329	4,178	0.08	332	20	0.13	34	513
Mongolia	2000	413	2,378	0.17	380	20	0.15	20	341
	2015	328	3,019	0.11	331	26	0.15	28	587
Mozambique	2000	2,396	15,705	0.18	1,881	38	0.08	38	252
	2015	2,768	22,614	0.15	3,045	170	0.13	125	471
Nepal	2000	3,167	22,851	0.17	3,588	43	0.07	43	185
	2015	3,736	32,546	0.14	4,110	164	0.13	129	338
Nicaragua	2000	841	5,044	0.16	848	49	0.13	49	469
	2015	897	6,930	0.13	987	83	0.13	79	709
Niger	2000	1,700	10,146	0.18	530	31	0.36	31	170
	2015	2,940	16,691	0.18	3,234	110	0.16	72	237
Nigeria	2000	20,457	126,910	0.16	17,411	772	0.14	772	324
	2015	29,585	169,441	0.17	29,881	2,100	0.15	1,537	504
Pakistan	2000	17,417	138,080	0.16	12,453	526	0.14	526	428
	2015	22,217	192,948	0.13	23,594	1,776	0.13	1,653	637
Rwanda	2000	1,336	8,508	0.16	1,351	26	0.09	26	211
	2015	1,978	11,149	0.18	2,176	90	0.14	68	334
Senegal	2000	1,596	9,530	0.17	1,109	65	0.14	65	460
	2015	2,192	13,342	0.16	2,411	220	0.15	146	683
Sierra Leone	2000	858	5,031	0.17	548	11	0.16	11	126
	2015	1,007	6,745	0.15	1,101	28	0.14	24	195
Sudan	2000	4,277	29,677	0.14	2,612	104	0.10	104	384
	2015	5,950	40,551	0.15	6,021	416	0.13	332	584
Tanzania	2000	5,589	32,923	0.17	3,710	89	0.10	89	239
	2015	6,984	43,556	0.16	7,210	339	0.13	241	395

(Continued)

155

Table A.5
(Continued)

Country	Year	School-age population (thousands)	Total population (thousands)	Demographic burden[a]	Number of students enrolled in primary school (5 or 6 years, thousands)	Recurrent public spending on primary education (millions of dollars)	Per-pupil spending on public education (PCGDP unit)	Total available resources for primary education (millions of dollars)	GDP per capita (2000 constant dollars)
Togo	2000	829	4,894	0.16	954	23	0.13	23	252
	2015	1,118	6,706	0.16	1,230	60	0.14	48	401
Uganda	2000	3,885	22,063	0.18	3,963	107	0.10	107	281
	2015	5,053	31,437	0.16	5,549	269	0.13	235	410
Yemen, Rep. of	2000	3,141	18,046	0.18	2,644	247	0.18	247	514
	2015	4,617	27,276	0.14	4,940	624	0.13	309	1,069
Zambia	2000	1,667	9,666	0.18	1,416	19	0.07	19	200
	2015	1,980	11,982	0.17	2,103	92	0.13	62	371
AFR	2000	94,716	572,121	0.17	70,642	2,334	0.13	2,335	304
	2015	127,925	786,919	0.16	136,492	7,583	0.14	5,595	478
EAP	2000	6,093	42,347	0.16	7,234	90	0.07	90	266
	2015	6,789	57,536	0.13	7,438	349	0.14	295	450
ECA	2000	1,411	13,560	0.10	1,191	48	0.10	48	447
	2015	982	13,588	0.07	987	113	0.13	215	952
LCR	2000	3,211	19,189	0.16	3,416	240	0.16	240	579
	2015	3,403	25,859	0.13	3,720	450	0.14	434	976
SAR	2000	146,135	1,265,349	0.15	143,731	4,477	0.10	4,477	382
	2015	134,504	1,580,952	0.11	147,110	12,501	0.13	15,318	624
MNA	2000	17,417	138,080	0.16	12,453	526	0.14	526	428
	2015	22,217	192,948	0.13	23,594	1,776	0.13	1,653	637
Total	**2000**	**254,707**	**1,930,612**	**n.a.**	**228,858**	**7,438**	**n.a.**	**7,438**	**n.a.**
	2015	**278,220**	**2,492,130**	**n.a.**	**300,688**	**21,620**	**n.a.**	**22,165**	**n.a.**
Average	**2000**	**n.a.**	**n.a.**	**0.16**	**n.a.**	**n.a.**	**0.12**	**n.a.**	**337**
	2015	**n.a.**	**n.a.**	**0.15**	**n.a.**	**n.a.**	**0.14**	**n.a.**	**559**

n.a. Not applicable.
a. Population aged 7–12 as a share of the total population.

Table A.6

Actual and Projected Expenditures on Primary Education, Domestic Financing, and Financing Gap, by Country, under Scenario C2

(millions of U.S. dollars per year)

| Country | Actual expenditures (circa 2000) | Domestic financing | PROJECTED UNDER SCENARIO C2 (ANNUAL AVERAGE FOR PERIOD 2001–2015) | | | | | | | |
| | | | Recurrent Expenditure | | Capital expenditure | Total expenditure | Recurrent Gap | | Capital | Total gap |
			Operation	AIDS			Operation	AIDS		
Angola	88	253	289	2	5	296	36	2	5	44
Armenia	24	33	47	0	0	47	15	0	0	15
Bangladesh	285	556	568	0	71	640	12	0	71	84
Benin	37	52	62	1	10	73	11	1	10	21
Burkina Faso	40	51	76	11	23	111	25	11	23	60
Burundi	11	12	18	5	11	34	6	5	11	21
Central African Republic	6	15	20	2	7	29	5	2	7	14
Cambodia	24	57	76	0	4	80	19	0	4	23
Cameroon	102	175	192	11	28	231	18	11	28	56
Chad	15	28	33	2	19	55	6	2	19	27
Congo, Dem. Rep. of	9	54	97	17	103	217	43	17	103	163
Congo, Rep. of	27	70	72	1	6	80	3	1	6	10
Côte d'Ivoire	218	307	347	16	16	379	40	16	16	72
Eritrea	10	13	17	0	6	23	3	0	6	10
Ethiopia	80	141	196	30	125	351	55	30	125	210
Gambia, The	7	9	11	0	1	13	2	0	1	4
Georgia	11	40	53	0	0	53	13	0	0	13

(Continued)

Table A.6
(Continued)

			PROJECTED UNDER SCENARIO C2 (ANNUAL AVERAGE FOR PERIOD 2001–2015)							
	Actual expenditures (circa 2000)	Domestic financing	RECURRENT EXPENDITURE		Capital expenditure	Total expenditure	RECURRENT GAP		Capital	Total gap
Country			Operation	AIDS			Operation	AIDS		
Ghana	111	100	107	6	14	127	7	6	14	27
Guinea	23	53	76	1	12	89	23	1	12	37
Guinea-Bissau	1	4	6	0	1	7	2	0	1	4
Haiti	23	65	76	0	23	99	11	0	23	34
Honduras	173	203	170	0	37	208	0	0	5	5
India	3,827	7,685	7,317	0	435	7,752	0	0	67	67
Kenya	295	316	429	21	0	450	113	21	0	134
Lao PDR	6	26	37	0	2	40	11	0	2	13
Lesotho	31	36	44	2	1	46	8	2	1	11
Madagascar	41	58	70	0	21	91	12	0	21	33
Malawi	32	33	42	10	9	62	9	10	9	29
Mali	25	45	68	2	28	98	23	2	28	53
Mauritania	18	23	27	0	3	30	4	0	3	8
Moldova	16	21	26	0	0	26	5	0	0	5
Mongolia	20	21	21	0	0	21	0	0	0	0
Mozambique	38	80	103	9	14	126	23	9	14	46
Nepal	46	89	119	0	14	133	30	0	14	44
Nicaragua	49	65	67	0	6	73	3	0	6	8
Niger	37	46	72	1	27	100	26	1	27	54

Nigeria	772	1,275	1,367	58	122	1,547	92	58	122	272
Pakistan	526	1,061	1,117	0	148	1,265	55	0	148	204
Rwanda	26	39	50	7	11	68	11	7	11	29
Senegal	65	103	122	2	19	142	19	2	19	40
Sierra Leone	11	15	19	2	6	27	4	2	6	12
Sudan	104	205	290	1	20	311	85	1	20	106
Tanzania	96	164	216	22	28	265	52	22	28	102
Togo	26	31	39	4	7	51	9	4	7	20
Uganda	107	146	195	24	14	233	49	24	14	87
Yemen, Rep. of	247	295	316	0	49	365	21	0	49	70
Zambia	32	41	58	15	9	81	16	15	9	40
Total	**7,818**	**14,210**	**14,840**	**285**	**1,515**	**16,645**	**1,035**	**285**	**1,115**	**2,441**

a. Excluding projected financial surpluses in three countries, this would total $17,751 million.

Table A.7
....
Domestic Resources Mobilized and Financing Gap, by Country, under Scenarios C1 and C3
(millions of U.S. dollars per year)

Country	SCENARIO C1					SCENARIO C3				
	Domestic resources	RECURRENT GAP		Capital gap	Total gap	Domestic resources	RECURRENT GAP		Capital gap	Total gap
		Operation	AIDS				Operation	AIDS		
Angola	253	37	2	5	44	479	0	0	0	0
Armenia	33	15	0	0	15	33	15	0	0	15
Bangladesh	556	12	0	71	84	556	12	0	71	84
Benin	52	11	1	10	21	52	11	1	10	21
Burkina Faso	51	25	11	23	60	52	23	11	23	58
Burundi	13	5	5	11	21	14	4	5	11	20
Central African Republic	15	5	2	7	14	15	5	2	7	14
Cambodia	57	19	0	4	23	57	19	0	4	23
Cameroon	175	18	11	28	56	175	18	11	28	56
Chad	29	5	2	19	26	28	5	2	19	27
Congo, Dem. Rep. of	54	43	17	103	163	54	43	17	103	163
Congo, Rep. of	70	3	1	6	10	89	0	0	0	0
Côte d' Ivoire	321	26	16	16	58	307	40	16	16	72
Eritrea	13	3	0	6	10	22	0	0	1	2
Ethiopia	141	55	30	125	210	164	32	30	125	187
Gambia, The	9	2	0	1	4	11	0	0	1	2
Georgia	40	13	0	0	13	40	13	0	0	13
Ghana	100	7	6	14	27	113	0	6	8	14
Guinea	53	23	1	12	37	53	23	1	12	37
Guinea-Bissau	4	2	0	1	4	5	1	0	1	3
Haiti	66	10	0	23	33	65	11	0	23	34
Honduras	208	0	0	0	0	204	0	0	3	3
India	7,685	0	0	67	67	7,724	0	0	28	28
Kenya	368	61	21	0	82	397	32	21	0	53
Lao PDR	26	11	0	2	13	33	4	0	2	6
Lesotho	38	6	2	1	9	51	0	0	0	0
Madagascar	58	12	0	21	33	58	12	0	21	33
Malawi	33	9	10	9	29	38	4	10	9	23
Mali	45	23	2	28	53	51	17	2	28	47
Mauritania	23	4	0	3	8	31	0	0	0	0

Table A.7
(Continued)

Country	SCENARIO C1					SCENARIO C3				
	Domestic resources	RECURRENT GAP		Capital gap	Total gap	Domestic resources	RECURRENT GAP		Capital gap	Total gap
		Operation	AIDS				Operation	AIDS		
Moldova	21	5	0	0	5	22	4	0	0	4
Mongolia	21	0	0	0	0	21	0	0	0	0
Mozambique	80	23	9	14	46	80	23	9	14	46
Nepal	89	30	0	14	44	89	30	0	14	44
Nicaragua	65	3	0	6	8	71	0	0	2	2
Niger	53	19	1	27	47	46	26	1	27	54
Nigeria	1,275	92	58	122	272	2,131	0	0	0	0
Pakistan	1,061	55	0	148	204	1,092	25	0	148	173
Rwanda	45	5	7	11	23	39	11	7	11	29
Senegal	103	19	2	19	40	111	11	2	19	32
Sierra Leone	17	2	2	6	9	15	4	2	6	12
Sudan	205	85	1	20	106	205	85	1	20	106
Tanzania	164	52	22	28	102	164	52	22	28	102
Togo	35	4	4	7	15	32	7	4	7	19
Uganda	168	27	24	14	65	146	49	24	14	87
Yemen, Rep. of	295	21	0	49	70	358	0	0	6	6
Zambia	41	16	15	9	40	50	8	15	9	31
Total	**14,327**	**923**	**285**	**1,110**	**2,323**	**15,643**	**679**	**222**	**879**	**1,785**

Table A.8

Estimated Annual Financing Gap, by Country, 2001–2015 (Scenario C2)

COUNTRY	REGION	2001	2002	2003	2004	2005	2006	2007	2008	2009	2010	2011	2012	2013	2014	2015	CUMULATIVE TOTAL	ANNUAL AVERAGE
Africa																		
Angola	AFR	100	86	72	58	46	34	24	15	9	10	14	22	36	49	75	649	43
Benin	AFR	6	9	11	12	13	15	17	19	21	25	28	32	36	41	32	318	21
Burkina Faso	AFR	26	29	33	38	43	48	54	61	69	68	75	82	90	95	78	890	60
Burundi	AFR	14	15	16	17	18	19	21	22	24	23	25	27	29	32	21	322	21
Cameroon	AFR	5	8	11	15	19	25	32	40	50	65	81	100	122	148	127	848	56
Central African Republic	AFR	6	7	7	8	9	10	11	13	14	15	17	20	23	25	17	203	14
Chad	AFR	9	10	11	13	15	18	20	23	27	33	38	45	53	52	33	400	27
Congo, Dem. Rep. of	AFR	125	132	139	146	154	162	171	181	191	171	180	189	199	180	122	2,440	163
Congo, Rep. of	AFR	5	4	4	4	4	4	5	5	6	9	12	16	21	22	21	144	10
Côte d'Ivoire	AFR	27	31	36	41	46	52	58	65	72	82	93	104	116	130	127	1,080	72
Eritrea	AFR	6	6	6	7	7	8	9	10	11	11	12	14	16	13	10	146	10
Ethiopia	AFR	106	116	128	141	156	173	191	212	236	239	264	293	326	343	226	3,150	210
Gambia, The	AFR	1	2	2	2	2	3	3	3	4	4	4	5	4	4	3	47	3
Ghana	AFR	18	19	21	22	24	25	27	29	31	29	30	32	34	32	30	403	27
Guinea	AFR	20	22	25	27	29	32	35	37	40	42	45	48	51	52	44	548	37
Guinea-Bissau	AFR	3	3	3	3	3	3	3	3	3	4	3	3	3	4	3	51	3
Kenya	AFR	34	44	56	68	80	94	109	124	141	158	178	198	220	245	268	2,017	134
Lesotho	AFR	2	3	3	4	5	6	8	9	10	13	15	17	20	26	28	169	11
Madagascar	AFR	10	17	19	21	22	24	27	29	31	41	46	52	58	62	37	495	33
Malawi	AFR	12	13	0	19	22	24	27	29	32	37	41	46	50	42	35	430	29
Mali	AFR	19	22	25	29	34	39	44	51	59	62	70	80	91	100	72	797	53
Mauritania	AFR	1	3	3	4	4	5	6	7	8	9	10	12	13	15	14	113	8

Mozambique	AFR	28	30	31	33	35	37	40	42	44	52	56	61	66	75	60	690	46
Niger	AFR	31	34	37	41	45	50	55	60	66	58	63	68	73	71	63	814	54
Nigeria	AFR	107	101	98	100	108	123	147	180	224	272	341	427	532	628	695	4,081	272
Rwanda	AFR	5	5	7	15	17	19	21	24	27	36	42	48	55	63	52	437	29
Senegal	AFR	8	10	14	17	21	26	31	37	44	48	55	63	72	82	69	599	40
Sierra Leone	AFR	6	8	9	10	10	11	12	13	14	12	13	14	15	16	15	179	12
Sudan	AFR	92	96	100	104	107	111	115	118	122	111	110	108	105	95	91	1,584	106
Tanzania	AFR	59	64	69	75	82	88	96	104	113	112	120	128	137	141	137	1,524	102
Togo	AFR	5	6	1	10	11	13	15	18	20	25	28	32	37	39	35	296	20
Uganda	AFR	52	56	59	63	68	72	77	83	89	97	104	112	121	128	130	1,311	87
Zambia	AFR	25	26	28	30	32	34	37	40	43	44	47	50	53	58	56	603	40
Subtotal	**AFR**	**971**	**1,037**	**1,084**	**1,197**	**1,295**	**1,410**	**1,547**	**1,708**	**1,896**	**2,017**	**2,262**	**2,547**	**2,878**	**3,111**	**2,832**	**27,791**	**1,853**
East Asia and the Pacific																		
Cambodia	EAP	30	29	27	25	23	22	21	20	18	23	24	24	25	22	18	351	23
Lao PDR	EAP	22	20	18	15	15	13	12	11	10	10	10	10	11	12	9	201	13
Mongolia	EAP	0	0	0	0	0	0	0	0	0	0	0	0	0	0	0	0	0
Subtotal	**EAP**	**52**	**49**	**45**	**41**	**39**	**35**	**33**	**31**	**28**	**34**	**34**	**35**	**36**	**34**	**27**	**552**	**37**
Europe and Central Asia																		
Armenia	ECA	67	52	39	28	19	11	4	0	0	0	0	0	0	0	0	221	15
Georgia	ECA	48	43	37	30	22	15	7	1	0	0	0	0	0	0	0	202	13
Moldova	ECA	23	19	15	11	7	4	2	0	0	0	0	0	0	0	0	80	5
Subtotal	**ECA**	**139**	**113**	**91**	**69**	**48**	**30**	**13**	**1**	**0**	**0**	**0**	**0**	**0**	**0**	**0**	**503**	**34**
Latin America and the Caribbean																		
Haiti	LCR	14	15	16	18	22	24	27	30	34	40	45	51	58	63	54	513	34
Honduras	LCR	0	0	0	0	0	0	0	0	0	0	3	6	10	14	37	71	5
Nicaragua	LCR	13	11	9	7	6	5	4	3	2	7	8	9	11	13	16	123	8
Subtotal	**LCR**	**27**	**26**	**25**	**28**	**29**	**31**	**33**	**36**	**47**	**56**	**67**	**79**	**90**	**96**	**96**	**696**	**46**

(Continued)

Table A.8
(Continued)

Country	Region	2001	2002	2003	2004	2005	2006	2007	2008	2009	2010	2011	2012	2013	2014	2015	Cumulative Total	Annual Average
Middle East and North Africa																		
Yemen, Rep. of	MNA	32	29	25	25	20	27	44	61	83	87	107	118	134	150	110	1,052	70
Subtotal	**MNA**	**32**	**29**	**25**	**25**	**20**	**27**	**44**	**61**	**83**	**87**	**107**	**118**	**134**	**150**	**110**	**1,052**	**70**
South Asia																		
Bangladesh	SAR	71	70	78	96	85	85	85	86	87	92	96	102	93	70	60	1,255	84
India	SAR	457	335	206	4	0	0	0	0	0	0	0	0	0	0	0	1,001	67
Nepal	SAR	37	34	32	29	35	42	44	46	47	49	52	54	57	60	49	667	44
Pakistan	SAR	106	111	120	145	155	172	193	217	246	232	243	266	297	294	256	3,053	204
Subtotal	**SAR**	**671**	**551**	**435**	**273**	**275**	**300**	**322**	**348**	**380**	**372**	**391**	**413**	**441**	**475**	**358**	**6,005**	**400**
Total		**1,892**	**1,805**	**1,705**	**1,629**	**1,704**	**1,832**	**1,990**	**2,181**	**2,423**	**2,557**	**2,850**	**3,180**	**3,568**	**3,858**	**3,416**	**36,591**	**2,439**

Note: Gross financing gaps are presented (not adjusted for any current or estimated ODA inflows). Financing gaps for African countries include the impact of HIV/AIDS. Totals differ slightly from totals presented elsewhere due to rounding.

Primary Completion Rate Estimates and Projections

FIGURE B.1 Global Progress in Primary Completion, 1990–2000 and Projected Trends, Country-Weighted

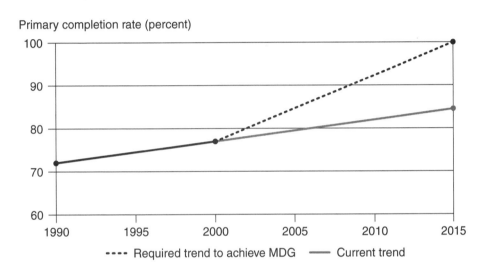

Primary completion rate (percent)

FIGURE B.2 Global Progress in Primary Completion, 1990–2000 and Projected Trends, Population-Weighted

Primary completion rate (percent)

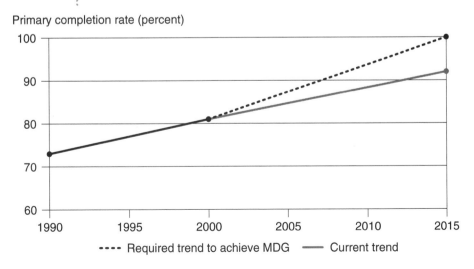

Primary Completion Progress by Region, 1990–2000 and Projected Trends, Country-Weighted

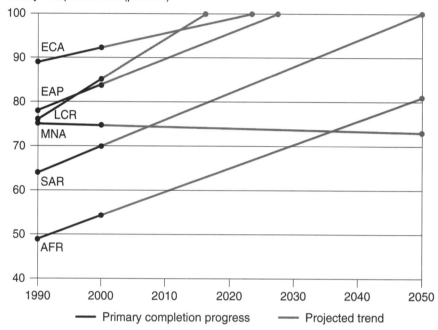

Primary completion rate (percent)

— Primary completion progress — Projected trend

FIGURE B.4 Primary Completion Progress by Region, 1990–2000 and Projected Trends, Population-Weighted

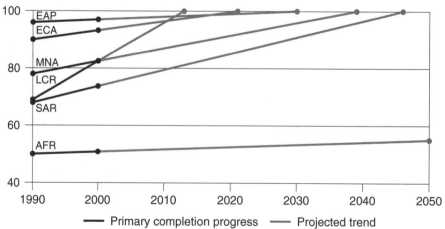

Primary completion rate (percent)

— Primary completion progress — Projected trend

Primary Completion Progress in Africa, Middle East and North Africa, and South Asia Regions, 1990–2015, Country-Weighted

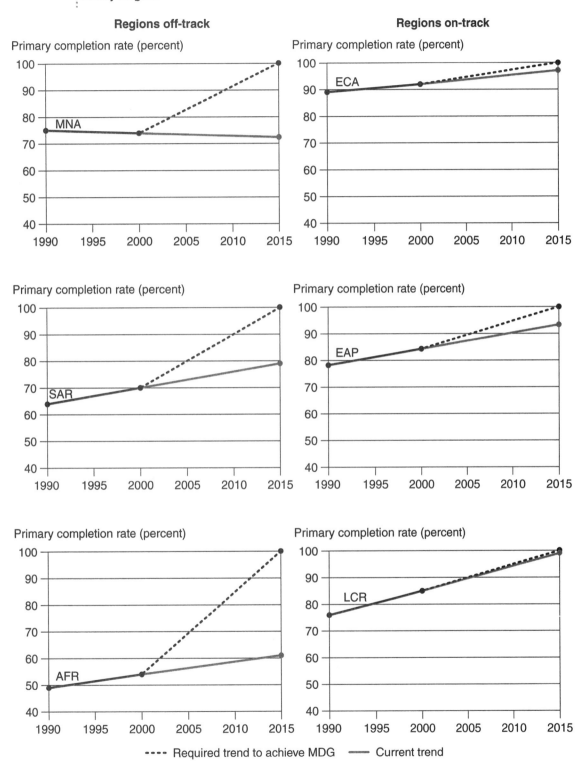

Regions off-track

Regions on-track

Primary completion rate (percent)

Primary completion rate (percent)

MNA

ECA

SAR

EAP

AFR

LCR

- - - - Required trend to achieve MDG ⸺ Current trend

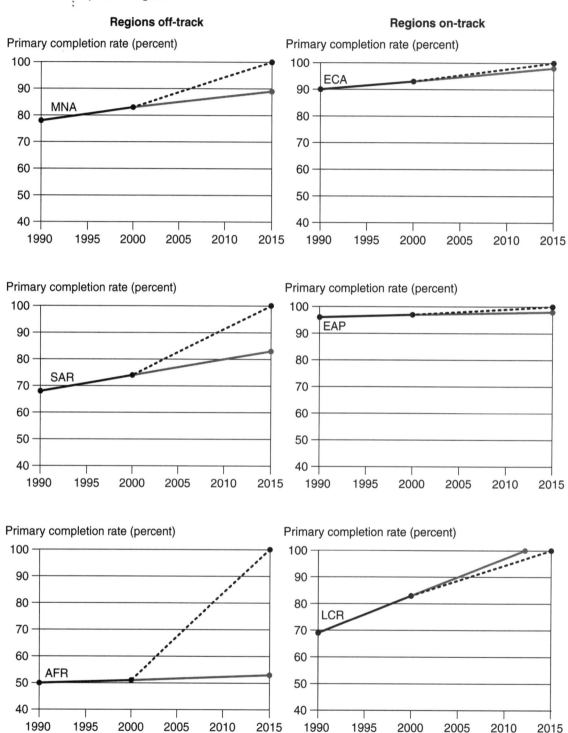

FIGURE B.6 Primary Completion Progress in Africa, Middle East and North Africa, and South Asia Regions, 1990–2015, Population-Weighted

Table B.1

Primary Completion Progress by Region, 1990–2000, Country-Weighted

	1990				Most Recent Year[a]			
	Mean	Median	Minimum	Maximum	Mean	Median	Minimum	Maximum
Africa	49	42	11	135	55	45	19	117
East Asia and the Pacific	78	89	39	99	84	90	54	108
Europe and Central Asia	89	90	67	100	92	93	77	109
Latin America and the Caribbean	76	86	28	112	85	89	40	110
Middle East and North Africa	75	75	32	102	74	76	30	104
South Asia	64	50	22	111	70	67	8	112
All developing countries	72	81	11	135	77	83	8	117
IDA	50	45	11	112	62	64	8	117
IBRD	84	89	43	135	87	92	44	111

a. Usually 1999/2000.

Table B.2
....
Primary Completion Progress by Region, 1990–2000, Population-Weighted

	1990			Most Recent Year[a]		
	Girls	Boys	Both	Girls	Boys	Both
Africa	43	57	50	46	56	51
East Asia and the Pacific	92	97	96	98	98	97
Europe and Central Asia	85	95	90	93	95	93
Latin America and the Caribbean	71	64	69	85	81	83
Middle East and North Africa	71	84	78	78	86	83
South Asia	59	77	68	63	84	74
All developing countries	65	79	73	76	85	81

Note: For population-weighted estimates, all PCRs over 100 were set to equal 100, in order to avoid distortions.
a. Usually 1999/2000.

Table B.3
....
Best Performers (IDA Countries) in Improving Primary Completion Rate, 1990 to Most Recent Year

Country	Years in Primary Cycle	Region	PRIMARY COMPLETION RATE			
			Level in 1990	Level in MRY[a]	Trend Rate (1990 to MRY)[b]	PCR 2015
Cambodia	6	EAP	39	70	7.63	100
Malawi	8	AFR	30	50	4.10	100
Gambia, The	6	AFR	40	70	3.35	100
Togo	6	AFR	41	63	2.51	100
Lao PDR	5	EAP	56	69	2.50	100
Serbia and Montenegro	8	ECA	72	96	2.40	100
Uganda	7	AFR	39	65	2.36	98
Zimbabwe	7	AFR	97	113	2.29	100
Nicaragua	6	LCR	45	65	2.03	96
Benin	6	AFR	23	39	1.96	72
Bangladesh	5	SAR	50	70	1.96	99
Guinea	6	AFR	16	34	1.75	60
Haiti	6	LCR	28	40	1.74	71
Eritrea	5	AFR	22	35	1.72	63
Bolivia	8	LCR	55	72	1.70	97
Tanzania	7	AFR	46	59	1.67	89
Moldova	4	ECA	67	79	1.51	100
Mali	6	AFR	11	23	1.51	49
Mauritania	6	AFR	34	46	1.47	71
Pakistan	5	SAR	44	59	1.39	80

a. Usually 1999/2000.
b. Trend rate is average annual percentage point change in primary completion rate from 1990 to most recent year.

Table B.4
....
Best Performers (IBRD Countries) in Improving Primary Completion Rate, 1990 to Most Recent Year

Country	Years in Primary Cycle	Region	PRIMARY COMPLETION RATE			
			Level in 1990	Level in MRY[a]	Trend Rate (1990 to MRY)[b]	PCR 2015
Czech Republic	4	ECA	89	109	6.55	100
South Africa	7	AFR	76	98	4.32	100
Egypt, Arab Rep. of	5	MNA	77	99	3.60	100
Namibia	7	AFR	70	90	2.85	100
Brazil	8	LCR	48	72	2.64	100
Tunisia	6	MNA	75	91	2.63	100
Latvia	4	ECA	76	86	2.39	100
Gabon	6	AFR	71	80	2.12	100
Lithuania	4	ECA	88	95	1.97	100
El Salvador	6	LCR	61	80	1.77	100
Morocco	6	MNA	47	55	1.65	87
Costa Rica	6	LAC	73	89	1.65	100
China	5	EAP	99	108	1.57	100
Hungary	4	ECA	93	102	1.48	100
Swaziland	7	AFR	71	81	1.46	100
Algeria	6	MNA	82	91	1.37	100
Colombia	5	LCR	72	85	1.36	100
Paraguay	6	LCR	65	78	1.34	98
Mexico	6	LCR	89	100	1.15	100
Croatia	8	ECA	86	96	1.11	100

a. Usually 1999/2000.
b. Trend rate is average annual percentage point change in primary completion rate from 1990 to most recent year.

Table B.5

···

IDA Countries with Declining Primary Completion Rate,1990 to Most Recent Year

Country	Years in Primary Cycle	Region	PRIMARY COMPLETION RATE			
			Level in 1990	Level in MRY[a]	Trend Rate (1990 to MRY)[b]	PCR 2015
Zambia	7	AFR	97	83	−2.10	41
Congo, Rep. of	6	AFR	61	44	−1.73	18
Albania	8	ECA	97	89	−1.55	58
Cameroon	6	AFR	57	43	−1.48	20
Afghanistan	6	SAR	22	8	−1.39	0
Vanuatu	6	EAP	89	86	−1.38	55
Comoros	6	AFR	35	33	−1.22	6
Kenya	8	AFR	63	58	−1.10	36
Madagascar	5	AFR	34	26	−0.93	11
Central African Republic	6	AFR	28	19	−0.87	6
Congo, Dem. Rep. of	6	AFR	48	40	−0.79	28
Nigeria	6	AFR	72	67	−0.56	58
Rwanda	6	AFR	34	28	−0.54	20
Senegal	6	AFR	45	41	−0.36	36
Côte d'Ivoire	6	AFR	44	40	−0.35	35

a. Usually 1999/2000.

b. Trend rate is average annual percentage point change in primary completion rate from 1990 to most recent year.

Table B.6
....
IBRD Countries with Declining Primary Completion Rate, 1990 to Most Recent Year

Country	Years in Primary Cycle	Region	PRIMARY COMPLETION RATE			
			Level in 1990	Level in MRY[a]	Trend Rate (1990 to MRY)[b]	PCR 2015
Qatar	6	MNA	74	44	−6.10	0
United Arab Emirates	6	MNA	94	80	−2.22	38
Estonia	6	ECA	93	88	−1.78	52
Bahrain	6	MNA	101	91	−1.55	62
Venezuela, RB	5	LCR	91	78	−1.52	54
Syrian Arab Rep.	6	MNA	98	90	−1.25	66
Iraq	6	MNA	63	57	−1.16	34
Belarus	4	ECA	97	93	−0.87	77
Belize	6	LCR	90	82	−0.87	68
Rwanda	6	AFR	34	28	−0.54	20
Iran, Islamic Rep. of	5	MNA	94	92	−0.41	84
Thailand	6	EAP	93	90	−0.26	86
Malaysia	6	EAP	91	90	−0.24	85

a. Usually 1999/2000.
b. Trend rate is average annual percentage point change in primary completion rate from 1990 to most recent year.

Table B.7
....
IDA Countries That Have Achieved Universal Primary Completion

Country	IDA/ IBRD	Region	Years in Primary Cycle	PCR 1990	Baseline Year	PCR MRY	MRY
Cape Verde	IDA	AFR	6	—	—	117	1997
Zimbabwe	IDA	AFR	7	97	1990	113	1997
Samoa	IDA	EAP	8	—	—	99	1997
Vietnam	IDA	EAP	5	—	—	101	2001
Azerbaijan	IDA	ECA	4	—	—	100	1998
Serbia and Montenegro	IDA	ECA	8	72	1990	96	2000
Dominica	IDA	LCR	6	—	—	103	2000
Grenada	IDA	LCR	7	—	—	106	2001
St. Lucia	IDA	LCR	7	112	1990	106	2001
Maldives	IDA	SAR	5	111	1992	112	1993
Sri Lanka	IDA	SAR	5	100	1990	111	2001

— Not available.
Note: Countries have ACHIEVED universal primary completion if the completion rate in the most recent year is 95 percent or higher.

Table B.8
....
IBRD Countries That Have Achieved Universal Primary Completion

Country	IDA/ IBRD	Region	Years in Primary Cycle	PCR 1990	Baseline Year	PCR MRY	MRY
Botswana	IBRD	AFR	7	114	1990	102	1996
Mauritius	IBRD	AFR	6	135	1990	111	1997
South Africa	IBRD	AFR	7	76	1990	98	1995
China	IBRD	EAP	5	99	1990	108	1996
Fiji	IBRD	EAP	6	—	—	95	1992
Korea, Rep. of	IBRD	EAP	6	96	1990	96	2000
Croatia	IBRD	ECA	8	86	1992	96	2001
Czech Republic	IBRD	ECA	4	89	1992	109	1995
Hungary	IBRD	ECA	4	93	1989	102	1995
Lithuania	IBRD	ECA	4	88	1992	95	1996
Poland	IBRD	ECA	8	100	1990	96	1995
Romania	IBRD	ECA	4	96	1989	98	1996
Russia	IBRD	ECA	3	—	—	96	2001
Slovak Republic	IBRD	ECA	4	96	1992	97	1996
Slovenia	IBRD	ECA	4	99	1992	—	—
Antigua and Barbuda	IBRD	LCR	7	—	—	95–100[a]	2000
Argentina	IBRD	LCR	7	—	—	96	2000
Chile	IBRD	LCR	6	94	1990	99	2000
Cuba	n. a.	LCR	6	—	—	95–100[a]	2001
Ecuador	IBRD	LCR	6	99	1992	96	1999
Mexico	IBRD	LCR	6	89	1990	100	2000
Peru	IBRD	LCR	6	85	1988	98	2000
St. Kitts and Nevis	IBRD	LCR	6	—	—	110	2001
Uruguay	IBRD	LCR	6	95	1990	98	2000
Egypt, Arab Rep. of	IBRD	MNA	5	77	1990	99	1996
Jordan	IBRD	MNA	6	102	1990	104	2000

n. a. Not applicable.
— Not available.
Note: Countries have ACHIEVED universal primary completion if the completion rate in the most recent year is 95 percent or higher.
a. Staff estimate.

Table B.9
....
IDA Countries "On Track" to Achieve Universal Primary Completion by 2015

Country	IDA/ IBRD	Region	Years in Primary Cycle	PCR 1990	Baseline Year	PCR MRY	MRY	PCR Annual Increase	PCR 2015
Gambia, The	IDA	AFR	6	40	1991	70	2000	3.35	100
Malawi	IDA	AFR	8	30	1990	50	1995	4.10	100
Togo	IDA	AFR	6	41	1990	63	1999	2.51	100
Uganda	IDA	AFR	7	39	1990	65	2001	2.36	98
Cambodia	IDA	EAP	6	39	1997	70	2001	7.63	100
Lao PDR	IDA	EAP	5	56	1995	69	2000	2.50	100
Bosnia and Herzegovina	IDA	ECA	4	—	—	88	1999	—	95–100[a]
Moldova	IDA	ECA	4	67	1991	79	1999	1.51	100
Bolivia	IDA	LCR	8	55	1990	72	2000	1.70	97
Nicaragua	IDA	LCR	6	45	1990	65	2000	2.03	96
Bangladesh	IDA	SAR	5	50	1990	70	2000	1.96	99

— Not available.

Note: Countries are ON TRACK if a projection of the observed trend results in a completion rate of 95 percent or higher by 2015. If a country does not have two data points, it is ON TRACK if the most recent year completion rate is 85–94 percent, inclusive.
a. Staff estimate.

Table B.10
....
IBRD Countries "On Track" to Achieve Universal Primary Completion by 2015

Country	IDA/ IBRD	Region	Years in Primary Cycle	PCR 1990	Baseline Year	PCR MRY	MRY	PCR Annual Increase	PCR 2015
Gabon	IBRD	AFR	6	71	1991	80	1995	2.12	100
Namibia	IBRD	AFR	7	70	1990	90	1997	2.85	100
Swaziland	IBRD	AFR	7	71	1990	81	1997	1.46	100
Philippines	IBRD	EAP	6	89	1989	92	1996	0.38	99
Bulgaria	IBRD	ECA	4	90	1990	92	1996	0.30	97
Latvia	IBRD	ECA	4	76	1992	86	1996	2.39	100
Macedonia, FYR	IBRD	ECA	8	89	1992	91	1996	0.44	99
Turkey	IBRD	ECA	5	90	1990	92	1994	0.52	100
Ukraine	IBRD	ECA	3	—	—	94[a]	2002	—	95–100[a]
Brazil	IBRD	LCR	8	48	1990	72	1999	2.64	100
Colombia	IBRD	LCR	5	72	1990	85	2000	1.36	100
Costa Rica	IBRD	LCR	6	73	1990	89	2000	1.65	100
El Salvador	IBRD	LCR	6	61	1989	80	2000	1.77	100
Jamaica	IBRD	LCR	6	90	1990	94	2000	0.40	100
Panama	IBRD	LCR	6	87	1990	94	2000	0.65	100
Paraguay	IBRD	LCR	6	65	1990	78	2000	1.34	98
Algeria	IBRD	MNA	6	82	1990	91	1996	1.37	100
Kuwait	n. a.	MNA	4	56	1991	70	1996	2.74	100
Oman	n. a.	MNA	6	67	1989	76	1996	1.31	100
Saudi Arabia	n. a.	MNA	6	60	1990	69	1996	1.50	97
Tunisia	IBRD	MNA	6	75	1990	91	1996	2.63	100

n. a. Not applicable.
— Not available.
Note: Countries are ON TRACK if a projection of the observed trend results in a completion rate of 95 percent or higher by 2015. If a country does not have two data points, it is ON TRACK if the most recent year completion rate is 85–94 percent, inclusive.
a. Staff estimate.

Table B.11

IDA Countries "Off Track" to Achieve Universal Primary Completion by 2015

Country	IDA/ IBRD	Region	Years in Primary Cycle	PCR 1990	Baseline Year	PCR MRY	MRY	PCR Annual Increase	PCR 2015
Benin	IDA	AFR	6	23	1990	39	1998	1.96	72
Eritrea	IDA	AFR	5	22	1991	35	1999	1.72	63
Ghana	IDA	AFR	6	63	1990	64	1999	0.11	65
Guinea	IDA	AFR	6	16	1990	34	2000	1.75	60
Lesotho	IDA	AFR	7	64	1990	69	1996	0.86	85
Mauritania	IDA	AFR	6	34	1990	46	1998	1.47	71
Mozambique	IDA	AFR	5	30	1990	36	1998	0.82	50
Nigeria	IDA	AFR	6	72	1990	67	2000	−0.56	58
São Tomé and Principe	IDA	AFR	4	—	—	84	2001	—	50–84[a]
Tanzania	IDA	AFR	7	46	1989	59	1997	1.67	89
Indonesia	IDA	EAP	6	92	1990	91	2000	−0.10	89
Mongolia	IDA	EAP	4	—	—	82	1998	—	50–84[a]
Solomon Islands	IDA	EAP	6	65	1990	66	1994	0.19	70
Timor-Leste, Dem. Rep.	IDA	EAP	6	—	—	54	2001	—	50–84[a]
Vanuatu	IDA	EAP	6	89	1990	86	1992	−1.38	55
Albania	IDA	ECA	8	97	1990	89	1995	−1.55	58
Armenia	IDA	ECA	4	—	—	82	1996	—	50–84[a]
Georgia	IDA	ECA	4	—	—	82	1998	—	50–84[a]
Tajikistan	IDA	ECA	4	—	—	77	1996	—	50–84[a]
Guyana	IDA	LCR	6	92	1990	89	2000	0.24	86
Haiti	IDA	LCR	6	28	1990	40	1997	1.74	71
Honduras	IDA	LCR	6	66	1991	67	2000	0.21	71
St. Vincent	IDA	LCR	6	—	—	84	2001	—	50–84[a]
Yemen, Rep. of	IDA	MNA	6	—	—	58	2000	—	50–84[a]
Bhutan	IDA	SAR	7	—	—	59	2001	—	50–84[a]
India	IDA	SAR	5	70	1992	76	1999	0.93	91
Nepal	IDA	SAR	5	49	1988	65	2000	1.33	85
Pakistan	IDA	SAR	5	44	1989	59	2000	1.39	80

— Not available.
Note: Countries are OFF TRACK if a projection of the observed trend results in a completion rate in 2015 of 50–94 percent, inclusive. If a country does not have two data points, it is OFF TRACK if the most recent year estimate is 50–84 percent, inclusive.
a. Staff estimate.

Table B.12
....
IBRD Countries "Off Track" to Achieve Universal Primary Completion by 2015

Country	IDA/ IBRD	Region	Years in Primary Cycle	PCR 1990	Baseline Year	PCR MRY	MRY	PCR Annual Increase	PCR 2015
Malaysia	IBRD	EAP	6	91	1990	90	1994	−0.24	85
Papua New Guinea	IBRD	EAP	6	53	1990	59	1995	1.04	79
Thailand	IBRD	EAP	6	93	1990	90	2000	−0.26	86
Belarus	IBRD	ECA	4	97	1992	93	1996	−0.87	77
Estonia	IBRD	ECA	6	93	1992	88	1995	−1.78	52
Belize	IBRD	LCR	6	90	1990	82	1999	−0.87	68
Dominican Republic	IBRD	LCR	8	—	—	62	2000	—	50–84[a]
Guatemala	IBRD	LCR	6	43	1991	52	2000	1.01	67
Trinidad and Tobago	IBRD	LCR	5	94	1990	94	2000	−0.01	94
Venezuela, RB	IBRD	LCR	5	91	1990	78	1999	−1.52	54
Bahrain	n. a.	MNA	6	101	1990	91	1996	−1.55	62
Iran, Islamic Rep. of	IBRD	MNA	5	94	1990	92	1996	−0.41	84
Lebanon	IBRD	MNA	5	—	—	70	1996	—	50–84[a]
Morocco	IBRD	MNA	6	47	1991	55	1996	1.65	87
Syrian Arab Rep.	IBRD	MNA	6	98	1990	90	1996	−1.25	66

n. a. Not applicable.
— Not available.
Note: Countries are OFF TRACK if a projection of the observed trend results in a completion rate in 2015 of 50–94 percent, inclusive. If a country does not have two data points, it is OFF TRACK if the most recent year estimate is 50–84 percent, inclusive.
a. Staff estimate.

Table B.13

IDA Countries "Seriously Off Track" to Achieve Universal Primary Completion by 2015

Country	IDA/ IBRD	Region	Years in Primary Cycle	PCR 1990	Baseline Year	PCR MRY	MRY	PCR Annual Increase	PCR 2015
Angola	IDA	AFR	4	39	1990	—	—	—	less than 50[a]
Burkina Faso	IDA	AFR	6	19	1990	25	1998	0.73	38
Burundi	IDA	AFR	6	46	1990	43	1998	−0.35	37
Cameroon	IDA	AFR	6	57	1990	43	1999	−1.48	20
Central African Rep.	IDA	AFR	6	28	1990	19	2000	−0.87	6
Chad	IDA	AFR	6	19	1990	19	2000	−0.04	18
Comoros	IDA	AFR	6	35	1991	33	1993	−1.22	6
Congo, Dem. Rep. of	IDA	AFR	6	48	1990	40	2000	−0.79	28
Congo, Rep. of	IDA	AFR	6	61	1990	44	2000	−1.73	18
Côte d'Ivoire	IDA	AFR	6	44	1990	40	1999	−0.35	35
Ethiopia	IDA	AFR	6	22	1990	24	1999	0.28	29
Guinea-Bissau	IDA	AFR	6	16	1988	31	2000	1.23	49
Kenya	IDA	AFR	8	63	1990	58	1995	−1.10	36
Madagascar	IDA	AFR	5	34	1990	26	1998	−0.93	11
Mali	IDA	AFR	6	11	1990	23	1998	1.51	49
Niger	IDA	AFR	6	18	1990	20	1998	0.25	25
Rwanda	IDA	AFR	6	34	1990	28	2000	−0.54	20
Senegal	IDA	AFR	6	45	1989	41	2000	−0.36	36
Sierra Leone	IDA	AFR	7	—	—	32	2000	—	less than 50[a]
Sudan	IDA	AFR	8	—	—	35	1996	—	less than 50[a]
Zambia	IDA	AFR	7	97	1988	83	1995	−2.10	41
Djibouti	IDA	MNA	6	32	1990	30	1999	−0.26	26
Afghanistan	IDA	SAR	6	22	1989	8	1999	−1.00	0

— Not available.

Note: Countries are SERIOUSLY OFF TRACK if a projection based on the observed trend results in a completion rate BELOW 50 percent in 2015. If a country does not have two data points, it is classed as SERIOUSLY OFF TRACK if the most recent year estimate is below 50 percent.

a. Staff estimate.

Table B.14
....
IBRD Countries "Seriously Off Track" to Achieve Universal Primary Completion by 2015

Country	IDA/ IBRD	Region	Years in Primary Cycle	PCR 1990	Baseline Year	PCR MRY	MRY	PCR Annual Increase	PCR 2015
Equatorial Guinea	IBRD	AFR	5	—	—	46	1993	—	less than 50[a]
Iraq	IBRD	MNA	6	63	1990	57	1995	−1.16	34
Qatar	n. a.	MNA	6	74	1990	44	1995	−6.10	0
United Arab Emirates	n. a.	MNA	6	94	1990	80	1996	−2.22	38

n. a. Not applicable.
— Not available.
Note: Countries are SERIOUSLY OFF TRACK if a projection based on the observed trend results in a completion rate BELOW 50 percent in 2015. If a country does not have two data points, it is classed as SERIOUSLY OFF TRACK if the most recent year estimate is below 50 percent.
a. Staff estimate.

Table B.15
....
Countries with No Data Available

Country	IDA/ IBRD	Region	Years in Primary Cycle
Korea, DPR	n.a.	EAP	4
Libya	n.a.	MNA	9
Seychelles	IBRD	AFR	6
Marshall Islands	IBRD	EAP	6
Micronesia, Fed. States of	IBRD	EAP	6
Palau	IBRD	EAP	8
Kazakhstan	IBRD	ECA	4
Turkmenistan	IBRD	ECA	4
Liberia	IDA	AFR	6
Somalia	IDA	AFR	8
Kiribati	IDA	EAP	7
Myanmar	IDA	EAP	5
Tonga	IDA	EAP	6
Kyrgyz Republic	IDA	ECA	4
Uzbekistan	IDA	ECA	4
West Bank/Gaza	IDA	MNA	10

n.a. Not applicable.
Note: Primary completion rates cannot be calculated for the countries listed because either enrollment or population data are not available.

Country Simulation Results

Table C.1

All 47 Countries: MDG-2015 Financing Gap under Alternative Policy Measures

Policy Scenario[a]		Pupils Per Teacher	Spending on Inputs Other than Teachers[b]	Average Annual Teacher Salary (as multiple of per capita GDP)	Average Repetition Rate	Government Revenues[c] As % of GDP	Government Revenues[c] % for Education	Primary Education Recurrent Spending[d]	Private Enrollments (as % of total)	Annual Financing Gap[e]
				A: Quality Measures	**B: Efficiency Measures**	**C: Financing Measures**				
Status quo		13 - 79	0.1 - 45	0.6 - 9.6	0 - 36%	8 - 56	1.4 - 32.6	26 - 66	0 - 77	
A only		36	33.7%	4.5						7,489
A + B		40	33.3%	3.8	8.2%					4,348
"Best practice": A + B +	C1	40	33.3%	3.7	8.2%	15.2%	21.1%	48.6%	10.0%	2,033
	C2					15.2%	20.0%			2,151
	C3					20.3%	20.0%			1,563

Note: Shaded cells denote no change from values directly above.
a. Policy scenarios are: A for quality improvement, B for efficiency improvement, and three alternative resource mobilization scenarios (C1, C2, and C3). The combination of scenarios A+B+C is considered "best practice."
b. As a share of primary education recurrent spending.
c. Current revenues, excluding grants.
d. As a share of total education recurrent spending.
e. In millions of 2000 U.S. dollars. Calculated as the difference between the total cost of service delivery under the specific policy scenario and the total resources for primary education mobilized domestically.

Table C.2

All 47 Countries: MDG-2015 Cost Estimates and Sources of Financing under "Best Practice" Policies and Alternative Resource Mobilization Scenarios
(millions of 2000 constant U.S. dollars)

Cost Item	Period	Scenario	Domestic Resources Mobilized	Cost of MDG-2015 Recurrent	Cost of MDG-2015 Capital	Cost of MDG-2015 Total	Domestic Resources Recurrent	Domestic Resources Capital	Domestic Resources Total	Gap for External Financing Recurrent	Gap for External Financing Capital	Gap for External Financing Total
										Financing Sources		
Education service delivery	Cumulative, 2001-2015	C1	214,897	222,665	22,728	245,393	208,811	6,085	214,896	13,853	16,643	30,496
		C2	213,124	222,665	22,728	245,393	207,109	6,014	213,123	15,556	16,714	32,270
		C3	234,632	222,665	22,728	245,393	212,430	9,521	221,951	10,234	13,208	23,442
	Annual	C1	14,326	14,844	1,515	16,360	13,921	406	14,326	924	1,110	2,033
		C2	14,208	14,844	1,515	16,360	13,807	401	14,208	1,037	1,114	2,151
		C3	15,642	14,844	1,515	16,360	14,162	635	14,797	682	881	1,563
AIDS-related costs	Annual	C1		286		286	0		0	286		286
		C2		286		286	0		0	285		286
		C3		286		286	63		63	223		286
Both items	Annual	C1		15,130	1,515	16,646	13,921	406	14,326	1,210	1,110	2,319
		C2		15,130	1,515	16,646	13,807	401	14,208	1,323	1,114	2,437
		C3		15,130	1,515	16,646	14,226	635	14,860	905	881	1,785

Note: "Best practice" policies refer to the combination of scenarios A+B+C. Shaded cells denote no change from values directly above.

Table C.3

World, Except Africa: Financing Gap under Alternative Policy Measures

Policy Scenario[a]		A: QUALITY MEASURES			B: EFFICIENCY MEASURES	C: FINANCING MEASURES				Annual Financing Gap[e]
						Government Revenues[c]		Primary Education Recurrent Spending[d]	Private Enrollments (as % of total)	
		Pupils Per Teacher	Spending on Inputs Other than Teachers[b]	Average Annual Teacher Salary (as multiple of per capita GDP)	Average Repetition Rate	As % of GDP	% for Education			
Status quo		34	25.7%	2.7	11.2%	20.5%	15.7%	42.8%	12.0%	538
A only		31	33.3%	3.9						3,967
A + B		40	33.3%	3.7	6.7%					2,428
"Best practice": A + B +	C1	40	33.3%	3.6	6.7%	15.7%	20.8%	47.1%	10.0%	579
	C2					15.7%	20.0%			585
	C3					20.8%	20.0%			438

Note: Shaded cells denote no change from values directly above.

a. Policy scenarios are: A for quality improvement, B for efficiency improvement, and three alternative resource mobilization scenarios (C1, C2, and C3). The combination of scenarios A+B+C is considered "best practice."
b. As a share of primary education recurrent spending.
c. Current revenues, excluding grants.
d. As a share of total education recurrent spending.
e. In millions of 2000 U.S. dollars. Calculated as the difference between the total cost of service delivery under the specific policy scenario and the total resources for primary education mobilized domestically.

Table C.4

World, Except Africa: MDG-2015 Cost Estimates and Sources of Financing under "Best Practice" Policies and Alternative Resource Mobilization Scenarios

(millions of 2000 U.S. dollars)

Cost Item	Period	Scenario	Domestic Resources Mobilized	COST OF MDG-2015			FINANCING SOURCES					
							DOMESTIC RESOURCES			GAP FOR EXTERNAL FINANCING		
				Recurrent	Capital	Total	Recurrent	Capital	Total	Recurrent	Capital	Total
Education service delivery	Cumulative, 2001–2015	C1	153,340	150,180	11,849	162,029	147,254	6,085	153,339	2,927	5,764	8,690
		C2	153,247	150,180	11,849	162,029	147,233	6,014	153,247	2,947	5,835	8,782
		C3	155,464	150,180	11,849	162,029	148,162	7,301	155,463	2,018	4,548	6,566
	Annual	C1	10,223	10,012	790	10,802	9,817	406	10,223	195	384	579
		C2	10,216	10,012	790	10,802	9,816	401	10,216	196	389	585
		C3	10,364	10,012	790	10,802	9,877	487	10,364	135	303	438
AIDS-related costs	Annual	C1		0		0	0		0	0		0
		C2		0		0	0		0	0		0
		C3		0		0	0		0	0		0
Both items	Annual	C1		10,012	790	10,802	9,817	406	10,223	195	384	579
		C2		10,012	790	10,802	9,816	401	10,216	197	389	586
		C3		10,012	790	10,802	9,877	487	10,364	135	303	438

Note: "Best practice" policies refer to the combination of scenarios A+B+C. Shaded cells denote no change from values directly above.

Table C.5

Africa: MDG-2015 Financing Gap under Alternative Policy Measures

		A: Quality Measures		B: Efficiency Measures		C: Financing Measures					
						Government Revenues[c]		Primary Education	Private Enrollments	Annual
Policy Scenario[a]		Pupils Per Teacher	Spending on Inputs Other than Teachers[b]	Average Annual Teacher Salary (as multiple of per capita GDP)	Average Repetition Rate	As % of GDP	% for Education	Recurrent Spending[d]	(as % of total)	Financing Gap[e]
Status quo		48	24.1%	4.4	18.2%	18.7%	17.5%	49.3%	8.1%	1,700
A only		38	33.8%	4.7						3,522
A + B		40	33.3%	3.8	8.9%					1,920
"Best practice": A + B +	C1	40	33.3%	3.8	8.9%	15.0%	21.2%	49.3%	10.0%	1,454
	C2					15.0%	20.0%			1,566
	C3					20.1%	20.0%			1,125

Note: Shaded cells denote no change from values directly above.

a. Policy scenarios are: A for quality improvement, B for efficiency improvement, and three alternative resource mobilization scenarios (C1, C2, and C3). The combination of scenarios A+B+C is considered "best practice."

b. As a share of primary education recurrent spending.

c. Current revenues, excluding grants.

d. As a share of total education recurrent spending.

e. In millions of 2000 U.S. dollars. Calculated as the difference between the total cost of service delivery under the specific policy scenario and the total resources for primary education mobilized domestically.

Table C.6

Africa: MDG-2015 Cost Estimates and Sources of Financing under "Best Practice" Policies and Alternative Resource Mobilization Scenarios

(millions of 2000 U.S. dollars)

Cost Item	Period	Scenario	Domestic Resources Mobilized	Cost of MDG-2015			Financing Sources					
							Domestic Resources			Gap for External Financing		
				Recurrent	Capital	Total	Recurrent	Capital	Total	Recurrent	Capital	Total
Education service delivery	Cumulative, 2001-2015	C1	61,558	72,484	10,880	83,364	61,558	0	61,558	10,927	10,880	21,806
		C2	59,876	72,484	10,880	83,364	59,876	0	59,876	12,608	10,880	23,488
		C3	79,168	72,484	10,880	83,364	64,268	2,220	66,488	8,216	8,660	16,876
	Annual	C1	4,104	4,832	725	5,558	4,104	0	4,104	728	725	1,454
		C2	3,992	4,832	725	5,558	3,992	0	3,992	841	725	1,566
		C3	5,278	4,832	725	5,558	4,285	148	4,433	548	577	1,125
AIDS-related costs	Annual	C1		286		286	0		0	286		286
		C2		286		286	0		0	285		286
		C3		286		286	63		63	222		286
Both items	Annual	C1		5,118	725	5,844	4,104	0	4,104	1,015	725	1,740
		C2		5,118	725	5,844	3,992	0	3,992	1,127	725	1,852
		C3		5,118	725	5,844	4,348	148	4,496	770	577	1,348

Note: "Best practice" policies refer to the combination of scenarios A+B+C. Shaded cells denote no change from values directly above.

Table C.7

Armenia: MDG-2015 Financing Gap under Alternative Policy Measures

Policy Scenario[a]		Pupils Per Teacher	Spending on Inputs Other than Teachers[b]	Average Annual Teacher Salary (as multiple of per capita GDP)	Average Repetition Rate	As % of GDP	% for Education	Primary Education Recurrent Spending[d]	Private Enrollments (as % of total)	Annual Financing Gap[e]
		A: Quality Measures			**B: Efficiency Measures**	**C: Financing Measures**				
						Government Revenues[c]		Primary Education	Private Enrollments	
Status quo		13	52.9%	0.6	0.1%	15.8%	15.1%	51.3%	0.0%	0
A only		13	33.3%	3.5						61
A + B		40	33.3%	3.5	0.1%					12
"Best practice": A + B +	C1	40	33.3%	3.5	0.1%	16.0%	20.0%	50.0%	10.0%	15
	C2					16.0%	20.0%			15
	C3					16.0%	20.0%			15

Note: Shaded cells denote no change from values directly above.
a. Policy scenarios are: A for quality improvement, B for efficiency improvement, and three alternative resource mobilization scenarios (C1, C2, and C3). The combination of scenarios A+B+C is considered "best practice."
b. As a share of primary education recurrent spending.
c. Current revenues, excluding grants.
d. As a share of total education recurrent spending.
e. In millions of 2000 U.S. dollars. Calculated as the difference between the total cost of service delivery under the specific policy scenario and the total resources for primary education mobilized domestically.

Table C.8

Armenia: MDG-2015 Cost Estimates and Sources of Financing under "Best Practice" Policies and Alternative Resource Mobilization Scenarios 195

(millions of 2000 U.S. dollars)

Cost Item	Period	Scenario	Domestic Resources Mobilized	Recurrent	Capital	Total	Recurrent	Capital	Total	Recurrent	Capital	Total
				Cost of MDG-2015			**Domestic Resources**			**Gap for External Financing**		
Education service delivery	Cumulative, 2001-2015	C1	491	712	0	712	491	0	491	221	0	221
		C2	491	712	0	712	491	0	491	221	0	221
		C3	491	712	0	712	491	0	491	221	0	221
	Annual	C1	33	47	0	47	33	0	33	15	0	15
		C2	33	47	0	47	33	0	33	15	0	15
		C3	33	47	0	47	33	0	33	15	0	15
AIDS-related costs	Annual	C1		0	0	0	0		0	0		0
		C2		0	0	0	0		0	0		0
		C3		0	0	0	0		0	0		0
Both items	Annual	C1		47	0	47	33	0	33	15	0	15
		C2		47	0	47	33	0	33	15	0	15
		C3		47	0	47	33	0	33	15	0	15

Note: "Best practice" policies refer to the combination of scenarios A+B+C. Shaded cells denote no change from values directly above.

Table C.9

Bangladesh: MDG-2015 Financing Gap under Alternative Policy Measures

Policy Scenario[a]		A: Quality Measures			B: Efficiency Measures	C: Financing Measures				Annual Financing Gap[e]
		Pupils Per Teacher	Spending on Inputs Other than Teachers[b]	Average Annual Teacher Salary (as multiple of per capita GDP)	Average Repetition Rate	Government Revenues[c] As % of GDP	% for Education	Primary Education Recurrent Spending[d]	Private Enrollments (as % of total)	
Status quo		55	25.0%	2.7	15.0%	12.8%	14.7%	41.6%	12.5%	0
A only		40	33.3%	3.5						224
A + B		40	33.3%	3.5	10.0%					195
"Best practice": A + B +	C1	40	33.3%	3.5	10.0%	14.0%	20.0%	42.0%	10.0%	84
	C2					14.0%	20.0%			84
	C3					14.0%	20.0%			84

Note: Shaded cells denote no change from values directly above.

a. Policy scenarios are: A for quality improvement, B for efficiency improvement, and three alternative resource mobilization scenarios (C1, C2, and C3). The combination of scenarios A+B+C is considered "best practice."

b. As a share of primary education recurrent spending.

c. Current revenues, excluding grants.

d. As a share of total education recurrent spending.

e. In millions of 2000 U.S. dollars. Calculated as the difference between the total cost of service delivery under the specific policy scenario and the total resources for primary education mobilized domestically.

Table C.10

Bangladesh: MDG-2015 Cost Estimates and Sources of Financing under "Best Practice" Policies and Alternative Resource Mobilization Scenarios 197

(millions of 2000 U.S. dollars)

Cost Item	Period	Scenario	Domestic Resources Mobilized	Cost of MDG-2015			Financing Sources					
							Domestic Resources			Gap for External Financing		
				Recurrent	Capital	Total	Recurrent	Capital	Total	Recurrent	Capital	Total
Education service delivery	Cumulative, 2001-2015	C1	8,342	8,527	1,070	9,597	8,342	0	8,342	185	1,070	1,255
		C2	8,342	8,527	1,070	9,597	8,342	0	8,342	185	1,070	1,255
		C3	8,342	8,527	1,070	9,597	8,342	0	8,342	185	1,070	1,255
	Annual	C1	556	568	71	640	556	0	556	12	71	84
		C2	556	568	71	640	556	0	556	12	71	84
		C3	556	568	71	640	556	0	556	12	71	84
AIDS-related costs	Annual	C1	0		0	0	0		0	0		0
		C2	0		0	0	0		0	0		0
		C3	0		0	0	0		0	0		0
Both items	Annual	C1		568	71	640	556	0	556	12	71	84
		C2		568	71	640	556	0	556	12	71	84
		C3		568	71	640	556	0	556	12	71	84

Note: "Best practice" policies refer to the combination of scenarios A+B+C. Shaded cells denote no change from values directly above.

Table C.11

Cambodia: MDG-2015 Financing Gap under Alternative Policy Measures

Policy Scenario[a]		A: Quality Measures			B: Efficiency Measures	C: Financing Measures				Annual Financing Gap[e]
		Pupils Per Teacher	Spending on Inputs Other than Teachers[b]	Average Annual Teacher Salary (as multiple of per capita GDP)	Average Repetition Rate	Government Revenues[c]		Primary Education Recurrent Spending[d]	Private Enrollments (as % of total)	
						As % of GDP	% for Education			
Status quo		53	20.0%	1.5	16.6%	11.5%	12.2%	51.0%	10.0%	0
A only		40	33.3%	3.5						45
A + B		40	33.3%	3.5	10.0%					40
"Best practice": A + B +	C1	40	33.3%	3.5	10.0%	14.0%	20.0%	50.0%	10.0%	23
	C2					14.0%	20.0%			23
	C3					14.0%	20.0%			23

Note: Shaded cells denote no change from values directly above.
a. Policy scenarios are: A for quality improvement, B for efficiency improvement, and three alternative resource mobilization scenarios (C1, C2, and C3). The combination of scenarios A+B+C is considered "best practice."
b. As a share of primary education recurrent spending.
c. Current revenues, excluding grants.
d. As a share of total education recurrent spending.
e. In millions of 2000 U.S. dollars. Calculated as the difference between the total cost of service delivery under the specific policy scenario and the total resources for primary education mobilized domestically.

Table C.12

Cambodia: MDG-2015 Cost Estimates and Sources of Financing under "Best Practice" Policies and Alternative Resource Mobilization Scenarios 199

(millions of 2000 U.S. dollars)

Cost Item	Period	Scenario	Domestic Resources Mobilized	Cost of MDG-2015			Financing Sources					
							Domestic Resources			Gap for External Financing		
				Recurrent	Capital	Total	Recurrent	Capital	Total	Recurrent	Capital	Total
Education service delivery	Cumulative, 2001-2015	C1	852	1,144	58	1,202	852	0	852	292	58	350
		C2	852	1,144	58	1,202	852	0	852	292	58	350
		C3	852	1,144	58	1,202	852	0	852	292	58	350
	Annual	C1	57	76	4	80	57	0	57	19	4	23
		C2	57	76	4	80	57	0	57	19	4	23
		C3	57	76	4	80	57	0	57	19	4	23
AIDS-related costs	Annual	C1		0		0	0		0	0		0
		C2		0		0	0		0	0		0
		C3		0		0	0		0	0		0
Both items	Annual	C1		76	4	80	57	0	57	19	4	23
		C2		76	4	80	57	0	57	19	4	23
		C3		76	4	80	57	0	57	19	4	23

Note: "Best practice" policies refer to the combination of scenarios A+B+C. Shaded cells denote no change from values directly above.

Table C.13

Georgia: MDG-2015 Financing Gap under Alternative Policy Measures

Policy Scenario[a]		A: Quality Measures			B: Efficiency Measures	C: Financing Measures				Annual Financing Gap[e]
		Pupils Per Teacher	Spending on Inputs Other than Teachers[b]	Average Annual Teacher Salary (as multiple of per capita GDP)	Average Repetition Rate	Government Revenues[c] As % of GDP	Government Revenues[c] % for Education	Primary Education Recurrent Spending[d]	Private Enrollments (as % of total)	
Status quo		17	16.0%	0.6	0.5%	13.7%	9.3%	26.0%	1.0%	0
A only		17	33.3%	3.5						129
A + B		40	33.3%	3.5	0.5%					39
"Best practice": A + B +	C1	40	33.3%	3.5	0.5%	16.0%	20.0%	50.0%	10.0%	13
	C2					16.0%	20.0%			13
	C3					16.0%	20.0%			13

Note: Shaded cells denote no change from values directly above.
a. Policy scenarios are: A for quality improvement, B for efficiency improvement, and three alternative resource mobilization scenarios (C1, C2, and C3). The combination of scenarios A+B+C is considered "best practice."
b. As a share of primary education recurrent spending.
c. Current revenues, excluding grants.
d. As a share of total education recurrent spending.
e. In millions of 2000 U.S. dollars. Calculated as the difference between the total cost of service delivery under the specific policy scenario and the total resources for primary education mobilized domestically.

Table C.14

Georgia: MDG-2015 Cost Estimates and Sources of Financing under "Best Practice" Policies and Alternative Resource Mobilization Scenarios
(millions of 2000 U.S. dollars)

Cost Item	Period	Scenario	Domestic Resources Mobilized	Cost of MDG-2015			Financing Sources					
							Domestic Resources			Gap for External Financing		
				Recurrent	Capital	Total	Recurrent	Capital	Total	Recurrent	Capital	Total
Education service delivery	Cumulative, 2001-2015	C1	599	801	0	801	599	0	599	202	0	202
		C2	599	801	0	801	599	0	599	202	0	202
		C3	599	801	0	801	599	0	599	202	0	202
	Annual	C1	40	53	0	53	40	0	40	13	0	13
		C2	40	53	0	53	40	0	40	13	0	13
		C3	40	53	0	53	40	0	40	13	0	13
AIDS-related costs	Annual	C1		0	0	0	0	0	0	0	0	0
		C2		0	0	0	0	0	0	0	0	0
		C3		0	0	0	0	0	0	0	0	0
Both items	Annual	C1		53	0	53	40	0	40	13	0	13
		C2		53	0	53	40	0	40	13	0	13
		C3		53	0	53	40	0	40	13	0	13

Note: "Best practice" policies refer to the combination of scenarios A+B+C. Shaded cells denote no change from values directly above.

Table C.15

Haiti: MDG-2015 Financing Gap under Alternative Policy Measures

Policy Scenario[a]		Pupils Per Teacher	Spending on Inputs Other than Teachers[b]	Average Annual Teacher Salary (as multiple of per capita GDP)	Average Repetition Rate	As % of GDP	% for Education	Primary Education Recurrent Spending[d]	Private Enrollments (as % of total)	Annual Financing Gap[e]
		A: Quality Measures			**B: Efficiency Measures**	**C: Financing Measures**				
						Government Revenues[c]		Primary Education Recurrent Spending[d]	Private Enrollments (as % of total)	Annual Financing Gap[e]
Status quo		46	10.0%	6.8	17.0%	9.3%	20.6%	38.7%	76.6%	0
A only		40	33.3%	6.8						7
A + B		40	33.3%	5.3	10.0%					0
"Best practice": A + B +	C1	40	33.3%	4.0	10.0%	16.0%	20.6%	50.0%	10.0%	33
	C2					16.0%	20.0%			34
	C3					16.0%	20.0%			34

Note: Shaded cells denote no change from values directly above.
a. Policy scenarios are: A for quality improvement, B for efficiency improvement, and three alternative resource mobilization scenarios (C1, C2, and C3). The combination of scenarios A+B+C is considered "best practice."
b. As a share of primary education recurrent spending.
c. Current revenues, excluding grants.
d. As a share of total education recurrent spending.
e. In millions of 2000 U.S. dollars. Calculated as the difference between the total cost of service delivery under the specific policy scenario and the total resources for primary education mobilized domestically.

Table C.16

Haiti: MDG-2015 Cost Estimates and Sources of Financing under "Best Practice" Policies and Alternative Resource Mobilization Scenarios
(millions of 2000 U.S. dollars)

Cost Item	Period	Scenario	Domestic Resources Mobilized	Recurrent	Capital	Total	Recurrent	Capital	Total	Recurrent	Capital	Total
				Cost of MDG-2015			**Domestic Resources**			**Gap for External Financing**		
Education service delivery	Cumulative, 2001-2015	C1	993	1,142	344	1,486	993	0	993	149	344	493
		C2	972	1,142	344	1,486	972	0	972	170	344	513
		C3	972	1,142	344	1,486	972	0	972	170	344	513
	Annual	C1	66	76	23	99	66	0	66	10	23	33
		C2	65	76	23	99	65	0	65	11	23	34
		C3	65	76	23	99	65	0	65	11	23	34
AIDS-related costs	Annual	C1		0		0	0		0	0		0
		C2		0		0	0		0	0		0
		C3		0		0	0		0	0		0
Both items	Annual	C1		76	23	99	66	0	66	10	23	33
		C2		76	23	99	65	0	65	11	23	34
		C3		76	23	99	65	0	65	11	23	34

Note: "Best practice" policies refer to the combination of scenarios A+B+C. Shaded cells denote no change from values directly above.

Table C.17

Honduras: MDG-2015 Financing Gap under Alternative Policy Measures

Policy Scenario[a]		A: Quality Measures			B: Efficiency Measures	C: Financing Measures				Annual Financing Gap[e]
		Pupils Per Teacher	Spending on Inputs Other than Teachers[b]	Average Annual Teacher Salary (as multiple of per capita GDP)	Average Repetition Rate	Government Revenues[c]		Primary Education Recurrent Spending[d]	Private Enrollments (as % of total)	
						As % of GDP	% for Education			
Status quo		32	12.1%	5.0	8.0%	18.5%	30.1%	49.6%	6.9%	17
A only		32	33.3%	5.0						169
A + B		40	33.3%	3.5	8.0%					0
"Best practice": A + B +	C1	40	33.3%	3.5	8.0%	18.0%	30.1%	50.0%	10.0%	0
	C2					18.0%	20.0%			5
	C3					18.5%	20.0%			3

Note: Shaded cells denote no change from values directly above.

a. Policy scenarios are: A for quality improvement, B for efficiency improvement, and three alternative resource mobilization scenarios (C1, C2, and C3). The combination of scenarios A+B+C is considered "best practice."

b. As a share of primary education recurrent spending.

c. Current revenues, excluding grants.

d. As a share of total education recurrent spending.

e. In millions of 2000 U.S. dollars. Calculated as the difference between the total cost of service delivery under the specific policy scenario and the total resources for primary education mobilized domestically.

Table C.18

Honduras: MDG-2015 Cost Estimates and Sources of Financing under "Best Practice" Policies and Alternative Resource Mobilization Scenarios

(millions of 2000 U.S. dollars)

Cost Item	Period	Scenario	Domestic Resources Mobilized	Cost of MDG-2015			Financing Sources					
							Domestic Resources			Gap for External Financing		
				Recurrent	Capital	Total	Recurrent	Capital	Total	Recurrent	Capital	Total
Education service delivery	Cumulative, 2001-2015	C1	3,114	2,553	561	3,114	2,553	561	3,114	0	0	0
		C2	3,043	2,553	561	3,114	2,553	490	3,043	0	71	71
		C3	3,063	2,553	561	3,114	2,553	510	3,063	0	51	51
	Annual	C1	208	170	37	208	170	37	208	0	0	0
		C2	203	170	37	208	170	33	203	0	5	5
		C3	204	170	37	208	170	34	204	0	3	3
AIDS-related costs	Annual	C1		0		0	0		0	0		0
		C2		0		0	0		0	0		0
		C3		0		0	0		0	0		0
Both items	Annual	C1		170	37	208	170	37	208	0	0	0
		C2		170	37	208	170	33	203	0	5	5
		C3		170	37	208	170	34	204	0	3	3

Note: "Best practice" policies refer to the combination of scenarios A+B+C. Shaded cells denote no change from values directly above.

Table C.19

India: MDG-2015 Financing Gap under Alternative Policy Measures

Policy Scenario[a]		Pupils Per Teacher	Spending on Inputs Other than Teachers[b]	Average Annual Teacher Salary (as multiple of per capita GDP)	Average Repetition Rate	As % of GDP	% for Education	Primary Education Recurrent Spending[d]	Private Enrollments (as % of total)	Annual Financing Gap[e]
		A: Quality Measures			**B: Efficiency Measures**	**C: Financing Measures**				
						Government Revenues[c]				
Status quo		52	23.2%	3.4	20.0%	21.2%	12.4%	32.1%	12.5%	146
A only		40	33.3%	3.5						2,470
A + B		40	33.3%	3.5	10.0%					1,782
"Best practice": A + B +	C1	40	33.3%	3.5	10.0%	16.0%	20.0%	42.0%	10.0%	67
	C2					16.0%	20.0%			67
	C3					21.2%	20.0%			28

Note: Shaded cells denote no change from values directly above.
a. Policy scenarios are: A for quality improvement, B for efficiency improvement, and three alternative resource mobilization scenarios (C1, C2, and C3). The combination of scenarios A+B+C is considered "best practice."
b. As a share of primary education recurrent spending.
c. Current revenues, excluding grants.
d. As a share of total education recurrent spending.
e. In millions of 2000 U.S. dollars. Calculated as the difference between the total cost of service delivery under the specific policy scenario and the total resources for primary education mobilized domestically.

Table C.20

India: MDG-2015 Cost Estimates and Sources of Financing under "Best Practice" Policies and Alternative Resource Mobilization Scenarios

(millions of 2000 U.S. dollars)

Cost Item	Period	Scenario	Domestic Resources Mobilized	Recurrent	Capital	Total	Recurrent	Capital	Total	Recurrent	Capital	Total
				Cost of MDG-2015			**Domestic Resources**			**Gap for External Financing**		
										Financing Sources		
Education service delivery	Cumulative, 2001-2015	C1	115,278	109,754	6,525	116,279	109,754	5,524	115,278	0	1,001	1,001
		C2	115,278	109,754	6,525	116,279	109,754	5,524	115,278	0	1,001	1,001
		C3	115,858	109,754	6,525	116,279	109,754	6,104	115,858	0	422	422
	Annual	C1	7,685	7,317	435	7,752	7,317	368	7,685	0	67	67
		C2	7,685	7,317	435	7,752	7,317	368	7,685	0	67	67
		C3	7,724	7,317	435	7,752	7,317	407	7,724	0	28	28
AIDS-related costs	Annual	C1		0		0	0		0	0		0
		C2		0		0	0		0	0		0
		C3		0		0	0		0	0		0
Both items	Annual	C1		7,317	435	7,752	7,317	368	7,685	0	67	67
		C2		7,317	435	7,752	7,317	368	7,685	0	67	67
		C3		7,317	435	7,752	7,317	407	7,724	0	28	28

Note: "Best practice" policies refer to the combination of scenarios A+B+C. Shaded cells denote no change from values directly above.

Table C.21
....

Lao PDR: MDG-2015 Financing Gap under Alternative Policy Measures

Policy Scenario[a]		Pupils Per Teacher	Spending on Inputs Other than Teachers[b]	Average Annual Teacher Salary (as multiple of per capita GDP)	Average Repetition Rate	As % of GDP	% for Education	Primary Education Recurrent Spending[d]	Private Enrollments (as % of total)	Annual Financing Gap[e]
		A: Quality Measures			**B: Efficiency Measures**	**C: Financing Measures**				
						Government Revenues[c]				
Status quo		31	19.6%	0.4	22.6%	38.1%	1.4%	48.8%	1.9%	2
A only		31	33.3%	3.5						49
A + B		40	33.3%	3.5	10.0%					33
"Best practice": A + B +	C1	40	33.3%	3.5	10.0%	16.0%	20.0%	42.0%	10.0%	13
	C2					16.0%	20.0%			13
	C3					38.1%	20.0%			6

Note: Shaded cells denote no change from values directly above.
a. Policy scenarios are: A for quality improvement, B for efficiency improvement, and three alternative resource mobilization scenarios (C1, C2, and C3). The combination of scenarios A+B+C is considered "best practice."
b. As a share of primary education recurrent spending.
c. Current revenues, excluding grants.
d. As a share of total education recurrent spending.
e. In millions of 2000 U.S. dollars. Calculated as the difference between the total cost of service delivery under the specific policy scenario and the total resources for primary education mobilized domestically.

Table C.22
....

Lao PDR: MDG-2015 Cost Estimates and Sources of Financing under "Best Practice" Policies and Alternative Resource Mobilization Scenarios
(millions of 2000 U.S. dollars)

Cost Item	Period	Scenario	Domestic Resources Mobilized	Recurrent	Capital	Total	Recurrent	Capital	Total	Recurrent	Capital	Total
				Cost of MDG-2015			**Domestic Resources**			**Gap for External Financing**		
								Financing Sources				
Education service delivery	Cumulative, 2001-2015	C1	393	558	36	594	393	0	393	165	36	201
		C2	393	558	36	594	393	0	393	165	36	201
		C3	500	558	36	594	500	0	500	57	36	94
	Annual	C1	26	37	2	40	26	0	26	11	2	13
		C2	26	37	2	40	26	0	26	11	2	13
		C3	33	37	2	40	33	0	33	4	2	6
AIDS-related costs	Annual	C1		0		0	0		0	0		0
		C2		0		0	0		0	0		0
		C3		0		0	0		0	0		0
Both items	Annual	C1		37	2	40	26	0	26	11	2	13
		C2		37	2	40	26	0	26	11	2	13
		C3		37	2	40	33	0	33	4	2	6

Note: "Best practice" policies refer to the combination of scenarios A+B+C. Shaded cells denote no change from values directly above.

Table C.23

Moldova: MDG-2015 Financing Gap under Alternative Policy Measures

Policy Scenario[a]		A: Quality Measures — Pupils Per Teacher	A: Quality Measures — Spending on Inputs Other than Teachers[b]	A: Quality Measures — Average Annual Teacher Salary (as multiple of per capita GDP)	B: Efficiency Measures — Average Repetition Rate	C: Financing Measures — Government Revenues[c] As % of GDP	C: Financing Measures — Government Revenues[c] % for Education	C: Financing Measures — Primary Education Recurrent Spending[d]	C: Financing Measures — Private Enrollments (as % of total)	Annual Financing Gap[e]
Status quo		21	67.8%	1.1	0.9%	29.8%	18.5%	25.5%	0.0%	0
A only		21	33.3%	3.5						17
A + B		40	33.3%	3.5	0.9%					5
"Best practice": A + B +	C1	40	33.3%	3.5	0.9%	16.0%	20.0%	50.0%	10.0%	5
	C2					16.0%	20.0%			5
	C3					29.8%	20.0%			4

Note: Shaded cells denote no change from values directly above.
a. Policy scenarios are: A for quality improvement, B for efficiency improvement, and three alternative resource mobilization scenarios (C1, C2, and C3). The combination of scenarios A+B+C is considered "best practice."
b. As a share of primary education recurrent spending.
c. Current revenues, excluding grants.
d. As a share of total education recurrent spending.
e. In millions of 2000 U.S. dollars. Calculated as the difference between the total cost of service delivery under the specific policy scenario and the total resources for primary education mobilized domestically.

Table C.24

Moldova: MDG-2015 Cost Estimates and Sources of Financing under "Best Practice" Policies and Alternative Resource Mobilization Scenarios
(millions of 2000 U.S. dollars)

Cost Item	Period	Scenario	Domestic Resources Mobilized	Cost of MDG-2015 Recurrent	Cost of MDG-2015 Capital	Cost of MDG-2015 Total	Financing Sources — Domestic Resources Recurrent	Financing Sources — Domestic Resources Capital	Financing Sources — Domestic Resources Total	Financing Sources — Gap for External Financing Recurrent	Financing Sources — Gap for External Financing Capital	Financing Sources — Gap for External Financing Total
Education service delivery	Cumulative, 2001–2015	C1	309	388	0	388	309	0	309	79	0	79
		C2	309	388	0	388	309	0	309	79	0	79
		C3	327	388	0	388	327	0	327	61	0	61
	Annual	C1	21	26	0	26	21	0	21	5	0	5
		C2	21	26	0	26	21	0	21	5	0	5
		C3	22	26	0	26	22	0	22	4	0	4
AIDS-related costs	Annual	C1		0		0	0		0	0		0
		C2		0		0	0		0	0		0
		C3		0		0	0		0	0		0
Both items	Annual	C1		26	0	26	21	0	21	5	0	5
		C2		26	0	26	21	0	21	5	0	5
		C3		26	0	26	22	0	22	4	0	4

Note: "Best practice" policies refer to the combination of scenarios A+B+C. Shaded cells denote no change from values directly above.

Table C.25

Mongolia: MDG-2015 Financing Gap under Alternative Policy Measures

Policy Scenario[a]		A: Quality Measures			B: Efficiency Measures	C: Financing Measures					Annual Financing Gap[e]
				Average Annual Teacher Salary (as multiple of per capita GDP)	Average Repetition Rate	Government Revenues[c]		Primary Education Recurrent Spending[d]	Private Enrollments (as % of total)		
		Pupils Per Teacher	Spending on Inputs Other than Teachers[b]			As % of GDP	% for Education				
Status quo		31	15.0%	3.9	0.9%	29.2%	24.6%	33.6%	0.5%		0
A only		31	33.3%	3.9							0
A + B		40	33.3%	3.9	0.9%						0
"Best practice": A + B +	C1	40	33.3%	3.9	0.9%	16.0%	20.0%	50.0%	10.0%		0
	C2					16.0%	20.0%				0
	C3					16.0%	20.0%				0

Note: Shaded cells denote no change from values directly above.
a. Policy scenarios are: A for quality improvement, B for efficiency improvement, and three alternative resource mobilization scenarios (C1, C2, and C3). The combination of scenarios A+B+C is considered "best practice."
b. As a share of primary education recurrent spending.
c. Current revenues, excluding grants.
d. As a share of total education recurrent spending.
e. In millions of 2000 U.S. dollars. Calculated as the difference between the total cost of service delivery under the specific policy scenario and the total resources for primary education mobilized domestically.

Table C.26

Mongolia: MDG-2015 Cost Estimates and Sources of Financing under "Best Practice" Policies and Alternative Resource Mobilization Scenarios
(millions of 2000 U.S. dollars)

Cost Item	Period	Scenario	Domestic Resources Mobilized	Cost of MDG-2015			Financing Sources					
							Domestic Resources			Gap for External Financing		
				Recurrent	Capital	Total	Recurrent	Capital	Total	Recurrent	Capital	Total
Education service delivery	Cumulative, 2001-2015	C1	319	318	0	318	318	0	318	0	0	0
		C2	319	318	0	318	318	0	318	0	0	0
		C3	319	318	0	318	318	0	318	0	0	0
	Annual	C1	21	21	0	21	21	0	21	0	0	0
		C2	21	21	0	21	21	0	21	0	0	0
		C3	21	21	0	21	21	0	21	0	0	0
AIDS-related costs	Annual	C1		0		0	0		0	0		0
		C2		0		0	0		0	0		0
		C3		0		0	0		0	0		0
Both items	Annual	C1		21	0	21	21	0	21	0	0	0
		C2		21	0	21	21	0	21	0	0	0
		C3		21	0	21	21	0	21	0	0	0

Note: "Best practice" policies refer to the combination of scenarios A+B+C. Shaded cells denote no change from values directly above.

Table C.27

Nepal: MDG-2015 Financing Gap under Alternative Policy Measures

Policy Scenario[a]		A: Quality Measures			B: Efficiency Measures	C: Financing Measures				Annual Financing Gap[e]
		Pupils Per Teacher	Spending on Inputs Other than Teachers[b]	Average Annual Teacher Salary (as multiple of per capita GDP)	Average Repetition Rate	Government Revenues[c] As % of GDP	% for Education	Primary Education Recurrent Spending[d]	Private Enrollments (as % of total)	
Status quo		36	20.0%	2.0	29.9%	10.4%	18.4%	53.2%	8.1%	5
A only		36	33.3%	3.5						97
A + B		40	33.3%	3.5	10.0%					54
"Best practice": A + B +	C1	40	33.3%	3.5	10.0%	14.0%	20.0%	42.0%	10.0%	44
	C2					14.0%	20.0%			44
	C3					14.0%	20.0%			44

Note: Shaded cells denote no change from values directly above.
a. Policy scenarios are: A for quality improvement, B for efficiency improvement, and three alternative resource mobilization scenarios (C1, C2, and C3). The combination of scenarios A+B+C is considered "best practice."
b. As a share of primary education recurrent spending.
c. Current revenues, excluding grants.
d. As a share of total education recurrent spending.
e. In millions of 2000 U.S. dollars. Calculated as the difference between the total cost of service delivery under the specific policy scenario and the total resources for primary education mobilized domestically.

Table C.28

Nepal: MDG-2015 Cost Estimates and Sources of Financing under "Best Practice" Policies and Alternative Resource Mobilization Scenarios

(millions of 2000 U.S. dollars)

Cost Item	Period	Scenario	Domestic Resources Mobilized	Cost of MDG-2015			Financing Sources					
							Domestic Resources			Gap for External Financing		
				Recurrent	Capital	Total	Recurrent	Capital	Total	Recurrent	Capital	Total
Education service delivery	Cumulative, 2001-2015	C1	1,333	1,787	213	2,000	1,333	0	1,333	454	213	667
		C2	1,333	1,787	213	2,000	1,333	0	1,333	454	213	667
		C3	1,333	1,787	213	2,000	1,333	0	1,333	454	213	667
	Annual	C1	89	119	14	133	89	0	89	30	14	44
		C2	89	119	14	133	89	0	89	30	14	44
		C3	89	119	14	133	89	0	89	30	14	44
AIDS-related costs	Annual	C1		0		0	0		0	0		0
		C2		0		0	0		0	0		0
		C3		0		0	0		0	0		0
Both items	Annual	C1		119	14	133	89	0	89	30	14	44
		C2		119	14	133	89	0	89	30	14	44
		C3		119	14	133	89	0	89	30	14	44

Note: "Best practice" policies refer to the combination of scenarios A+B+C. Shaded cells denote no change from values directly above.

Table C.29

Nicaragua: MDG-2015 Financing Gap under Alternative Policy Measures

Policy Scenario[a]		A: Quality Measures — Pupils Per Teacher	Spending on Inputs Other than Teachers[b]	Average Annual Teacher Salary (as multiple of per capita GDP)	B: Efficiency Measures — Average Repetition Rate	C: Financing Measures — Government Revenues[c] As % of GDP	% for Education	Primary Education Recurrent Spending[d]	Private Enrollments (as % of total)	Annual Financing Gap[e]
Status quo		36	32.7%	3.2	12.0%	25.3%	16.8%	48.7%	6.8%	0
A only		36	33.3%	3.5						19
A + B		40	33.3%	3.5	10.0%					1
"Best practice": A + B +	C1	40	33.3%	3.5	10.0%	16.0%	20.0%	50.0%	10.0%	8
	C2					16.0%	20.0%			8
	C3					25.3%	20.0%			2

Note: Shaded cells denote no change from values directly above.
a. Policy scenarios are: A for quality improvement, B for efficiency improvement, and three alternative resource mobilization scenarios (C1, C2, and C3). The combination of scenarios A+B+C is considered "best practice."
b. As a share of primary education recurrent spending.
c. Current revenues, excluding grants.
d. As a share of total education recurrent spending.
e. In millions of 2000 U.S. dollars. Calculated as the difference between the total cost of service delivery under the specific policy scenario and the total resources for primary education mobilized domestically.

Table C.30

Nicaragua: MDG-2015 Cost Estimates and Sources of Financing under "Best Practice" Policies and Alternative Resource Mobilization Scenarios

(millions of 2000 U.S. dollars)

Cost Item	Period	Scenario	Domestic Resources Mobilized	Cost of MDG-2015 Recurrent	Capital	Total	Domestic Resources Recurrent	Capital	Total	Gap for External Financing Recurrent	Capital	Total
Education service delivery	Cumulative, 2001-2015	C1	974	1,012	85	1,097	974	0	974	38	85	123
		C2	974	1,012	85	1,097	974	0	974	38	85	123
		C3	1,062	1,012	85	1,097	1,012	50	1,062	0	35	35
	Annual	C1	65	67	6	73	65	0	65	3	6	8
		C2	65	67	6	73	65	0	65	3	6	8
		C3	71	67	6	73	67	3	71	0	2	2
AIDS-related costs	Annual	C1	0		0	0	0		0	0		0
		C2	0		0	0	0		0	0		0
		C3	0		0	0	0		0	0		0
Both items	Annual	C1		67	6	73	65	0	65	3	6	8
		C2		67	6	73	65	0	65	3	6	8
		C3		67	6	73	67	3	71	0	2	2

Note: "Best practice" policies refer to the combination of scenarios A+B+C. Shaded cells denote no change from values directly above.

Table C.31

Pakistan: MDG-2015 Financing Gap under Alternative Policy Measures

Policy Scenario[a]		Pupils Per Teacher	Spending on Inputs Other than Teachers[b]	Average Annual Teacher Salary (as multiple of per capita GDP)	Average Repetition Rate	As % of GDP	% for Education	Primary Education Recurrent Spending[d]	Private Enrollments (as % of total)	Annual Financing Gap[e]
		A: Quality Measures			**B: Efficiency Measures**	**C: Financing Measures**				
						Government Revenues[c]				
Status quo		32	19.3%	3.6	6.2%	16.7%	10.2%	51.8%	29.4%	285
A only		32	33.3%	3.5						450
A + B		40	33.3%	3.5	6.2%					261
"Best practice": A + B +	C1	40	33.3%	3.5	6.2%	16.0%	20.0%	42.0%	10.0%	204
	C2					16.0%	20.0%			204
	C3					16.7%	20.0%			173

Note: Shaded cells denote no change from values directly above.
a. Policy scenarios are: A for quality improvement, B for efficiency improvement, and three alternative resource mobilization scenarios (C1, C2, and C3). The combination of scenarios A+B+C is considered "best practice."
b. As a share of primary education recurrent spending.
c. Current revenues, excluding grants.
d. As a share of total education recurrent spending.
e. In millions of 2000 U.S. dollars. Calculated as the difference between the total cost of service delivery under the specific policy scenario and the total resources for primary education mobilized domestically.

Table C.32

Pakistan: MDG-2015 Cost Estimates and Sources of Financing under "Best Practice" Policies and Alternative Resource Mobilization Scenarios

(millions of 2000 U.S. dollars)

Cost Item	Period	Scenario	Domestic Resources Mobilized	Recurrent	Capital	Total	Recurrent	Capital	Total	Recurrent	Capital	Total
				Cost of MDG-2015			**Domestic Resources**			**Gap for External Financing**		
Education service delivery	Cumulative, 2001-2015	C1	15,919	16,748	2,224	18,972	15,919	0	15,919	829	2,224	3,053
		C2	15,919	16,748	2,224	18,972	15,919	0	15,919	829	2,224	3,053
		C3	16,373	16,748	2,224	18,972	16,373	0	16,373	375	2,224	2,599
	Annual	C1	1,061	1,117	148	1,265	1,061	0	1,061	55	148	204
		C2	1,061	1,117	148	1,265	1,061	0	1,061	55	148	204
		C3	1,092	1,117	148	1,265	1,092	0	1,092	25	148	173
AIDS-related costs	Annual	C1		0		0	0		0	0		0
		C2		0		0	0		0	0		0
		C3		0		0	0		0	0		0
Both items	Annual	C1		1,117	148	1,265	1,061	0	1,061	55	148	204
		C2		1,117	148	1,265	1,061	0	1,061	55	148	204
		C3		1,117	148	1,265	1,092	0	1,092	25	148	173

Note: "Best practice" policies refer to the combination of scenarios A+B+C. Shaded cells denote no change from values directly above.

Table C.33

Yemen: MDG-2015 Financing Gap under Alternative Policy Measures

Policy Scenario[a]		A: Quality Measures			B: Efficiency Measures	C: Financing Measures				Annual Financing Gap[e]
		Pupils Per Teacher	Spending on Inputs Other than Teachers[b]	Average Annual Teacher Salary (as multiple of per capita GDP)	Average Repetition Rate	Government Revenues[c]		Primary Education Recurrent Spending[d]	Private Enrollments (as % of total)	
						As % of GDP	% for Education			
Status quo		25	26.7%	3.4	7.0%	35.2%	15.8%	48.0%	1.4%	82
A only		25	33.3%	3.5						231
A + B		40	33.3%	3.5	7.0%					6
"Best practice": A + B +	C1	40	33.3%	3.5	7.0%	16.0%	20.0%	50.0%	10.0%	70
	C2					16.0%	20.0%			70
	C3					35.2%	20.0%			6

Note: Shaded cells denote no change from values directly above.
a. Policy scenarios are: A for quality improvement, B for efficiency improvement, and three alternative resource mobilization scenarios (C1, C2, and C3). The combination of scenarios A+B+C is considered "best practice."
b. As a share of primary education recurrent spending.
c. Current revenues, excluding grants.
d. As a share of total education recurrent spending.
e. In millions of 2000 U.S. dollars. Calculated as the difference between the total cost of service delivery under the specific policy scenario and the total resources for primary education mobilized domestically.

Table C.34

Yemen: MDG-2015 Cost Estimates and Sources of Financing under "Best Practice" Policies and Alternative Resource Mobilization Scenarios
(millions of 2000 U.S. dollars)

Cost Item	Period	Scenario	Domestic Resources Mobilized	Cost of MDG-2015			Financing Sources					
							Domestic Resources			Gap for External Financing		
				Recurrent	Capital	Total	Recurrent	Capital	Total	Recurrent	Capital	Total
Education service delivery	Cumulative, 2001-2015	C1	4,423	4,736	732	5,468	4,423	0	4,423	313	732	1,045
		C2	4,423	4,736	732	5,468	4,423	0	4,423	313	732	1,045
		C3	5,373	4,736	732	5,468	4,736	637	5,373	0	95	95
	Annual	C1	295	316	49	365	295	0	295	21	49	70
		C2	295	316	49	365	295	0	295	21	49	70
		C3	358	316	49	365	316	42	358	0	6	6
AIDS-related costs	Annual	C1		0		0	0		0	0		0
		C2		0		0	0		0	0		0
		C3		0		0	0		0	0		0
Both items	Annual	C1		316	49	365	295	0	295	21	49	70
		C2		316	49	365	295	0	295	21	49	70
		C3		316	49	365	316	42	358	0	6	6

Note: "Best practice" policies refer to the combination of scenarios A+B+C. Shaded cells denote no change from values directly above.

Table C.35
....
Angola: MDG-2015 Financing Gap under Alternative Policy Measures

Policy Scenario[a]		A: Quality Measures			B: Efficiency Measures	C: Financing Measures				Annual Financing Gap[e]
		Pupils Per Teacher	Spending on Inputs Other than Teachers[b]	Average Annual Teacher Salary (as multiple of per capita GDP)	Average Repetition Rate	Government Revenues[c]		Primary Education Recurrent Spending[d]	Private Enrollments (as % of total)	
						As % of GDP	% for Education			
Status quo		24	19.0%	1.5	25.0%	55.7%	4.3%	41.6%	6.0%	87
A only		24	33.3%	3.5						354
A + B		40	33.3%	3.5	10.0%					161
"Best practice": A + B +	C1	40	33.3%	3.5	10.0%	18.0%	20.0%	50.0%	10.0%	41
	C2					18.0%	20.0%			41
	C3					55.7%	20.0%			0

Note: Shaded cells denote no change from values directly above.
a. Policy scenarios are: A for quality improvement, B for efficiency improvement, and three alternative resource mobilization scenarios (C1, C2, and C3). The combination of scenarios A+B+C is considered "best practice."
b. As a share of primary education recurrent spending.
c. Current revenues, excluding grants.
d. As a share of total education recurrent spending.
e. In millions of 2000 U.S. dollars. Calculated as the difference between the total cost of service delivery under the specific policy scenario and the total resources for primary education mobilized domestically.

Table C.36
....
Angola: MDG-2015 Cost Estimates and Sources of Financing under "Best Practice" Policies and Alternative Resource Mobilization Scenarios
(millions of 2000 U.S. dollars)

Cost Item	Period	Scenario	Domestic Resources Mobilized	Cost of MDG-2015			Financing Sources					
							Domestic Resources			Gap for External Financing		
				Recurrent	Capital	Total	Recurrent	Capital	Total	Recurrent	Capital	Total
Education service delivery	Cumulative, 2001-2015	C1	3,793	4,337	75	4,412	3,793	0	3,793	544	75	619
		C2	3,793	4,337	75	4,412	3,793	0	3,793	544	75	619
		C3	7,191	4,337	75	4,412	4,337	75	4,412	0	0	0
	Annual	C1	253	289	5	294	253	0	253	36	5	41
		C2	253	289	5	294	253	0	253	36	5	41
		C3	479	289	5	294	289	5	294	0	0	0
AIDS-related costs	Annual	C1		2		2	0		0	2		2
		C2		2		2	0		0	2		2
		C3		2		2	2		2	0		2
Both items	Annual	C1		292	5	296	253	0	253	39	5	44
		C2		292	5	296	253	0	253	39	5	44
		C3		292	5	296	292	5	296	0	0	0

Note: "Best practice" policies refer to the combination of scenarios A+B+C. Shaded cells denote no change from values directly above.

Table C.37

Benin: MDG-2015 Financing Gap under Alternative Policy Measures

Policy Scenario[a]		A: Quality Measures			B: Efficiency Measures	C: Financing Measures				Annual Financing Gap[e]
		Pupils Per Teacher	Spending on Inputs Other than Teachers[b]	Average Annual Teacher Salary (as multiple of per capita GDP)	Average Repetition Rate	Government Revenues[c] As % of GDP	% for Education	Primary Education Recurrent Spending[d]	Private Enrollments (as % of total)	
Status quo		54	26.4%	4.6	25.0%	15.3%	16.5%	62.6%	10.8%	16
A only		40	33.3%	4.6						39
A + B		40	33.3%	3.8	10.0%					21
"Best practice": A + B +	C1	40	33.3%	3.8	10.0%	16.0%	20.0%	50.0%	10.0%	20
	C2					16.0%	20.0%			20
	C3					16.0%	20.0%			20

Note: Shaded cells denote no change from values directly above.

a. Policy scenarios are: A for quality improvement, B for efficiency improvement, and three alternative resource mobilization scenarios (C1, C2, and C3). The combination of scenarios A+B+C is considered "best practice."

b. As a share of primary education recurrent spending.

c. Current revenues, excluding grants.

d. As a share of total education recurrent spending.

e. In millions of 2000 U.S. dollars. Calculated as the difference between the total cost of service delivery under the specific policy scenario and the total resources for primary education mobilized domestically.

Table C.38

Benin: MDG-2015 Cost Estimates and Sources of Financing under "Best Practice" Policies and Alternative Resource Mobilization Scenarios

(millions of 2000 U.S. dollars)

Cost Item	Period	Scenario	Domestic Resources Mobilized	Cost of MDG-2015			Financing Sources					
							Domestic Resources			Gap for External Financing		
				Recurrent	Capital	Total	Recurrent	Capital	Total	Recurrent	Capital	Total
Education service delivery	Cumulative, 2001-2015	C1	778	936	145	1,081	778	0	778	158	145	303
		C2	778	936	145	1,081	778	0	778	158	145	303
		C3	778	936	145	1,081	778	0	778	158	145	303
	Annual	C1	52	62	10	72	52	0	52	11	10	20
		C2	52	62	10	72	52	0	52	11	10	20
		C3	52	62	10	72	52	0	52	11	10	20
AIDS-related costs	Annual	C1		1		1	0		0	1		1
		C2		1		1	0		0	1		1
		C3		1		1	0		0	1		1
Both items	Annual	C1		63	10	73	52	0	52	11	10	21
		C2		63	10	73	52	0	52	11	10	21
		C3		63	10	73	52	0	52	11	10	21

Note: "Best practice" policies refer to the combination of scenarios A+B+C. Shaded cells denote no change from values directly above.

Table C.39

Burkina Faso: MDG-2015 Financing Gap under Alternative Policy Measures

Policy Scenario[a]		A: Quality Measures			B: Efficiency Measures	C: Financing Measures				Annual Financing Gap[e]
		Pupils Per Teacher	Spending on Inputs Other than Teachers[b]	Average Annual Teacher Salary (as multiple of per capita GDP)	Average Repetition Rate	Government Revenues[c] As % of GDP	Government Revenues[c] % for Education	Primary Education Recurrent Spending[d]	Private Enrollments (as % of total)	
Status quo		49	30.7%	8.0	17.7%	14.7%	17.1%	64.0%	10.8%	79
A only		40	33.3%	8.0						106
A + B		40	33.3%	4.2	10.0%					44
"Best practice": A + B +	C1	40	33.3%	4.2	10.0%	14.0%	20.0%	50.0%	10.0%	48
	C2					14.0%	20.0%			48
	C3					14.7%	20.0%			47

Note: Shaded cells denote no change from values directly above.
a. Policy scenarios are: A for quality improvement, B for efficiency improvement, and three alternative resource mobilization scenarios (C1, C2, and C3). The combination of scenarios A+B+C is considered "best practice."
b. As a share of primary education recurrent spending.
c. Current revenues, excluding grants.
d. As a share of total education recurrent spending.
e. In millions of 2000 U.S. dollars. Calculated as the difference between the total cost of service delivery under the specific policy scenario and the total resources for primary education mobilized domestically.

Table C.40

Burkina Faso: MDG-2015 Cost Estimates and Sources of Financing under "Best Practice" Policies and Alternative Resource Mobilization Scenarios

(millions of 2000 U.S. dollars)

Cost Item	Period	Scenario	Domestic Resources Mobilized	Cost of MDG-2015			Financing Sources					
							Domestic Resources			Gap for External Financing		
				Recurrent	Capital	Total	Recurrent	Capital	Total	Recurrent	Capital	Total
Education service delivery	Cumulative, 2001–2015	C1	764	1,138	351	1,489	764	0	764	374	351	725
		C2	764	1,138	351	1,489	764	0	764	374	351	725
		C3	787	1,138	351	1,489	787	0	787	351	351	703
	Annual	C1	51	76	23	99	51	0	51	25	23	48
		C2	51	76	23	99	51	0	51	25	23	48
		C3	52	76	23	99	52	0	52	23	23	47
AIDS-related costs	Annual	C1		11		11	0		0	11		11
		C2		11		11	0		0	11		11
		C3		11		11	0		0	11		11
Both items	Annual	C1		87	23	111	51	0	51	36	23	60
		C2		87	23	111	51	0	51	36	23	60
		C3		87	23	111	52	0	52	35	23	58

Note: "Best practice" policies refer to the combination of scenarios A+B+C. Shaded cells denote no change from values directly above.

Table C.41

Burundi: MDG-2015 Financing Gap under Alternative Policy Measures

Policy Scenario[a]		A: Quality Measures			B: Efficiency Measures	C: Financing Measures				Annual Financing Gap[e]
		Pupils Per Teacher	Spending on Inputs Other than Teachers[b]	Average Annual Teacher Salary (as multiple of per capita GDP)	Average Repetition Rate	Government Revenues[c]		Primary Education Recurrent Spending[d]	Private Enrollments (as % of total)	
						As % of GDP	% for Education			
Status quo		55	22.1%	5.3	27.5%	17.4%	20.4%	35.5%	0.0%	18
A only		40	33.3%	5.3						33
A + B		40	33.3%	3.9	10.0%					17
"Best practice": A + B +	C1	40	33.3%	3.9	10.0%	14.0%	20.4%	50.0%	10.0%	16
	C2					14.0%	20.0%			16
	C3					17.4%	20.0%			15

Note: Shaded cells denote no change from values directly above.
a. Policy scenarios are: A for quality improvement, B for efficiency improvement, and three alternative resource mobilization scenarios (C1, C2, and C3). The combination of scenarios A+B+C is considered "best practice."
b. As a share of primary education recurrent spending.
c. Current revenues, excluding grants.
d. As a share of total education recurrent spending.
e. In millions of 2000 U.S. dollars. Calculated as the difference between the total cost of service delivery under the specific policy scenario and the total resources for primary education mobilized domestically.

Table C.42

Burundi: MDG-2015 Cost Estimates and Sources of Financing under "Best Practice" Policies and Alternative Resource Mobilization Scenarios
(millions of 2000 U.S. dollars)

Cost Item	Period	Scenario	Domestic Resources Mobilized	Cost of MDG-2015			Financing Sources					
							Domestic Resources			Gap for External Financing		
				Recurrent	Capital	Total	Recurrent	Capital	Total	Recurrent	Capital	Total
Education service delivery	Cumulative, 2001-2015	C1	189	270	163	433	189	0	189	81	163	244
		C2	187	270	163	433	187	0	187	84	163	247
		C3	214	270	163	433	214	0	214	56	163	219
	Annual	C1	13	18	11	29	13	0	13	5	11	16
		C2	12	18	11	29	12	0	12	6	11	16
		C3	14	18	11	29	14	0	14	4	11	15
AIDS-related costs	Annual	C1		5		5	0		0	5		5
		C2		5		5	0		0	5		5
		C3		5		5	0		0	5		5
Both items	Annual	C1		23	11	34	13	0	13	10	11	21
		C2		23	11	34	12	0	12	11	11	21
		C3		23	11	34	14	0	14	9	11	20

Note: "Best practice" policies refer to the combination of scenarios A+B+C. Shaded cells denote no change from values directly above.

Table C.43

Cameroon: MDG-2015 Financing Gap under Alternative Policy Measures

Policy Scenario[a]		A: Quality Measures			B: Efficiency Measures	C: Financing Measures				Annual Financing Gap[e]
		Pupils Per Teacher	Spending on Inputs Other than Teachers[b]	Average Annual Teacher Salary (as multiple of per capita GDP)	Average Repetition Rate	Government Revenues[c]		Primary Education Recurrent Spending[d]	Private Enrollments (as % of total)	
						As % of GDP	% for Education			
Status quo		65	32.5%	3.4	25.9%	15.5%	10.8%	66.3%	19.0%	24
A only		40	33.3%	3.5						100
A + B		40	33.3%	3.5	10.0%					89
"Best practice": A + B +	C1	40	33.3%	3.5	10.0%	16.0%	20.0%	50.0%	10.0%	46
	C2					16.0%	20.0%			46
	C3					16.0%	20.0%			46

Note: Shaded cells denote no change from values directly above.
a. Policy scenarios are: A for quality improvement, B for efficiency improvement, and three alternative resource mobilization scenarios (C1, C2, and C3). The combination of scenarios A+B+C is considered "best practice."
b. As a share of primary education recurrent spending.
c. Current revenues, excluding grants.
d. As a share of total education recurrent spending.
e. In millions of 2000 U.S. dollars. Calculated as the difference between the total cost of service delivery under the specific policy scenario and the total resources for primary education mobilized domestically.

Table C.44

Cameroon: MDG-2015 Cost Estimates and Sources of Financing under "Best Practice" Policies and Alternative Resource Mobilization Scenarios

(millions of 2000 U.S. dollars)

Cost Item	Period	Scenario	Domestic Resources Mobilized	Cost of MDG-2015			Financing Sources					
							Domestic Resources			Gap for External Financing		
				Recurrent	Capital	Total	Recurrent	Capital	Total	Recurrent	Capital	Total
Education service delivery	Cumulative, 2001-2015	C1	2,625	2,887	420	3,308	2,625	0	2,625	263	420	683
		C2	2,625	2,887	420	3,308	2,625	0	2,625	263	420	683
		C3	2,625	2,887	420	3,308	2,625	0	2,625	263	420	683
	Annual	C1	175	192	28	221	175	0	175	18	28	46
		C2	175	192	28	221	175	0	175	18	28	46
		C3	175	192	28	221	175	0	175	18	28	46
AIDS-related costs	Annual	C1		11		11	0		0	11		11
		C2		11		11	0		0	11		11
		C3		11		11	0		0	11		11
Both items	Annual	C1		203	28	231	175	0	175	28	28	56
		C2		203	28	231	175	0	175	28	28	56
		C3		203	28	231	175	0	175	28	28	56

Note: "Best practice" policies refer to the combination of scenarios A+B+C. Shaded cells denote no change from values directly above.

Table C.45

Central African Republic: MDG-2015 Financing Gap under Alternative Policy Measures

Policy Scenario[a]		A: Quality Measures			B: Efficiency Measures	C: Financing Measures				Annual Financing Gap[e]
		Pupils Per Teacher	Spending on Inputs Other than Teachers[b]	Average Annual Teacher Salary (as multiple of per capita GDP)	Average Repetition Rate	Government Revenues[c]		Primary Education Recurrent Spending[d]	Private Enrollments (as % of total)	
						As % of GDP	% for Education			
Status quo		79	28.5%	4.9	32.8%	9.6%	12.5%	52.4%	3.3%	14
A only		40	33.3%	4.9						32
A + B		40	33.3%	3.7	10.0%					18
"Best practice": A + B +	C1	40	33.3%	3.7	10.0%	14.0%	20.0%	50.0%	10.0%	12
	C2					14.0%	20.0%			12
	C3					14.0%	20.0%			12

Note: Shaded cells denote no change from values directly above.

a. Policy scenarios are: A for quality improvement, B for efficiency improvement, and three alternative resource mobilization scenarios (C1, C2, and C3). The combination of scenarios A+B+C is considered "best practice."

b. As a share of primary education recurrent spending.

c. Current revenues, excluding grants.

d. As a share of total education recurrent spending.

e. In millions of 2000 U.S. dollars. Calculated as the difference between the total cost of service delivery under the specific policy scenario and the total resources for primary education mobilized domestically.

Table C.46

Central African Republic: MDG-2015 Cost Estimates and Sources of Financing under "Best Practice" Policies and Alternative Resource Mobilization Scenarios

(millions of 2000 U.S. dollars)

Cost Item	Period	Scenario	Domestic Resources Mobilized	Cost of MDG-2015			Financing Sources					
							Domestic Resources			Gap for External Financing		
				Recurrent	Capital	Total	Recurrent	Capital	Total	Recurrent	Capital	Total
Education service delivery	Cumulative, 2001-2015	C1	232	302	103	405	232	0	232	70	103	173
		C2	232	302	103	405	232	0	232	70	103	173
		C3	232	302	103	405	232	0	232	70	103	173
	Annual	C1	15	20	7	27	15	0	15	5	7	12
		C2	15	20	7	27	15	0	15	5	7	12
		C3	15	20	7	27	15	0	15	5	7	12
AIDS-related costs	Annual	C1		2		2	0		0	2		2
		C2		2		2	0		0	2		2
		C3		2		2	0		0	2		2
Both items	Annual	C1		22	7	29	15	0	15	7	7	14
		C2		22	7	29	15	0	15	7	7	14
		C3		22	7	29	15	0	15	7	7	14

Note: "Best practice" policies refer to the combination of scenarios A+B+C. Shaded cells denote no change from values directly above.

Table C.47

Chad: MDG-2015 Financing Gap under Alternative Policy Measures

Policy Scenario[a]		A: Quality Measures			B: Efficiency Measures	C: Financing Measures					
		Pupils Per Teacher	Spending on Inputs Other than Teachers[b]	Average Annual Teacher Salary (as multiple of per capita GDP)	Average Repetition Rate	Government Revenues[c] As % of GDP	% for Education	Primary Education Recurrent Spending[d]	Private Enrollments (as % of total)	Annual Financing Gap[e]
Status quo		72	34.2%	4.8	24.6%	8.0%	20.9%	65.5%	8.8%	21
A only		40	34.2%	4.8						48
A + B		40	33.3%	3.6	10.0%					29
"Best practice": A + B +	C1	40	33.3%	3.6	10.0%	14.0%	20.9%	50.0%	10.0%	24
	C2					14.0%	20.0%			25
	C3					14.0%	20.0%			25

Note: Shaded cells denote no change from values directly above.
a. Policy scenarios are: A for quality improvement, B for efficiency improvement, and three alternative resource mobilization scenarios (C1, C2, and C3). The combination of scenarios A+B+C is considered "best practice."
b. As a share of primary education recurrent spending.
c. Current revenues, excluding grants.
d. As a share of total education recurrent spending.
e. In millions of 2000 U.S. dollars. Calculated as the difference between the total cost of service delivery under the specific policy scenario and the total resources for primary education mobilized domestically.

Table C.48

Chad: MDG-2015 Cost Estimates and Sources of Financing under "Best Practice" Policies and Alternative Resource Mobilization Scenarios
(millions of 2000 U.S. dollars)

Cost Item	Period	Scenario	Domestic Resources Mobilized	Cost of MDG-2015			Financing Sources					
							Domestic Resources			Gap for External Financing		
				Recurrent	Capital	Total	Recurrent	Capital	Total	Recurrent	Capital	Total
Education service delivery	Cumulative, 2001–2015	C1	430	498	290	788	430	0	430	69	290	358
		C2	418	498	290	788	418	0	418	80	290	370
		C3	418	498	290	788	418	0	418	80	290	370
	Annual	C1	29	33	19	53	29	0	29	5	19	24
		C2	28	33	19	53	28	0	28	5	19	25
		C3	28	33	19	53	28	0	28	5	19	25
AIDS-related costs	Annual	C1		2		2	0		0	2		2
		C2		2		2	0		0	2		2
		C3		2		2	0		0	2		2
Both items	Annual	C1		36	19	55	29	0	29	7	19	26
		C2		36	19	55	28	0	28	8	19	27
		C3		36	19	55	28	0	28	8	19	27

Note: "Best practice" policies refer to the combination of scenarios A+B+C. Shaded cells denote no change from values directly above.

Table C.49
....
Congo, Democratic Republic: MDG-2015 Financing Gap under Alternative Policy Measures

| | | A: QUALITY MEASURES | | | B: EFFICIENCY MEASURES | C: FINANCING MEASURES | | | | |
| | | | | | | Government Revenues[c] | | Primary Education | Private Enrollments | Annual |
Policy Scenario[a]		Pupils Per Teacher	Spending on Inputs Other than Teachers[b]	Average Annual Teacher Salary (as multiple of per capita GDP)	Average Repetition Rate	As % of GDP	% for Education	Recurrent Spending[d]	(as % of total)	Financing Gap[e]
Status quo		42	10.3%	0.9	15.0%	10.6%	3.2%	65.1%	10.0%	109
A only		40	33.3%	3.5						198
A + B		40	33.3%	3.5	10.0%					187
"Best	C1	40	33.3%	3.5	10.0%	14.0%	20.0%	50.0%	10.0%	146
practice":	C2					14.0%	20.0%			146
A + B +	C3					14.0%	20.0%			146

Note: Shaded cells denote no change from values directly above.
a. Policy scenarios are: A for quality improvement, B for efficiency improvement, and three alternative resource mobilization scenarios (C1, C2, and C3). The combination of scenarios A+B+C is considered "best practice."
b. As a share of primary education recurrent spending.
c. Current revenues, excluding grants.
d. As a share of total education recurrent spending.
e. In millions of 2000 U.S. dollars. Calculated as the difference between the total cost of service delivery under the specific policy scenario and the total resources for primary education mobilized domestically.

Table C.50
....
Congo, Democratic Republic: MDG-2015 Cost Estimates and Sources of Financing under "Best Practice" Policies and Alternative Resource Mobilization Scenarios
(millions of 2000 U.S. dollars)

| | | | | | | | FINANCING SOURCES | | | | | |
| Cost Item | Period | Scenario | Domestic Resources Mobilized | COST OF MDG-2015 | | | DOMESTIC RESOURCES | | | GAP FOR EXTERNAL FINANCING | | |
				Recurrent	Capital	Total	Recurrent	Capital	Total	Recurrent	Capital	Total
Education service delivery	Cumulative, 2001-2015	C1	814	1,456	1,542	2,998	814	0	814	642	1,542	2,185
		C2	814	1,456	1,542	2,998	814	0	814	642	1,542	2,185
		C3	814	1,456	1,542	2,998	814	0	814	642	1,542	2,185
	Annual	C1	54	97	103	200	54	0	54	43	103	146
		C2	54	97	103	200	54	0	54	43	103	146
		C3	54	97	103	200	54	0	54	43	103	146
AIDS-related costs	Annual	C1		17		17	0		0	17		17
		C2		17		17	0		0	17		17
		C3		17		17	0		0	17		17
Both items	Annual	C1		114	103	217	54	0	54	60	103	163
		C2		114	103	217	54	0	54	60	103	163
		C3		114	103	217	54	0	54	60	103	163

Note: "Best practice" policies refer to the combination of scenarios A+B+C. Shaded cells denote no change from values directly above.

Table C.51
....

Congo, Republic: MDG-2015 Financing Gap under Alternative Policy Measures

Policy Scenario[a]		A: Quality Measures		B: Efficiency Measures		C: Financing Measures					
		Pupils Per Teacher	Spending on Inputs Other than Teachers[b]	Average Annual Teacher Salary (as multiple of per capita GDP)	Average Repetition Rate	Government Revenues[c]		Primary Education Recurrent Spending[d]	Private Enrollments (as % of total)	Annual Financing Gap[e]
						As % of GDP	% for Education			
Status quo		61	20.3%	3.4	31.1%	26.7%	8.6%	36.6%	15.2%	17
A only		40	33.3%	3.5						47
A + B		40	33.3%	3.5	10.0%					38
"Best practice": A + B +	C1	40	33.3%	3.5	10.0%	18.0%	20.0%	50.0%	10.0%	9
	C2					18.0%	20.0%			9
	C3					26.7%	20.0%			0

Note: Shaded cells denote no change from values directly above.

a. Policy scenarios are: A for quality improvement, B for efficiency improvement, and three alternative resource mobilization scenarios (C1, C2, and C3). The combination of scenarios A+B+C is considered "best practice."

b. As a share of primary education recurrent spending.

c. Current revenues, excluding grants.

d. As a share of total education recurrent spending.

e. In millions of 2000 U.S. dollars. Calculated as the difference between the total cost of service delivery under the specific policy scenario and the total resources for primary education mobilized domestically.

Table C.52
....

Congo, Republic: MDG-2015 Cost Estimates and Sources of Financing under "Best Practice" Policies and Alternative Resource Mobilization Scenarios

(millions of 2000 U.S. dollars)

Cost Item	Period	Scenario	Domestic Resources Mobilized	Cost of MDG-2015			Financing Sources					
							Domestic Resources			Gap for External Financing		
				Recurrent	Capital	Total	Recurrent	Capital	Total	Recurrent	Capital	Total
Education service delivery	Cumulative, 2001-2015	C1	1,046	1,086	89	1,175	1,046	0	1,046	40	89	129
		C2	1,046	1,086	89	1,175	1,046	0	1,046	40	89	129
		C3	1,342	1,086	89	1,175	1,086	89	1,175	0	0	0
	Annual	C1	70	72	6	78	70	0	70	3	6	9
		C2	70	72	6	78	70	0	70	3	6	9
		C3	89	72	6	78	72	6	78	0	0	0
AIDS-related costs	Annual	C1		1		1	0		0	1		1
		C2		1		1	0		0	1		1
		C3		1		1	1		1	0		1
Both items	Annual	C1		74	6	80	70	0	70	4	6	10
		C2		74	6	80	70	0	70	4	6	10
		C3		74	6	80	74	6	80	0	0	0

Note: "Best practice" policies refer to the combination of scenarios A+B+C. Shaded cells denote no change from values directly above.

Table C.53

Côte d'Ivoire: MDG-2015 Financing Gap under Alternative Policy Measures

Policy Scenario[a]		A: Quality Measures			B: Efficiency Measures	C: Financing Measures				Annual Financing Gap[e]
						Government Revenues[c]		Primary Education Recurrent Spending[d]	Private Enrollments (as % of total)	
		Pupils Per Teacher	Spending on Inputs Other than Teachers[b]	Average Annual Teacher Salary (as multiple of per capita GDP)	Average Repetition Rate	As % of GDP	% for Education			
Status quo		46	22.5%	5.7	24.7%	16.5%	21.5%	49.0%	11.6%	102
A only		40	33.3%	5.7						187
A + B		40	33.3%	4.3	10.0%					63
"Best practice": A + B +	C1	40	33.3%	4.3	10.0%	18.0%	21.5%	50.0%	10.0%	42
	C2					18.0%	20.0%			56
	C3					18.0%	20.0%			56

Note: Shaded cells denote no change from values directly above.

a. Policy scenarios are: A for quality improvement, B for efficiency improvement, and three alternative resource mobilization scenarios (C1, C2, and C3). The combination of scenarios A+B+C is considered "best practice."

b. As a share of primary education recurrent spending.

c. Current revenues, excluding grants.

d. As a share of total education recurrent spending.

e. In millions of 2000 U.S. dollars. Calculated as the difference between the total cost of service delivery under the specific policy scenario and the total resources for primary education mobilized domestically.

Table C.54

Côte d'Ivoire: MDG-2015 Cost Estimates and Sources of Financing under "Best Practice" Policies and Alternative Resource Mobilization Scenarios

(millions of 2000 U.S. dollars)

Cost Item	Period	Scenario	Domestic Resources Mobilized	Cost of MDG-2015			Financing Sources					
							Domestic Resources			Gap for External Financing		
				Recurrent	Capital	Total	Recurrent	Capital	Total	Recurrent	Capital	Total
Education service delivery	Cumulative, 2001-2015	C1	4,815	5,205	237	5,442	4,815	0	4,815	391	237	628
		C2	4,603	5,205	237	5,442	4,603	0	4,603	603	237	840
		C3	4,603	5,205	237	5,442	4,603	0	4,603	603	237	840
	Annual	C1	321	347	16	363	321	0	321	26	16	42
		C2	307	347	16	363	307	0	307	40	16	56
		C3	307	347	16	363	307	0	307	40	16	56
AIDS-related costs	Annual	C1	16		16	16	0		0	16		16
		C2	16		16	16	0		0	16		16
		C3	16		16	16	0		0	16		16
Both items	Annual	C1		363	16	379	321	0	321	42	16	58
		C2		363	16	379	307	0	307	56	16	72
		C3		363	16	379	307	0	307	56	16	72

Note: "Best practice" policies refer to the combination of scenarios A+B+C. Shaded cells denote no change from values directly above.

Table C.55

Eritrea: MDG-2015 Financing Gap under Alternative Policy Measures

Policy Scenario[a]		A: Quality Measures			B: Efficiency Measures	C: Financing Measures				Annual Financing Gap[e]
						Government Revenues[c]		Primary Education Recurrent Spending[d]	Private Enrollments (as % of total)	
		Pupils Per Teacher	Spending on Inputs Other than Teachers[b]	Average Annual Teacher Salary (as multiple of per capita GDP)	Average Repetition Rate	As % of GDP	% for Education			
Status quo		49	29.6%	7.7	19.4%	34.6%	8.0%	53.6%	10.1%	16
A only		40	33.3%	7.7						22
A + B		40	33.3%	4.3	10.0%					10
"Best practice": A + B +	C1	40	33.3%	4.3	10.0%	14.0%	20.0%	42.0%	10.0%	10
	C2					14.0%	20.0%			10
	C3					34.6%	20.0%			1

Note: Shaded cells denote no change from values directly above.
a. Policy scenarios are: A for quality improvement, B for efficiency improvement, and three alternative resource mobilization scenarios (C1, C2, and C3). The combination of scenarios A+B+C is considered "best practice."
b. As a share of primary education recurrent spending.
c. Current revenues, excluding grants.
d. As a share of total education recurrent spending.
e. In millions of 2000 U.S. dollars. Calculated as the difference between the total cost of service delivery under the specific policy scenario and the total resources for primary education mobilized domestically.

Table C.56

Eritrea: MDG-2015 Cost Estimates and Sources of Financing under "Best Practice" Policies and Alternative Resource Mobilization Scenarios

(millions of 2000 U.S. dollars)

Cost Item	Period	Scenario	Domestic Resources Mobilized	Cost of MDG-2015			Financing Sources					
							Domestic Resources			Gap for External Financing		
				Recurrent	Capital	Total	Recurrent	Capital	Total	Recurrent	Capital	Total
Education service delivery	Cumulative, 2001-2015	C1	198	250	94	344	198	0	198	52	94	146
		C2	198	250	94	344	198	0	198	52	94	146
		C3	325	250	94	344	250	75	325	0	19	19
	Annual	C1	13	17	6	23	13	0	13	3	6	10
		C2	13	17	6	23	13	0	13	3	6	10
		C3	22	17	6	23	17	5	22	0	1	1
AIDS-related costs	Annual	C1		0		0	0		0	0		0
		C2		0		0	0		0	0		0
		C3		0		0	0		0	0		0
Both items	Annual	C1		17	6	23	13	0	13	4	6	10
		C2		17	6	23	13	0	13	4	6	10
		C3		17	6	23	17	5	22	0	1	2

Note: "Best practice" policies refer to the combination of scenarios A+B+C. Shaded cells denote no change from values directly above.

Table C.57

Ethiopia: MDG-2015 Financing Gap under Alternative Policy Measures

Policy Scenario[a]		A: Quality Measures			B: Efficiency Measures	C: Financing Measures				Annual Financing Gap[e]
		Pupils Per Teacher	Spending on Inputs Other than Teachers[b]	Average Annual Teacher Salary (as multiple of per capita GDP)	Average Repetition Rate	Government Revenues[c] As % of GDP	% for Education	Primary Education Recurrent Spending[d]	Private Enrollments (as % of total)	
Status quo		61	20.5%	6.8	8.0%	17.8%	15.0%	46.2%	5.0%	146
A only		40	33.3%	6.8						312
A + B		40	33.3%	4.1	8.0%					192
"Best practice": A + B +	C1	40	33.3%	4.1	8.0%	14.0%	20.0%	50.0%	10.0%	180
	C2					14.0%	20.0%			180
	C3					17.8%	20.0%			157

Note: Shaded cells denote no change from values directly above.
a. Policy scenarios are: A for quality improvement, B for efficiency improvement, and three alternative resource mobilization scenarios (C1, C2, and C3). The combination of scenarios A+B+C is considered "best practice."
b. As a share of primary education recurrent spending.
c. Current revenues, excluding grants.
d. As a share of total education recurrent spending.
e. In millions of 2000 U.S. dollars. Calculated as the difference between the total cost of service delivery under the specific policy scenario and the total resources for primary education mobilized domestically.

Table C.58

Ethiopia: MDG-2015 Cost Estimates and Sources of Financing under "Best Practice" Policies and Alternative Resource Mobilization Scenarios

(millions of 2000 U.S. dollars)

Cost Item	Period	Scenario	Domestic Resources Mobilized	Cost of MDG-2015			Financing Sources					
							Domestic Resources			Gap for External Financing		
				Recurrent	Capital	Total	Recurrent	Capital	Total	Recurrent	Capital	Total
Education service delivery	Cumulative, 2001–2015	C1	2,113	2,940	1,872	4,811	2,113	0	2,113	827	1,872	2,699
		C2	2,113	2,940	1,872	4,811	2,113	0	2,113	827	1,872	2,699
		C3	2,454	2,940	1,872	4,811	2,454	0	2,454	486	1,872	2,358
	Annual	C1	141	196	125	321	141	0	141	55	125	180
		C2	141	196	125	321	141	0	141	55	125	180
		C3	164	196	125	321	164	0	164	32	125	157
AIDS-related costs	Annual	C1	30		30	0		0	30		30
		C2	30		30	0		0	30		30
		C3	30		30	0		0	30		30
Both items	Annual	C1	226	125	351	141	0	141	85	125	210
		C2	226	125	351	141	0	141	85	125	210
		C3	226	125	351	164	0	164	62	125	187

Note: "Best practice" policies refer to the combination of scenarios A+B+C. Shaded cells denote no change from values directly above.

Table C.59

The Gambia: MDG-2015 Financing Gap under Alternative Policy Measures

Policy Scenario[a]		A: Quality Measures		Average Annual Teacher Salary (as multiple of per capita GDP)	B: Efficiency Measures	C: Financing Measures				Annual Financing Gap[e]
						Government Revenues[c]		Primary Education Recurrent Spending[d]	Private Enrollments (as % of total)	
		Pupils Per Teacher	Spending on Inputs Other than Teachers[b]		Average Repetition Rate	As % of GDP	% for Education			
Status quo		37	24.9%	3.7	10.6%	18.5%	16.6%	51.7%	8.5%	3
A only		37	33.3%	3.7						4
A + B		40	33.3%	3.6	10.0%					3
"Best practice": A + B +	C1	40	33.3%	3.6	10.0%	14.0%	20.0%	50.0%	10.0%	3
	C2					14.0%	20.0%			3
	C3					18.5%	20.0%			2

Note: Shaded cells denote no change from values directly above.
a. Policy scenarios are: A for quality improvement, B for efficiency improvement, and three alternative resource mobilization scenarios (C1, C2, and C3). The combination of scenarios A+B+C is considered "best practice."
b. As a share of primary education recurrent spending.
c. Current revenues, excluding grants.
d. As a share of total education recurrent spending.
e. In millions of 2000 U.S. dollars. Calculated as the difference between the total cost of service delivery under the specific policy scenario and the total resources for primary education mobilized domestically.

Table C.60

The Gambia: MDG-2015 Cost Estimates and Sources of Financing under "Best Practice" Policies and Alternative Resource Mobilization Scenarios

(millions of 2000 U.S. dollars)

Cost Item	Period	Scenario	Domestic Resources Mobilized	Cost of MDG-2015			Financing Sources					
							Domestic Resources			Gap for External Financing		
				Recurrent	Capital	Total	Recurrent	Capital	Total	Recurrent	Capital	Total
Education service delivery	Cumulative, 2001-2015	C1	140	170	17	187	140	0	140	31	17	47
		C2	140	170	17	187	140	0	140	31	17	47
		C3	164	170	17	187	164	0	164	7	17	23
	Annual	C1	9	11	1	12	9	0	9	2	1	3
		C2	9	11	1	12	9	0	9	2	1	3
		C3	11	11	1	12	11	0	11	0	1	2
AIDS-related costs	Annual	C1		0		0	0		0	0		0
		C2		0		0	0		0	0		0
		C3		0		0	0		0	0		0
Both items	Annual	C1		12	1	13	9	0	9	2	1	4
		C2		12	1	13	9	0	9	2	1	4
		C3		12	1	13	11	0	11	1	1	2

Note: "Best practice" policies refer to the combination of scenarios A+B+C. Shaded cells denote no change from values directly above.

Table C.61
Ghana: MDG-2015 Financing Gap under Alternative Policy Measures

Policy Scenario[a]		Pupils Per Teacher	Spending on Inputs Other than Teachers[b]	Average Annual Teacher Salary (as multiple of per capita GDP)	Average Repetition Rate	As % of GDP	% for Education	Primary Education Recurrent Spending[d]	Private Enrollments (as % of total)	Annual Financing Gap[e]
		A: Quality Measures			**B: Efficiency Measures**	**C: Financing Measures**				
						Government Revenues[c]		Primary Education	Private Enrollments	Annual
Status quo		34	17.7%	3.6	5.0%	21.8%	17.6%	37.2%	18.0%	29
A only		34	33.3%	3.6						44
A + B		40	33.3%	3.5	5.0%					35
"Best practice": A + B +	C1	40	33.3%	3.5	5.0%	18.0%	20.0%	50.0%	10.0%	21
	C2					18.0%	20.0%			21
	C3					21.8%	20.0%			8

Note: Shaded cells denote no change from values directly above.

a. Policy scenarios are: A for quality improvement, B for efficiency improvement, and three alternative resource mobilization scenarios (C1, C2, and C3). The combination of scenarios A+B+C is considered "best practice."

b. As a share of primary education recurrent spending.

c. Current revenues, excluding grants.

d. As a share of total education recurrent spending.

e. In millions of 2000 U.S. dollars. Calculated as the difference between the total cost of service delivery under the specific policy scenario and the total resources for primary education mobilized domestically.

Table C.62
Ghana: MDG-2015 Cost Estimates and Sources of Financing under "Best Practice" Policies and Alternative Resource Mobilization Scenarios
(millions of 2000 U.S. dollars)

Cost Item	Period	Scenario	Domestic Resources Mobilized	Recurrent	Capital	Total	Recurrent	Capital	Total	Recurrent	Capital	Total
				Cost of MDG-2015			**Financing Sources**					
							Domestic Resources			**Gap for External Financing**		
Education service delivery	Cumulative, 2001-2015	C1	1,499	1,604	207	1,812	1,499	0	1,499	105	207	312
		C2	1,499	1,604	207	1,812	1,499	0	1,499	105	207	312
		C3	1,692	1,604	207	1,812	1,604	88	1,692	0	120	120
	Annual	C1	100	107	14	121	100	0	100	7	14	21
		C2	100	107	14	121	100	0	100	7	14	21
		C3	113	107	14	121	107	6	113	0	8	8
AIDS-related costs	Annual	C1		6		6	0		0	6		6
		C2		6		6	0		0	6		6
		C3		6		6	0		0	6		6
Both items	Annual	C1		113	14	127	100	0	100	13	14	27
		C2		113	14	127	100	0	100	13	14	27
		C3		113	14	127	107	6	113	6	8	14

Note: "Best practice" policies refer to the combination of scenarios A+B+C. Shaded cells denote no change from values directly above.

Table C.63

Guinea: MDG-2015 Financing Gap under Alternative Policy Measures

Policy Scenario[a]		Pupils Per Teacher	Spending on Inputs Other than Teachers[b]	Average Annual Teacher Salary (as multiple of per capita GDP)	Average Repetition Rate	As % of GDP	% for Education	Primary Education Recurrent Spending[d]	Private Enrollments (as % of total)	Annual Financing Gap[e]
		A: Quality Measures			**B: Efficiency Measures**	**C: Financing Measures**				
						Government Revenues[c]				
Status quo		49	34.7%	2.7	23.3%	11.1%	18.1%	37.2%	16.1%	28
A only		40	34.7%	3.5						58
A + B		40	33.3%	3.5	10.0%					53
"Best practice": A + B +	C1	40	33.3%	3.5	10.0%	14.0%	20.0%	50.0%	10.0%	35
	C2					14.0%	20.0%			35
	C3					14.0%	20.0%			35

Note: Shaded cells denote no change from values directly above.

a. Policy scenarios are: A for quality improvement, B for efficiency improvement, and three alternative resource mobilization scenarios (C1, C2, and C3). The combination of scenarios A+B+C is considered "best practice."

b. As a share of primary education recurrent spending.

c. Current revenues, excluding grants.

d. As a share of total education recurrent spending.

e. In millions of 2000 U.S. dollars. Calculated as the difference between the total cost of service delivery under the specific policy scenario and the total resources for primary education mobilized domestically.

Table C.64

Guinea: MDG-2015 Cost Estimates and Sources of Financing under "Best Practice" Policies and Alternative Resource Mobilization Scenarios

(millions of 2000 U.S. dollars)

Cost Item	Period	Scenario	Domestic Resources Mobilized	Recurrent	Capital	Total	Recurrent	Capital	Total	Recurrent	Capital	Total
				Cost of MDG-2015			**Financing Sources**					
							Domestic Resources			**Gap for External Financing**		
Education service delivery	Cumulative, 2001-2015	C1	790	1,141	181	1,322	790	0	790	351	181	532
		C2	790	1,141	181	1,322	790	0	790	351	181	532
		C3	790	1,141	181	1,322	790	0	790	351	181	532
	Annual	C1	53	76	12	88	53	0	53	23	12	35
		C2	53	76	12	88	53	0	53	23	12	35
		C3	53	76	12	88	53	0	53	23	12	35
AIDS-related costs	Annual	C1		1		1	0		0	1		1
		C2		1		1	0		0	1		1
		C3	1	1		1	0		0	1		1
Both items	Annual	C1		77	12	89	53	0	53	24	12	37
		C2		77	12	89	53	0	53	24	12	37
		C3		77	12	89	53	0	53	24	12	37

Note: "Best practice" policies refer to the combination of scenarios A+B+C. Shaded cells denote no change from values directly above.

Table C.65

Guinea-Bissau: MDG-2015 Financing Gap under Alternative Policy Measures

Policy Scenario[a]		A: Quality Measures			B: Efficiency Measures	C: Financing Measures					
		Pupils Per Teacher	Spending on Inputs Other than Teachers[b]	Average Annual Teacher Salary (as multiple of per capita GDP)	Average Repetition Rate	Government Revenues[c]		Primary Education Recurrent Spending[d]	Private Enrollments (as % of total)	Annual Financing Gap[e]
						As % of GDP	% for Education			
Status quo		37	34.3%	1.6	27.1%	19.6%	9.8%	35.0%	8.5%	3
A only		37	34.3%	3.5						7
A + B		40	33.3%	3.5	10.0%					5
"Best practice": A + B +	C1	40	33.3%	3.5	10.0%	14.0%	20.0%	50.0%	10.0%	3
	C2					14.0%	20.0%			3
	C3					19.6%	20.0%			2

Note: Shaded cells denote no change from values directly above.

a. Policy scenarios are: A for quality improvement, B for efficiency improvement, and three alternative resource mobilization scenarios (C1, C2, and C3). The combination of scenarios A+B+C is considered "best practice."

b. As a share of primary education recurrent spending.

c. Current revenues, excluding grants.

d. As a share of total education recurrent spending.

e. In millions of 2000 U.S. dollars. Calculated as the difference between the total cost of service delivery under the specific policy scenario and the total resources for primary education mobilized domestically.

Table C.66

Guinea-Bissau: MDG-2015 Cost Estimates and Sources of Financing under "Best Practice" Policies and Alternative Resource Mobilization Scenarios

(millions of 2000 U.S. dollars)

Cost Item	Period	Scenario	Domestic Resources Mobilized	Cost of MDG-2015			Financing Sources					
							Domestic Resources			Gap for External Financing		
				Recurrent	Capital	Total	Recurrent	Capital	Total	Recurrent	Capital	Total
Education service delivery	Cumulative, 2001-2015	C1	55	87	18	105	55	0	55	32	18	50
		C2	55	87	18	105	55	0	55	32	18	50
		C3	68	87	18	105	68	0	68	19	18	37
	Annual	C1	4	6	1	7	4	0	4	2	1	3
		C2	4	6	1	7	4	0	4	2	1	3
		C3	5	6	1	7	5	0	5	1	1	2
AIDS-related costs	Annual	C1		0		0	0		0	0		0
		C2		0		0	0		0	0		0
		C3		0		0	0		0	0		0
Both items	Annual	C1		6	1	7	4	0	4	2	1	4
		C2		6	1	7	4	0	4	2	1	4
		C3		6	1	7	5	0	5	1	1	3

Note: "Best practice" policies refer to the combination of scenarios A+B+C. Shaded cells denote no change from values directly above.

Table C.67

Kenya: MDG-2015 Financing Gap under Alternative Policy Measures

Policy Scenario[a]		A: Quality Measures — Pupils Per Teacher	Spending on Inputs Other than Teachers[b]	Average Annual Teacher Salary (as multiple of per capita GDP)	B: Efficiency Measures — Average Repetition Rate	C: Financing Measures — Government Revenues[c] As % of GDP	% for Education	Primary Education Recurrent Spending[d]	Private Enrollments (as % of total)	Annual Financing Gap[e]
Status quo		31	4.2%	5.3	14.2%	24.2%	26.2%	44.2%	2.2%	53
A only		31	33.3%	5.3						178
A + B		40	33.3%	4.8	10.0%					−3
"Best practice":	C1	40	33.3%	4.8	10.0%	16.0%	26.2%	50.0%	10.0%	61
A + B +	C2					16.0%	20.0%			113
	C3					24.2%	20.0%			32

Note: Shaded cells denote no change from values directly above.
a. Policy scenarios are: A for quality improvement, B for efficiency improvement, and three alternative resource mobilization scenarios (C1, C2, and C3). The combination of scenarios A+B+C is considered "best practice."
b. As a share of primary education recurrent spending.
c. Current revenues, excluding grants.
d. As a share of total education recurrent spending.
e. In millions of 2000 U.S. dollars. Calculated as the difference between the total cost of service delivery under the specific policy scenario and the total resources for primary education mobilized domestically.

Table C.68

Kenya: MDG-2015 Cost Estimates and Sources of Financing under "Best Practice" Policies and Alternative Resource Mobilization Scenarios

(millions of 2000 U.S. dollars)

Cost Item	Period	Scenario	Domestic Resources Mobilized	Cost of MDG-2015 — Recurrent	Capital	Total	Financing Sources — Domestic Resources — Recurrent	Capital	Total	Gap for External Financing — Recurrent	Capital	Total
Education service delivery	Cumulative, 2001-2015	C1	5,517	6,436	0	6,436	5,517	0	5,517	919	0	919
		C2	4,734	6,436	0	6,436	4,734	0	4,734	1,702	0	1,702
		C3	5,959	6,436	0	6,436	5,959	0	5,959	477	0	477
	Annual	C1	368	429	0	429	368	0	368	61	0	61
		C2	316	429	0	429	316	0	316	113	0	113
		C3	397	429	0	429	397	0	397	32	0	32
AIDS-related costs	Annual	C1		21		21	0		0	21		21
		C2		21		21	0		0	21		21
		C3		21		21	0		0	21		21
Both items	Annual	C1		450	0	450	368	0	368	82	0	82
		C2		450	0	450	316	0	316	134	0	134
		C3		450	0	450	397	0	397	53	0	53

Note: "Best practice" policies refer to the combination of scenarios A+B+C. Shaded cells denote no change from values directly above.

Table C.69

Lesotho: MDG-2015 Financing Gap under Alternative Policy Measures

Policy Scenario[a]		A: Quality Measures			B: Efficiency Measures	C: Financing Measures				Annual Financing Gap[e]
		Pupils Per Teacher	Spending on Inputs Other than Teachers[b]	Average Annual Teacher Salary (as multiple of per capita GDP)	Average Repetition Rate	Government Revenues[c] As % of GDP	% for Education	Primary Education Recurrent Spending[d]	Private Enrollments (as % of total)	
Status quo		45	29.9%	6.6	18.3%	35.9%	22.2%	40.2%	0.0%	5
A only		40	33.3%	6.6						12
A + B		40	33.3%	5.2	10.0%					−2
"Best practice": A + B +	C1	40	33.3%	5.2	10.0%	18.0%	22.2%	50.0%	10.0%	7
	C2					18.0%	20.0%			9
	C3					35.9%	20.0%			0

Note: Shaded cells denote no change from values directly above.
a. Policy scenarios are: A for quality improvement, B for efficiency improvement, and three alternative resource mobilization scenarios (C1, C2, and C3). The combination of scenarios A+B+C is considered "best practice."
b. As a share of primary education recurrent spending.
c. Current revenues, excluding grants.
d. As a share of total education recurrent spending.
e. In millions of 2000 U.S. dollars. Calculated as the difference between the total cost of service delivery under the specific policy scenario and the total resources for primary education mobilized domestically.

Table C.70

Lesotho: MDG-2015 Cost Estimates and Sources of Financing under "Best Practice" Policies and Alternative Resource Mobilization Scenarios

(millions of 2000 U.S. dollars)

Cost Item	Period	Scenario	Domestic Resources Mobilized	Cost of MDG-2015			Financing Sources					
							Domestic Resources			Gap for External Financing		
				Recurrent	Capital	Total	Recurrent	Capital	Total	Recurrent	Capital	Total
Education service delivery	Cumulative, 2001-2015	C1	565	659	15	674	565	0	565	94	15	108
		C2	534	659	15	674	534	0	534	125	15	140
		C3	763	659	15	674	659	15	674	0	0	0
	Annual	C1	38	44	1	45	38	0	38	6	1	7
		C2	36	44	1	45	36	0	36	8	1	9
		C3	51	44	1	45	44	1	45	0	0	0
AIDS-related costs	Annual	C1		2		2	0		0	2		2
		C2		2		2	0		0	2		2
		C3		2		2	2		2	0		2
Both items	Annual	C1		45	1	46	38	0	38	8	1	9
		C2		45	1	46	36	0	36	10	1	11
		C3		45	1	46	45	1	46	0	0	0

Note: "Best practice" policies refer to the combination of scenarios A+B+C. Shaded cells denote no change from values directly above.

Table C.71

Madagascar: MDG-2015 Financing Gap under Alternative Policy Measures

Policy Scenario[a]		A: Quality Measures		B: Efficiency Measures		C: Financing Measures				Annual Financing Gap[e]
		Pupils Per Teacher	Spending on Inputs Other than Teachers[b]	Average Annual Teacher Salary (as multiple of per capita GDP)	Average Repetition Rate	Government Revenues[c]		Primary Education Recurrent Spending[d]	Private Enrollments (as % of total)	
						As % of GDP	% for Education			
Status quo		54	42.4%	3.3	33.0%	10.6%	18.8%	54.7%	22.0%	23
A only		40	42.4%	3.5						50
A + B		40	33.3%	3.5	10.0%					36
"Best practice": A + B +	C1	40	33.3%	3.5	10.0%	14.0%	20.0%	42.0%	10.0%	33
	C2					14.0%	20.0%			33
	C3					14.0%	20.0%			33

Note: Shaded cells denote no change from values directly above.
a. Policy scenarios are: A for quality improvement, B for efficiency improvement, and three alternative resource mobilization scenarios (C1, C2, and C3). The combination of scenarios A+B+C is considered "best practice."
b. As a share of primary education recurrent spending.
c. Current revenues, excluding grants.
d. As a share of total education recurrent spending.
e. In millions of 2000 U.S. dollars. Calculated as the difference between the total cost of service delivery under the specific policy scenario and the total resources for primary education mobilized domestically.

Table C.72

Madagascar: MDG-2015 Cost Estimates and Sources of Financing under "Best Practice" Policies and Alternative Resource Mobilization Scenarios

(millions of 2000 U.S. dollars)

Cost Item	Period	Scenario	Domestic Resources Mobilized	Cost of MDG-2015			Financing Sources					
							Domestic Resources			Gap for External Financing		
				Recurrent	Capital	Total	Recurrent	Capital	Total	Recurrent	Capital	Total
Education service delivery	Cumulative, 2001-2015	C1	874	1,053	314	1,367	874	0	874	180	314	494
		C2	874	1,053	314	1,367	874	0	874	180	314	494
		C3	874	1,053	314	1,367	874	0	874	180	314	494
	Annual	C1	58	70	21	91	58	0	58	12	21	33
		C2	58	70	21	91	58	0	58	12	21	33
		C3	58	70	21	91	58	0	58	12	21	33
AIDS-related costs	Annual	C1		0		0	0		0	0		0
		C2		0		0	0		0	0		0
		C3		0		0	0		0	0		0
Both items	Annual	C1		70	21	91	58	0	58	12	21	33
		C2		70	21	91	58	0	58	12	21	33
		C3		70	21	91	58	0	58	12	21	33

Note: "Best practice" policies refer to the combination of scenarios A+B+C. Shaded cells denote no change from values directly above.

Table C.73

Malawi: MDG-2015 Financing Gap under Alternative Policy Measures

Policy Scenario[a]		A: Quality Measures			B: Efficiency Measures	C: Financing Measures				Annual Financing Gap[e]
		Pupils Per Teacher	Spending on Inputs Other than Teachers[b]	Average Annual Teacher Salary (as multiple of per capita GDP)	Average Repetition Rate	Government Revenues[c]		Primary Education Recurrent Spending[d]	Private Enrollments (as % of total)	
						As % of GDP	% for Education			
Status quo		53	14.0%	4.0	14.7%	18.1%	19.8%	49.2%	2.0%	2
A only		40	33.3%	4.0						24
A + B		40	33.3%	3.7	10.0%					14
"Best practice": A + B +	C1	40	33.3%	3.7	10.0%	14.0%	20.0%	50.0%	10.0%	19
	C2					14.0%	20.0%			19
	C3					18.1%	20.0%			13

Note: Shaded cells denote no change from values directly above.
a. Policy scenarios are: A for quality improvement, B for efficiency improvement, and three alternative resource mobilization scenarios (C1, C2, and C3). The combination of scenarios A+B+C is considered "best practice."
b. As a share of primary education recurrent spending.
c. Current revenues, excluding grants.
d. As a share of total education recurrent spending.
e. In millions of 2000 U.S. dollars. Calculated as the difference between the total cost of service delivery under the specific policy scenario and the total resources for primary education mobilized domestically.

Table C.74

Malawi: MDG-2015 Cost Estimates and Sources of Financing under "Best Practice" Policies and Alternative Resource Mobilization Scenarios

(millions of 2000 U.S. dollars)

Cost Item	Period	Scenario	Domestic Resources Mobilized	Cost of MDG-2015			Financing Sources					
							Domestic Resources			Gap for External Financing		
				Recurrent	Capital	Total	Recurrent	Capital	Total	Recurrent	Capital	Total
Education service delivery	Cumulative, 2001-2015	C1	491	633	136	769	491	0	491	142	136	278
		C2	491	633	136	769	491	0	491	142	136	278
		C3	571	633	136	769	571	0	571	62	136	198
	Annual	C1	33	42	9	51	33	0	33	9	9	19
		C2	33	42	9	51	33	0	33	9	9	19
		C3	38	42	9	51	38	0	38	4	9	13
AIDS-related costs	Annual	C1		10		10	0		0	10		10
		C2		10		10	0		0	10		10
		C3		10		10	0		0	10		10
Both items	Annual	C1		52	9	62	33	0	33	20	9	29
		C2		52	9	62	33	0	33	20	9	29
		C3		52	9	62	38	0	38	14	9	23

Note: "Best practice" policies refer to the combination of scenarios A+B+C. Shaded cells denote no change from values directly above.

Table C.75

Mali: MDG-2015 Financing Gap under Alternative Policy Measures

Policy Scenario[a]		A: Quality Measures			B: Efficiency Measures	C: Financing Measures				Annual Financing Gap[e]
		Pupils Per Teacher	Spending on Inputs Other than Teachers[b]	Average Annual Teacher Salary (as multiple of per capita GDP)	Average Repetition Rate	Government Revenues[c]		Primary Education Recurrent Spending[d]	Private Enrollments (as % of total)	
						As % of GDP	% for Education			
Status quo		61	31.1%	6.1	17.9%	16.8%	13.7%	42.1%	21.2%	54
A only		40	33.3%	6.1						91
A + B		40	33.3%	3.8	10.0%					62
"Best practice": A + B +	C1	40	33.3%	3.8	10.0%	14.0%	20.0%	50.0%	10.0%	51
	C2					14.0%	20.0%			51
	C3					16.8%	20.0%			45

Note: Shaded cells denote no change from values directly above.
a. Policy scenarios are: A for quality improvement, B for efficiency improvement, and three alternative resource mobilization scenarios (C1, C2, and C3). The combination of scenarios A+B+C is considered "best practice."
b. As a share of primary education recurrent spending.
c. Current revenues, excluding grants.
d. As a share of total education recurrent spending.
e. In millions of 2000 U.S. dollars. Calculated as the difference between the total cost of service delivery under the specific policy scenario and the total resources for primary education mobilized domestically.

Table C.76

Mali: MDG-2015 Cost Estimates and Sources of Financing under "Best Practice" Policies and Alternative Resource Mobilization Scenarios

(millions of 2000 U.S. dollars)

Cost Item	Period	Scenario	Domestic Resources Mobilized	Cost of MDG-2015			Financing Sources					
							Domestic Resources			Gap for External Financing		
				Recurrent	Capital	Total	Recurrent	Capital	Total	Recurrent	Capital	Total
Education service delivery	Cumulative, 2001-2015	C1	676	1,014	427	1,442	676	0	676	339	427	766
		C2	676	1,014	427	1,442	676	0	676	339	427	766
		C3	762	1,014	427	1,442	762	0	762	252	427	679
	Annual	C1	45	68	28	96	45	0	45	23	28	51
		C2	45	68	28	96	45	0	45	23	28	51
		C3	51	68	28	96	51	0	51	17	28	45
AIDS-related costs	Annual	C1		2		2	0		0	2		2
		C2		2		2	0		0	2		2
		C3		2		2	0		0	2		2
Both items	Annual	C1		69	28	98	45	0	45	24	28	53
		C2		69	28	98	45	0	45	24	28	53
		C3		69	28	98	51	0	51	19	28	47

Note: "Best practice" policies refer to the combination of scenarios A+B+C. Shaded cells denote no change from values directly above.

Table C.77

Mauritania: MDG-2015 Financing Gap under Alternative Policy Measures

Policy Scenario[a]		A: Quality Measures — Pupils Per Teacher	A: Quality Measures — Spending on Inputs Other than Teachers[b]	A: Quality Measures — Average Annual Teacher Salary (as multiple of per capita GDP)	B: Efficiency Measures — Average Repetition Rate	C: Financing Measures — Government Revenues[c] As % of GDP	C: Financing Measures — Government Revenues[c] % for Education	C: Financing Measures — Primary Education Recurrent Spending[d]	C: Financing Measures — Private Enrollments (as % of total)	Annual Financing Gap[e]
Status quo		48	18.2%	5.1	16.0%	26.5%	13.7%	49.0%	1.8%	6
A only		40	33.3%	5.1						16
A + B		40	33.3%	4.0	10.0%					7
"Best practice": A + B +	C1	40	33.3%	4.0	10.0%	16.0%	20.0%	50.0%	10.0%	7
	C2					16.0%	20.0%			7
	C3					26.5%	20.0%			0

Note: Shaded cells denote no change from values directly above.

a. Policy scenarios are: A for quality improvement, B for efficiency improvement, and three alternative resource mobilization scenarios (C1, C2, and C3). The combination of scenarios A+B+C is considered "best practice."

b. As a share of primary education recurrent spending.

c. Current revenues, excluding grants.

d. As a share of total education recurrent spending.

e. In millions of 2000 U.S. dollars. Calculated as the difference between the total cost of service delivery under the specific policy scenario and the total resources for primary education mobilized domestically.

Table C.78

Mauritania: MDG-2015 Cost Estimates and Sources of Financing under "Best Practice" Policies and Alternative Resource Mobilization Scenarios

(millions of 2000 U.S. dollars)

Cost Item	Period	Scenario	Domestic Resources Mobilized	Cost of MDG-2015 — Recurrent	Cost of MDG-2015 — Capital	Cost of MDG-2015 — Total	Domestic Resources — Recurrent	Domestic Resources — Capital	Domestic Resources — Total	Gap for External Financing — Recurrent	Gap for External Financing — Capital	Gap for External Financing — Total
Education service delivery	Cumulative, 2001-2015	C1	343	406	48	454	343	0	343	63	48	111
		C2	343	406	48	454	343	0	343	63	48	111
		C3	466	406	48	454	406	48	454	0	0	0
	Annual	C1	23	27	3	30	23	0	23	4	3	7
		C2	23	27	3	30	23	0	23	4	3	7
		C3	31	27	3	30	27	3	30	0	0	0
AIDS-related costs	Annual	C1		0		0	0		0	0		0
		C2		0		0	0		0	0		0
		C3		0		0	0		0	0		0
Both items	Annual	C1		27	3	30	23	0	23	4	3	8
		C2		27	3	30	23	0	23	4	3	8
		C3		27	3	30	27	3	30	0	0	0

Note: "Best practice" policies refer to the combination of scenarios A+B+C. Shaded cells denote no change from values directly above.

Table C.79

Mozambique: MDG-2015 Financing Gap under Alternative Policy Measures

Policy Scenario[a]		A: Quality Measures			B: Efficiency Measures	C: Financing Measures					Annual Financing Gap[e]
						Government Revenues[c]		Primary Education Recurrent Spending[d]	Private Enrollments (as % of total)		
		Pupils Per Teacher	Spending on Inputs Other than Teachers[b]	Average Annual Teacher Salary (as multiple of per capita GDP)	Average Repetition Rate	As % of GDP	% for Education				
Status quo		54	26.1%	3.2	23.7%	11.3%	18.1%	46.4%	0.0%		27
A only		40	33.3%	3.5							75
A + B		40	33.3%	3.5	10.0%						48
"Best practice": A + B +	C1	40	33.3%	3.5	10.0%	14.0%	20.0%	42.0%	10.0%		37
	C2					14.0%	20.0%				37
	C3					14.0%	20.0%				37

Note: Shaded cells denote no change from values directly above.
a. Policy scenarios are: A for quality improvement, B for efficiency improvement, and three alternative resource mobilization scenarios (C1, C2, and C3). The combination of scenarios A+B+C is considered "best practice."
b. As a share of primary education recurrent spending.
c. Current revenues, excluding grants.
d. As a share of total education recurrent spending.
e. In millions of 2000 U.S. dollars. Calculated as the difference between the total cost of service delivery under the specific policy scenario and the total resources for primary education mobilized domestically.

Table C.80

Mozambique: MDG-2015 Cost Estimates and Sources of Financing under "Best Practice" Policies and Alternative Resource Mobilization Scenarios
(millions of 2000 U.S. dollars)

Cost Item	Period	Scenario	Domestic Resources Mobilized	Cost of MDG-2015			Financing Sources					
							Domestic Resources			Gap for External Financing		
				Recurrent	Capital	Total	Recurrent	Capital	Total	Recurrent	Capital	Total
Education service delivery	Cumulative, 2001-2015	C1	1,206	1,552	209	1,761	1,206	0	1,206	346	209	555
		C2	1,206	1,552	209	1,761	1,206	0	1,206	346	209	555
		C3	1,206	1,552	209	1,761	1,206	0	1,206	346	209	555
	Annual	C1	80	103	14	117	80	0	80	23	14	37
		C2	80	103	14	117	80	0	80	23	14	37
		C3	80	103	14	117	80	0	80	23	14	37
AIDS-related costs	Annual	C1		9		9	0		0	9		9
		C2		9		9	0		0	9		9
		C3		9		9	0		0	9		9
Both items	Annual	C1		112	14	126	80	0	80	32	14	46
		C2		112	14	126	80	0	80	32	14	46
		C3		112	14	126	80	0	80	32	14	46

Note: "Best practice" policies refer to the combination of scenarios A+B+C. Shaded cells denote no change from values directly above.

Table C.81

Niger: MDG-2015 Financing Gap under Alternative Policy Measures

Policy Scenario[a]		A: Quality Measures			B: Efficiency Measures	C: Financing Measures				Annual Financing Gap[e]
		Pupils Per Teacher	Spending on Inputs Other than Teachers[b]	Average Annual Teacher Salary (as multiple of per capita GDP)	Average Repetition Rate	Government Revenues[c]		Primary Education Recurrent Spending[d]	Private Enrollments (as % of total)	
						As % of GDP	% for Education			
Status quo		37	25.9%	9.6	13.0%	9.1%	31.5%	62.0%	4.0%	135
A only		37	33.3%	9.6						146
A + B		40	33.3%	4.3	10.0%					48
"Best practice": A + B +	C1	40	33.3%	4.3	10.0%	14.0%	26.0%	50.0%	10.0%	46
	C2					14.0%	20.0%			53
	C3					14.0%	20.0%			53

Note: Shaded cells denote no change from values directly above.
a. Policy scenarios are: A for quality improvement, B for efficiency improvement, and three alternative resource mobilization scenarios (C1, C2, and C3). The combination of scenarios A+B+C is considered "best practice."
b. As a share of primary education recurrent spending.
c. Current revenues, excluding grants.
d. As a share of total education recurrent spending.
e. In millions of 2000 U.S. dollars. Calculated as the difference between the total cost of service delivery under the specific policy scenario and the total resources for primary education mobilized domestically.

Table C.82

Niger: MDG-2015 Cost Estimates and Sources of Financing under "Best Practice" Policies and Alternative Resource Mobilization Scenarios
(millions of 2000 U.S. dollars)

Cost Item	Period	Scenario	Domestic Resources Mobilized	Cost of MDG-2015			Financing Sources					
							Domestic Resources			Gap for External Financing		
				Recurrent	Capital	Total	Recurrent	Capital	Total	Recurrent	Capital	Total
Education service delivery	Cumulative, 2001–2015	C1	796	1,078	403	1,481	796	0	796	282	403	685
		C2	684	1,078	403	1,481	684	0	684	394	403	797
		C3	684	1,078	403	1,481	684	0	684	394	403	797
	Annual	C1	53	72	27	99	53	0	53	19	27	46
		C2	46	72	27	99	46	0	46	26	27	53
		C3	46	72	27	99	46	0	46	26	27	53
AIDS-related costs	Annual	C1		1		1	0		0	1		1
		C2		1		1	0		0	1		1
		C3		1		1	0		0	1		1
Both items	Annual	C1		73	27	100	53	0	53	20	27	47
		C2		73	27	100	46	0	46	28	27	54
		C3		73	27	100	46	0	46	28	27	54

Note: "Best practice" policies refer to the combination of scenarios A+B+C. Shaded cells denote no change from values directly above.

Table C.83

Nigeria: MDG-2015 Financing Gap under Alternative Policy Measures

Policy Scenario[a]		A: Quality Measures			B: Efficiency Measures	C: Financing Measures				
		Pupils Per Teacher	Spending on Inputs Other than Teachers[b]	Average Annual Teacher Salary (as multiple of per capita GDP)	Average Repetition Rate	Government Revenues[c] As % of GDP	Government Revenues[c] % for Education	Primary Education Recurrent Spending[d]	Private Enrollments (as % of total)	Annual Financing Gap[e]
Status quo		39	9.1%	4.9	1.0%	46.1%	9.9%	41.0%	1.0%	352
A only		39	33.3%	4.9						654
A + B		40	33.3%	4.1	1.0%					323
"Best practice": A + B +	C1	40	33.3%	4.1	1.0%	18.0%	20.0%	50.0%	10.0%	214
	C2					18.0%	20.0%			214
	C3					46.1%	20.0%			0

Note: Shaded cells denote no change from values directly above.
a. Policy scenarios are: A for quality improvement, B for efficiency improvement, and three alternative resource mobilization scenarios (C1, C2, and C3). The combination of scenarios A+B+C is considered "best practice."
b. As a share of primary education recurrent spending.
c. Current revenues, excluding grants.
d. As a share of total education recurrent spending.
e. In millions of 2000 U.S. dollars. Calculated as the difference between the total cost of service delivery under the specific policy scenario and the total resources for primary education mobilized domestically.

Table C.84

Nigeria: MDG-2015 Cost Estimates and Sources of Financing under "Best Practice" Policies and Alternative Resource Mobilization Scenarios
(millions of 2000 U.S. dollars)

Cost Item	Period	Scenario	Domestic Resources Mobilized	Cost of MDG-2015			Financing Sources					
							Domestic Resources			Gap for External Financing		
				Recurrent	Capital	Total	Recurrent	Capital	Total	Recurrent	Capital	Total
Education service delivery	Cumulative, 2001-2015	C1	19,123	20,502	1,831	22,333	19,123	0	19,123	1,380	1,831	3,210
		C2	19,123	20,502	1,831	22,333	19,123	0	19,123	1,380	1,831	3,210
		C3	31,966	20,502	1,831	22,333	20,502	1,831	22,333	0	0	0
	Annual	C1	1,275	1,367	122	1,489	1,275	0	1,275	92	122	214
		C2	1,275	1,367	122	1,489	1,275	0	1,275	92	122	214
		C3	2,131	1,367	122	1,489	1,367	122	1,489	0	0	0
AIDS-related costs	Annual	C1		58		58	0		0	58		58
		C2		58		58	0		0	58		58
		C3		58		58	58		58	0		58
Both items	Annual	C1		1,425	122	1,547	1,275	0	1,275	150	122	272
		C2		1,425	122	1,547	1,275	0	1,275	150	122	272
		C3		1,425	122	1,547	1,425	122	1,547	0	0	0

Note: "Best practice" policies refer to the combination of scenarios A+B+C. Shaded cells denote no change from values directly above.

Table C.85

Rwanda: MDG-2015 Financing Gap under Alternative Policy Measures

Policy Scenario[a]		A: Quality Measures			B: Efficiency Measures	C: Financing Measures				
		Pupils Per Teacher	Spending on Inputs Other than Teachers[b]	Average Annual Teacher Salary (as multiple of per capita GDP)	Average Repetition Rate	Government Revenues[c] As % of GDP	% for Education	Primary Education Recurrent Spending[d]	Private Enrollments (as % of total)	Annual Financing Gap[e]
Status quo		48	8.6%	4.0	36.1%	9.8%	32.6%	44.7%	0.8%	24
A only		40	33.3%	4.0						48
A + B		40	33.3%	3.7	10.0%					23
"Best practice": A + B +	C1	40	33.3%	3.7	10.0%	14.0%	26.0%	50.0%	10.0%	16
	C2						14.0%	20.0%		22
	C3						14.0%	20.0%		22

Note: Shaded cells denote no change from values directly above.

a. Policy scenarios are: A for quality improvement, B for efficiency improvement, and three alternative resource mobilization scenarios (C1, C2, and C3). The combination of scenarios A+B+C is considered "best practice."

b. As a share of primary education recurrent spending.

c. Current revenues, excluding grants.

d. As a share of total education recurrent spending.

e. In millions of 2000 U.S. dollars. Calculated as the difference between the total cost of service delivery under the specific policy scenario and the total resources for primary education mobilized domestically.

Table C.86

Rwanda: MDG-2015 Cost Estimates and Sources of Financing under "Best Practice" Policies and Alternative Resource Mobilization Scenarios

(millions of 2000 U.S. dollars)

Cost Item	Period	Scenario	Domestic Resources Mobilized	Cost of MDG-2015			Domestic Resources			Gap for External Financing		
				Recurrent	Capital	Total	Recurrent	Capital	Total	Recurrent	Capital	Total
Education service delivery	Cumulative, 2001-2015	C1	682	756	166	922	682	0	682	75	166	240
		C2	591	756	166	922	591	0	591	165	166	331
		C3	591	756	166	922	591	0	591	165	166	331
	Annual	C1	45	50	11	61	45	0	45	5	11	16
		C2	39	50	11	61	39	0	39	11	11	22
		C3	39	50	11	61	39	0	39	11	11	22
AIDS-related costs	Annual	C1		7		7	0		0	7		7
		C2		7		7	0		0	7		7
		C3		7		7	0		0	7		7
Both items	Annual	C1		57	11	68	45	0	45	12	11	23
		C2		57	11	68	39	0	39	18	11	29
		C3		57	11	68	39	0	39	18	11	29

Note: "Best practice" policies refer to the combination of scenarios A+B+C. Shaded cells denote no change from values directly above.

Table C.87

Senegal: MDG-2015 Financing Gap under Alternative Policy Measures

Policy Scenario[a]		A: Quality Measures			B: Efficiency Measures	C: Financing Measures				Annual Financing Gap[e]
						Government Revenues[c]		Primary Education	Private Enrollments	
		Pupils Per Teacher	Spending on Inputs Other than Teachers[b]	Average Annual Teacher Salary (as multiple of per capita GDP)	Average Repetition Rate	As % of GDP	% for Education	Recurrent Spending[d]	(as % of total)	
Status quo		55	36.6%	4.9	13.6%	18.1%	18.6%	43.9%	10.7%	48
A only		40	36.6%	4.9						85
A + B		40	33.3%	3.7	10.0%					43
"Best practice": A + B +	C1	40	33.3%	3.7	10.0%	16.0%	20.0%	50.0%	10.0%	38
	C2					16.0%	20.0%			38
	C3					18.1%	20.0%			30

Note: Shaded cells denote no change from values directly above.
a. Policy scenarios are: A for quality improvement, B for efficiency improvement, and three alternative resource mobilization scenarios (C1, C2, and C3). The combination of scenarios A+B+C is considered "best practice."
b. As a share of primary education recurrent spending.
c. Current revenues, excluding grants.
d. As a share of total education recurrent spending.
e. In millions of 2000 U.S. dollars. Calculated as the difference between the total cost of service delivery under the specific policy scenario and the total resources for primary education mobilized domestically.

Table C.88

Senegal: MDG-2015 Cost Estimates and Sources of Financing under "Best Practice" Policies and Alternative Resource Mobilization Scenarios 275

(millions of 2000 U.S. dollars)

Cost Item	Period	Scenario	Domestic Resources Mobilized	Cost of MDG-2015			Financing Sources					
							Domestic Resources			Gap for External Financing		
				Recurrent	Capital	Total	Recurrent	Capital	Total	Recurrent	Capital	Total
Education service delivery	Cumulative, 2001-2015	C1	1,543	1,830	282	2,112	1,543	0	1,543	288	282	569
		C2	1,543	1,830	282	2,112	1,543	0	1,543	288	282	569
		C3	1,658	1,830	282	2,112	1,658	0	1,658	172	282	454
	Annual	C1	103	122	19	141	103	0	103	19	19	38
		C2	103	122	19	141	103	0	103	19	19	38
		C3	111	122	19	141	111	0	111	11	19	30
AIDS-related costs	Annual	C1		2		2	0		0	2		2
		C2		2		2	0		0	2		2
		C3	2	2		2	0		0	2		2
Both items	Annual	C1		124	19	142	103	0	103	21	19	40
		C2		124	19	142	103	0	103	21	19	40
		C3		124	19	142	111	0	111	13	19	32

Note: "Best practice" policies refer to the combination of scenarios A+B+C. Shaded cells denote no change from values directly above.

Table C.89

Sierra Leone: MDG-2015 Financing Gap under Alternative Policy Measures

Policy Scenario[a]		A: Quality Measures		B: Efficiency Measures		C: Financing Measures				Annual Financing Gap[e]
		Pupils Per Teacher	Spending on Inputs Other than Teachers[b]	Average Annual Teacher Salary (as multiple of per capita GDP)	Average Repetition Rate	Government Revenues[c]		Primary Education Recurrent Spending[d]	Private Enrollments (as % of total)	
						As % of GDP	% for Education			
Status quo		40	33.1%	4.3	9.3%	11.4%	30.4%	51.3%	0.0%	13
A only		40	33.3%	4.3						13
A + B		40	33.3%	3.8	9.3%					8
"Best practice": A + B +	C1	40	33.3%	3.8	9.3%	14.0%	26.0%	50.0%	10.0%	8
	C2					14.0%	20.0%			10
	C3					14.0%	20.0%			10

Note: Shaded cells denote no change from values directly above.
a. Policy scenarios are: A for quality improvement, B for efficiency improvement, and three alternative resource mobilization scenarios (C1, C2, and C3). The combination of scenarios A+B+C is considered "best practice."
b. As a share of primary education recurrent spending.
c. Current revenues, excluding grants.
d. As a share of total education recurrent spending.
e. In millions of 2000 U.S. dollars. Calculated as the difference between the total cost of service delivery under the specific policy scenario and the total resources for primary education mobilized domestically.

Table C.90

Sierra Leone: MDG-2015 Cost Estimates and Sources of Financing under "Best Practice" Policies and Alternative Resource Mobilization Scenarios

(millions of 2000 U.S. dollars)

Cost Item	Period	Scenario	Domestic Resources Mobilized	Cost of MDG-2015			Financing Sources					
							Domestic Resources			Gap for External Financing		
				Recurrent	Capital	Total	Recurrent	Capital	Total	Recurrent	Capital	Total
Education service delivery	Cumulative, 2001-2015	C1	261	288	88	376	261	0	261	27	88	115
		C2	227	288	88	376	227	0	227	62	88	150
		C3	227	288	88	376	227	0	227	62	88	150
	Annual	C1	17	19	6	25	17	0	17	2	6	8
		C2	15	19	6	25	15	0	15	4	6	10
		C3	15	19	6	25	15	0	15	4	6	10
AIDS-related costs	Annual	C1		2		2	0		0	2		2
		C2		2		2	0		0	2		2
		C3		2		2	0		0	2		2
Both items	Annual	C1	21		6	27	17	0	17	4	6	9
		C2	21		6	27	15	0	15	6	6	12
		C3	21		6	27	15	0	15	6	6	12

Note: "Best practice" policies refer to the combination of scenarios A+B+C. Shaded cells denote no change from values directly above.

Table C.91
....

Sudan: MDG-2015 Financing Gap under Alternative Policy Measures

		A: Quality Measures			B: Efficiency Measures	C: Financing Measures				
Policy Scenario[a]		Pupils Per Teacher	Spending on Inputs Other than Teachers[b]	Average Annual Teacher Salary (as multiple of per capita GDP)	Average Repetition Rate	Government Revenues[c]		Primary Education Recurrent Spending[d]	Private Enrollments (as % of total)	Annual Financing Gap[e]
						As % of GDP	% for Education			
Status quo		28	22.5%	2.2	1.2%	11.1%	16.2%	50.5%	0.0%	131
A only		28	33.3%	3.5						301
A + B		40	33.3%	3.5	1.2%					153
"Best practice": A + B +	C1	40	33.3%	3.5	1.2%	14.0%	20.0%	50.0%	10.0%	105
	C2					14.0%	20.0%			105
	C3					14.0%	20.0%			105

Note: Shaded cells denote no change from values directly above.
a. Policy scenarios are: A for quality improvement, B for efficiency improvement, and three alternative resource mobilization scenarios (C1, C2, and C3). The combination of scenarios A+B+C is considered "best practice."
b. As a share of primary education recurrent spending.
c. Current revenues, excluding grants.
d. As a share of total education recurrent spending.
e. In millions of 2000 U.S. dollars. Calculated as the difference between the total cost of service delivery under the specific policy scenario and the total resources for primary education mobilized domestically.

Table C.92
....

Sudan: MDG-2015 Cost Estimates and Sources of Financing under "Best Practice" Policies and Alternative Resource Mobilization Scenarios
(millions of 2000 U.S. dollars)

Cost Item	Period	Scenario	Domestic Resources Mobilized	Cost of MDG-2015			Financing Sources					
							Domestic Resources			Gap for External Financing		
				Recurrent	Capital	Total	Recurrent	Capital	Total	Recurrent	Capital	Total
Education service delivery	Cumulative, 2001-2015	C1	3,078	4,349	297	4,646	3,078	0	3,078	1,271	297	1,568
		C2	3,078	4,349	297	4,646	3,078	0	3,078	1,271	297	1,568
		C3	3,078	4,349	297	4,646	3,078	0	3,078	1,271	297	1,568
	Annual	C1	205	290	20	310	205	0	205	85	20	105
		C2	205	290	20	310	205	0	205	85	20	105
		C3	205	290	20	310	205	0	205	85	20	105
AIDS-related costs	Annual	C1		1		1	0		0	1		1
		C2		1		1	0		0	1		1
		C3	1		1	0		0	1		1
Both items	Annual	C1		291	20	311	205	0	205	86	20	106
		C2		291	20	311	205	0	205	86	20	106
		C3		291	20	311	205	0	205	86	20	106

Note: "Best practice" policies refer to the combination of scenarios A+B+C. Shaded cells denote no change from values directly above.

Table C.93

Tanzania: MDG-2015 Financing Gap under Alternative Policy Measures

Policy Scenario[a]		Pupils Per Teacher	Spending on Inputs Other than Teachers[b]	Average Annual Teacher Salary (as multiple of per capita GDP)	Average Repetition Rate	Government Revenues[c] As % of GDP	Government Revenues[c] % for Education	Primary Education Recurrent Spending[d]	Private Enrollments (as % of total)	Annual Financing Gap[e]
		A: Quality Measures			**B: Efficiency Measures**	**C: Financing Measures**				
Status quo		40	11.2%	3.6	3.2%	10.9%	16.4%	63.0%	0.0%	87
A only		40	33.3%	3.6						128
A + B		40	33.3%	3.5	3.2%					102
"Best practice": A + B +	C1	40	33.3%	3.5	3.2%	14.0%	20.0%	50.0%	10.0%	80
	C2					14.0%	20.0%			80
	C3					14.0%	20.0%			80

Note: Shaded cells denote no change from values directly above.
a. Policy scenarios are: A for quality improvement, B for efficiency improvement, and three alternative resource mobilization scenarios (C1, C2, and C3). The combination of scenarios A+B+C is considered "best practice."
b. As a share of primary education recurrent spending.
c. Current revenues, excluding grants.
d. As a share of total education recurrent spending.
e. In millions of 2000 U.S. dollars. Calculated as the difference between the total cost of service delivery under the specific policy scenario and the total resources for primary education mobilized domestically.

Table C.94

Tanzania: MDG-2015 Cost Estimates and Sources of Financing under "Best Practice" Policies and Alternative Resource Mobilization Scenarios

(millions of 2000 U.S. dollars)

Cost Item	Period	Scenario	Domestic Resources Mobilized	Cost of MDG-2015 Recurrent	Cost of MDG-2015 Capital	Cost of MDG-2015 Total	Domestic Resources Recurrent	Domestic Resources Capital	Domestic Resources Total	Gap for External Financing Recurrent	Gap for External Financing Capital	Gap for External Financing Total
							Financing Sources					
Education service delivery	Cumulative, 2001-2015	C1	2,454	3,234	413	3,646	2,454	0	2,454	780	413	1,193
		C2	2,454	3,234	413	3,646	2,454	0	2,454	780	413	1,193
		C3	2,454	3,234	413	3,646	2,454	0	2,454	780	413	1,193
	Annual	C1	164	216	28	243	164	0	164	52	28	80
		C2	164	216	28	243	164	0	164	52	28	80
		C3	164	216	28	243	164	0	164	52	28	80
AIDS-related costs	Annual	C1		22		22	0		0	22		22
		C2		22		22	0		0	22		22
		C3		22		22	0		0	22		22
Both items	Annual	C1		238	28	265	164	0	164	74	28	102
		C2		238	28	265	164	0	164	74	28	102
		C3		238	28	265	164	0	164	74	28	102

Note: "Best practice" policies refer to the combination of scenarios A+B+C. Shaded cells denote no change from values directly above.

Table C.95

Togo: MDG-2015 Financing Gap under Alternative Policy Measures

	A: Quality Measures			B: Efficiency Measures	C: Financing Measures				Annual Financing Gap[e]
					Government Revenues[c]		Primary Education Recurrent Spending[d]	Private Enrollments (as % of total)	
Policy Scenario[a]	Pupils Per Teacher	Spending on Inputs Other than Teachers[b]	Average Annual Teacher Salary (as multiple of per capita GDP)	Average Repetition Rate	As % of GDP	% for Education			
Status quo	45	25.2%	4.5	27.0%	14.9%	25.6%	48.3%	35.6%	3
A only	40	33.3%	4.5						10
A + B	40	33.3%	3.9	10.0%					12
"Best practice": A + B + C1	40	33.3%	3.9	10.0%	14.0%	25.6%	50.0%	10.0%	11
C2					14.0%	20.0%			16
C3					14.9%	20.0%			15

Note: Shaded cells denote no change from values directly above.
a. Policy scenarios are: A for quality improvement, B for efficiency improvement, and three alternative resource mobilization scenarios (C1, C2, and C3). The combination of scenarios A+B+C is considered "best practice."
b. As a share of primary education recurrent spending.
c. Current revenues, excluding grants.
d. As a share of total education recurrent spending.
e. In millions of 2000 U.S. dollars. Calculated as the difference between the total cost of service delivery under the specific policy scenario and the total resources for primary education mobilized domestically.

Table C.96

Togo: MDG-2015 Cost Estimates and Sources of Financing under "Best Practice" Policies and Alternative Resource Mobilization Scenarios

(millions of 2000 U.S. dollars)

Cost Item	Scenario	Mobilized Domestic Resources Recurrent	Cost of MDG-2015			Financing Sources				Gap for External Financing		
						Domestic Resources						
			Capital	Total	Recurrent	Capital	Total	Recurrent	Capital	Total	Recurrent	
Education service delivery	Cumulative, 2001-2015	C1	531	589	107	696	531	0	531	58	107	165
		C2	460	589	107	696	460	0	460	129	107	236
		C3	478	589	107	696	478	0	478	112	107	219
	Annual	C1	35	39	7	46	35	0	35	4	7	11
		C2	31	39	7	46	31	0	31	9	7	16
		C3	32	39	7	46	32	0	32	7	7	15
AIDS-related costs	Annual	C1		4		4	0		0	4		4
		C2		4		4	0		0	4		4
		C3		4		4	0		0	4		4
Both items	Annual	C1		43	7	51	35	0	35	8	7	15
		C2		43	7	51	31	0	31	13	7	20
		C3		43	7	51	32	0	32	12	7	19

Note: "Best practice" policies refer to the combination of scenarios A+B+C. Shaded cells denote no change from values directly above.

Table C.97

Uganda: MDG-2015 Financing Gap under Alternative Policy Measures

Policy Scenario[a]		Pupils Per Teacher	Spending on Inputs Other than Teachers[b]	Average Annual Teacher Salary (as multiple of per capita GDP)	Average Repetition Rate	As % of GDP	% for Education	Primary Education Recurrent Spending[d]	Private Enrollments (as % of total)	Annual Financing Gap[e]
		A: Quality Measures			**B: Efficiency Measures**	**C: Financing Measures**				
						Government Revenues[c]				
Status quo		41	26.2%	2.9	9.8%	10.8%	30.1%	53.2%	2.0%	14
A only		40	33.3%	3.5						63
A + B		40	33.3%	3.5	9.8%					48
"Best practice": A + B +	C1	40	33.3%	3.5	9.8%	14.0%	26.0%	50.0%	10.0%	41
	C2					14.0%	20.0%			63
	C3					14.0%	20.0%			63

Note: Shaded cells denote no change from values directly above.
a. Policy scenarios are: A for quality improvement, B for efficiency improvement, and three alternative resource mobilization scenarios (C1, C2, and C3). The combination of scenarios A+B+C is considered "best practice."
b. As a share of primary education recurrent spending.
c. Current revenues, excluding grants.
d. As a share of total education recurrent spending.
e. In millions of 2000 U.S. dollars. Calculated as the difference between the total cost of service delivery under the specific policy scenario and the total resources for primary education mobilized domestically.

Table C.98

Uganda: MDG-2015 Cost Estimates and Sources of Financing under "Best Practice" Policies and Alternative Resource Mobilization Scenarios

(millions of 2000 U.S. dollars)

Cost Item	Period	Scenario	Domestic Resources Mobilized	Recurrent	Capital	Total	Recurrent	Capital	Total	Recurrent	Capital	Total
				Cost of MDG-2015			**Domestic Resources**			**Gap for External Financing**		
Education service delivery	Cumulative, 2001–2015	C1	2,523	2,930	210	3,140	2,523	0	2,523	407	210	617
		C2	2,189	2,930	210	3,140	2,189	0	2,189	741	210	951
		C3	2,189	2,930	210	3,140	2,189	0	2,189	741	210	951
	Annual	C1	168	195	14	209	168	0	168	27	14	41
		C2	146	195	14	209	146	0	146	49	14	63
		C3	146	195	14	209	146	0	146	49	14	63
AIDS-related costs	Annual	C1		24		24	0		0	24		24
		C2		24		24	0		0	24		24
		C3		24		24	0		0	24		24
Both items	Annual	C1		219	14	233	168	0	168	51	14	65
		C2		219	14	233	146	0	146	73	14	87
		C3		219	14	233	146	0	146	73	14	87

Note: "Best practice" policies refer to the combination of scenarios A+B+C. Shaded cells denote no change from values directly above.

Table C.99

Zambia: MDG-2015 Financing Gap under Alternative Policy Measures

Policy Scenario[a]		Pupils Per Teacher	Spending on Inputs Other than Teachers[b]	Average Annual Teacher Salary (as multiple of per capita GDP)	Average Repetition Rate	As % of GDP	% for Education	Primary Education Recurrent Spending[d]	Private Enrollments (as % of total)	Annual Financing Gap[e]
		A: Quality Measures			**B: Efficiency Measures**	**C: Financing Measures**				
						Government Revenues[c]		Primary Education	Private Enrollments	
Status quo		50	21.7%	2.7	6.2%	18.8%	12.3%	43.2%	1.6%	10
A only		40	33.3%	3.5						40
A + B		40	33.3%	3.5	6.2%					34
"Best practice": A + B +	C1	40	33.3%	3.5	6.2%	14.0%	20.0%	50.0%	10.0%	25
	C2					14.0%	20.0%			25
	C3					18.8%	20.0%			17

Note: Shaded cells denote no change from values directly above.
a. Policy scenarios are: A for quality improvement, B for efficiency improvement, and three alternative resource mobilization scenarios (C1, C2, and C3). The combination of scenarios A+B+C is considered "best practice."
b. As a share of primary education recurrent spending.
c. Current revenues, excluding grants.
d. As a share of total education recurrent spending.
e. In millions of 2000 U.S. dollars. Calculated as the difference between the total cost of service delivery under the specific policy scenario and the total resources for primary education mobilized domestically.

Table C.100

Zambia: MDG-2015 Cost Estimates and Sources of Financing under "Best Practice" Policies and Alternative Resource Mobilization Scenarios
(millions of 2000 U.S. dollars)

Cost Item	Period	Scenario	Domestic Resources Mobilized	Recurrent	Capital	Total	Recurrent	Capital	Total	Recurrent	Capital	Total
				Cost of MDG-2015			**Domestic Resources**			**Gap for External Financing**		
Education service delivery	Cumulative, 2001-2015	C1	619	866	131	996	619	0	619	247	131	378
		C2	619	866	131	996	619	0	619	247	131	378
		C3	747	866	131	996	747	0	747	119	131	249
	Annual	C1	41	58	9	66	41	0	41	16	9	25
		C2	41	58	9	66	41	0	41	16	9	25
		C3	50	58	9	66	50	0	50	8	9	17
AIDS-related costs	Annual	C1		15		15	0		0	15		15
		C2		15		15	0		0	15		15
		C3		15		15	0		0	15		15
Both items	Annual	C1		72	9	81	41	0	41	31	9	40
		C2		72	9	81	41	0	41	31	9	40
		C3		72	9	81	50	0	50	23	9	31

Note: "Best practice" policies refer to the combination of scenarios A+B+C. Shaded cells denote no change from values directly above.

Aid for Primary Education

D

Table D.1
....
Development Assistance Committee and Multilateral Official Commitments for Education and Basic Education, 1997–2000
(millions of current U.S. dollars)

Donor	1997	1998	1999	2000	Annual Average
IBRD, total education	739.3	1,927.8	799.4	215.3	920.5
o/w basic education	163.2	612.7	363.5	76.6	304.0
IDA, total education	255.1	1,201.5	534.8	468.7	615.0
o/w basic education	96.3	1,018.8	283.4	298.7	424.3
World Bank, total education	994.4	3,129.3	1,334.2	684.0	1,535.5
o/w basic education	259.5	1,631.5	646.9	375.3	728.3
Other multilateral, total education	486.1	1,274.7	773.7	1,335.5	967.5
o/w basic education	184.7	181.0	184.1	199.7	187.4
All MDBs, total education	1,480.5	4,404.0	2,107.9	2,019.5	2,503.0
o/w basic education	444.2	1,812.5	831.0	575.0	915.7
G-7, total education	3,838.2	3,568.5	4,093.9	2,639.7	3,535.1
o/w basic education	356.5	218.0	345.9	432.5	338.2
EU members, total education	3,278.3	3,229.1	3,066.0	2,155.0	2,932.1
o/w basic education	241.5	306.9	293.8	379.1	305.3
All DAC countries, total education	4,804.3	4,459.2	5,014.3	3,541.7	4,454.9
o/w basic education	534.0	434.3	599.7	684.4	563.1
Grand total, all education donors	**6,284.8**	**8,863.2**	**7,122.2**	**5,561.2**	**6,957.8**
o/w basic education	**978.3**	**2,246.3**	**1,430.6**	**1,259.4**	**1,478.7**

Sources: World Bank Business Warehouse and OECD DAC Database.

Table D.2

Official Commitments for Basic Education as a Percentage of Total Education Commitments, 1997–2000

Donor	1997	1998	1999	2000	Annual Average
IBRD	22	32	45	36	34
IDA	38	85	53	64	60
World Bank	26	52	48	55	45
Other multilateral	38	14	24	15	23
All MDBs	30	41	39	28	35
G-7	9	6	8	16	10
EU members	7	10	10	18	11
All DAC countries	11	10	12	19	13
Total, all sources	**16**	**25**	**20**	**23**	**21**

Table D.3

Multilateral Official Commitments for Education and Basic Education, by Donor and Region, 1997–2000

(millions of current U.S. dollars)

Donor	1997	1998	1999	2000	Annual Average
World Bank, total education	**994.4**	**3,129.3**	**1,334.2**	**684.0**	**1,535.5**
o/w basic education	**259.5**	**1,631.5**	**646.9**	**375.3**	**728.3**
AFR education	75.1	372.3	194.1	159.7	200.3
o/w AFR basic education	21.3	218.3	131.0	58.8	107.4
LCR education	61.5	1,199.9	393.6	77.5	433.1
o/w LCR basic education	33.0	387.7	243.2	72.5	184.1
EAP education	645.0	103.5	557.2	5.0	327.7
o/w EAP basic education	113.4	..	138.4	5.0	85.6
ECA education	137.8	592.4	36.1	22.6	197.2
o/w ECA basic education	16.8	321.0	36.1	..	124.6
SAR education	0.0	718.2	98.2	200.0	254.1
o/w SAR basic education	0.0	704.5	98.2	182.4	246.3
MNA education	75.0	143.0	50.0	219.2	121.8
o/w MNA basic education	75.0	..	..	56.6	65.8
Other multilateral, total education	**486.1**	**1,274.7**	**773.7**	**1,335.5**	**967.5**
o/w basic education	**184.7**	**181.0**	**184.1**	**199.7**	**187.4**
AFR education	161.2	868.9	309.5	1,041.3	595.2
o/w AFR basic education	33.3	28.2	110.7	116.2	72.1
LCR education	150.0	165.9	89.8	64.1	117.5
o/w LCR basic education	110.0	72.6	73.6	11.1	66.8
EAP education	150.4	203.5	144.7	90.3	147.2
o/w EAP basic education	85.0	29.0	36.1	6.2	39.1
ECA education	21.0	0.0	0.1	85.7	26.7
o/w ECA basic education	..	..	..	0.1	0.1
SAR education	46.6	45.7	38.0	54.0	46.1
o/w SAR basic education	20.2	17.9	12.8	10.0	15.2
MNA education	..	..	50.6	321.5	186.0
o/w MNA basic education	..	..	30.4	56.1	43.3
All MDBs, total education	**1,480.5**	**4,404.0**	**2,107.9**	**2,019.5**	**2,503.0**
o/w basic education	**444.2**	**1,812.5**	**831.0**	**575.0**	**915.7**
AFR education	236.3	1,241.2	503.6	1,201.0	795.5
o/w AFR basic education	54.6	246.5	241.7	175.0	179.4
LCR education	211.5	1,365.8	483.4	141.6	550.6
o/w LCR basic education	143.0	460.3	316.8	83.6	250.9
EAP education	795.4	307.0	701.9	95.3	474.9
o/w EAP basic education	198.4	29.0	174.5	11.2	103.3
ECA education	158.8	592.4	36.2	108.3	223.9
o/w ECA basic education	16.8	321.0	36.1	0.1	93.5
SAR education	46.6	763.9	136.2	254.0	300.2
o/w SAR basic education	20.2	722.4	111.0	192.4	261.5
MNA education	75.0	143.0	100.6	540.7	214.8
o/w MNA basic education	75.0	..	30.4	112.7	72.7

.. Negligible.

Sources: World Bank Business Warehouse and OECD DAC Database.

Table D.4
....
Bilateral Official Commitments for Education and Basic Education, by Donor and Region, 1997–2000

Donor	1997	1998	1999	2000	Annual Average
All DAC countries, total education	**4,804.3**	**4,459.2**	**5,014.3**	**3,541.7**	**4,454.9**
o/w basic education	**534.0**	**434.3**	**599.7**	**684.4**	**563.1**
AFR education	1,781.8	2,328.4	1,259.2	1,405.6	1,693.7
o/w AFR basic education	210.2	422.2	326.1	378.8	334.3
LCR education	880.1	590.4	571.2	517.1	639.7
o/w LCR basic education	74.5	69.0	106.9	116.3	91.7
EAP education	771.8	722.1	1,846.7	502.7	960.8
o/w EAP basic education	128.0	48.6	76.0	64.4	79.2
ECA education	139.3	47.8	253.6	230.5	167.8
o/w ECA basic education	1.7	5.4	1.9	12.7	5.4
SAR education	701.0	428.9	466.8	339.3	484.0
o/w SAR basic education	92.0	113.4	136.6	102.9	111.2
MNA education	530.4	341.7	616.9	546.4	508.9
o/w MNA basic education	52.2	61.2	44.7	73.8	58.0
G-7, total education	**3,838.2**	**3,568.5**	**4,093.9**	**2,639.7**	**3,535.1**
o/w basic education	**356.5**	**218.0**	**345.9**	**432.5**	**338.2**
AFR education	1,584.1	2,099.5	912.3	1,050.0	1,411.5
o/w AFR basic education	154.6	339.4	224.1	270.6	247.2
LCR education	741.9	384.3	391.9	319.1	459.3
o/w LCR basic education	61.0	47.7	80.7	90.2	69.9
EAP education	584.6	413.6	1,609.5	366.5	743.6
o/w EAP basic education	122.2	39.0	60.5	25.7	61.8
ECA education	42.9	32.1	196.2	161.3	108.1
o/w ECA basic education	0.5	0.5	0.4	7.5	2.2
SAR education	355.8	360.2	395.3	247.7	339.7
o/w SAR basic education	27.9	82.7	106.5	65.0	70.5
MNA education	528.9	278.8	588.8	495.2	472.9
o/w MNA basic education	7.5	42.0	35.0	60.8	36.3
EU members, total education	**3,278.3**	**3,229.1**	**3,066.0**	**2,155.0**	**2,932.1**
o/w basic education	**241.5**	**306.9**	**293.8**	**379.1**	**305.3**
AFR education	1,453.0	1,851.2	1,014.9	889.0	1,302.0
o/w AFR basic education	77.9	260.0	185.7	247.9	192.9
LCR education	648.6	448.0	433.3	306.7	459.2
o/w LCR basic education	48.2	49.0	53.7	39.0	47.5
EAP education	165.4	301.8	564.2	242.9	318.6
o/w EAP basic education	9.1	24.5	32.1	37.1	25.7
ECA education	168.1	44.5	256.2	152.1	155.2
o/w ECA basic education	0.7	5.4	1.4	5.6	3.3
SAR education	495.0	287.4	285.2	203.5	317.8
o/w SAR basic education	62.5	82.9	84.4	72.9	75.7
MNA education	348.2	296.3	512.2	360.7	379.3
o/w MNA basic education	4.7	40.9	17.2	31.1	23.5

Sources: World Bank Business Warehouse and OECD DAC Database.

Table D.5

Total Official Commitments for Education and Basic Education, by Region, 1997–2000

Donor	1997	1998	1999	2000	Annual Average
Education, all sources	**6,284.8**	**8,863.2**	**7,122.2**	**5,561.2**	**6,957.8**
o/w basic education	**978.3**	**2,246.8**	**1,430.6**	**1,259.4**	**1,478.8**
AFR education	2,018.1	3,243.7	1,762.8	1,840.8	2,216.4
o/w AFR basic education	264.7	668.7	567.8	468.8	492.5
LCR education	1,091.6	1,894.0	1,054.6	611.6	1,162.9
o/w LCR basic education	217.5	529.3	423.6	199.8	342.6
EAP education	1,567.1	952.8	2,548.6	531.6	1,400.0
o/w EAP basic education	326.4	77.6	250.5	75.6	182.5
ECA education	298.1	640.2	289.8	275.8	376.0
o/w ECA basic education	18.5	326.4	38.0	12.7	98.9
SAR education	747.5	1,175.7	603.1	553.6	770.0
o/w SAR basic education	112.2	835.8	247.7	295.3	372.7
MNA education	605.4	484.7	717.5	850.7	664.6
o/w MNA basic education	127.2	61.2	75.1	186.6	112.5

Sources: World Bank Business Warehouse and OECD DAC Database.

Table D.6

Official Development Assistance to Education by Region, All Sources, 1998–2000
(commitments basis, millions of current U.S. dollars)

Donor	1998	AFR	EAP	ECA	LCR	MNA	SAR	1999	AFR
IBRD, total education	1,927.8							799.4	
o/w basic education	612.7							363.5	
IDA, total education	1,201.5							534.8	
o/w basic education	1,018.8							283.4	
World Bank, total education	3,129.3	372.3	103.5	592.4	1,199.9	143.0	718.2	1,334.2	194.1
o/w basic education	1,631.5	218.3		321.0	387.7		704.5	646.9	131.0
Other multilateral, total education	1,274.7	868.9	203.5		165.9		45.7	773.7	309.5
o/w basic education	180.9	28.2	29.0		72.6		17.9	184.0	110.6
All MDBs, total education	4,404.0	1,241.2	307.0	592.4	1,365.8	143.0	763.9	2,107.9	503.6
o/w basic education	1,812.5	246.5	29.0	321.0	460.3		722.4	830.9	241.6
G-7, total education	3,568.4	2,099.5	413.6	32.1	384.3	278.8	360.2	4,093.9	912.3
o/w basic education	217.9	339.4	38.9	0.5	47.7	42.0	82.7	345.9	224.1
EU, total education	3,229.1	1,851.2	301.8	44.5	448.0	296.3	287.4	3,065.9	1,014.9
o/w basic education	306.9	260.0	24.5	5.4	49.0	40.8	82.9	293.8	185.7
All DAC countries, total education	4,459.2	2,328.4	722.0	47.8	590.4	341.7	428.9	5,014.3	1,259.2
o/w basic education	434.3	422.2	48.6	5.4	68.9	61.2	113.4	599.7	326.1
Grand total, education	**8,863.2**	**3,243.7**	**952.8**	**640.2**	**1,893.9**	**484.7**	**1,175.7**	**7,122.2**	**1,762.8**
o/w basic education	**2,246.8**	**668.7**	**77.6**	**326.4**	**529.3**	**61.2**	**835.8**	**1,430.6**	**567.8**

Note: The World Bank (IBRD and IDA) reports flows to "primary education" whereas the DAC reports flows to "basic education." Regional breakdowns could not be obtained for some multilateral sources; hence, regional totals may be underreported. Regional classifications reported by the DAC are not consistent with those reported by the World Bank. Distribution across regions subject to authors' estimates. Grand total estimates include some flows that could not be attributed to individual regions.

Sources: World Bank (IBRD and IDA) figures from World Bank Business Warehouse; all other figures from OECD DAC Database.

EAP	ECA	LCR	MNA	SAR	2000	AFR	EAP	ECA	LCR	MNA	SAR
					215.3						
					76.6						
					468.7						
					298.7						
557.2	36.1	393.6	50.0	98.2	**684.0**	159.7	5.0	22.6	77.5	219.2	200.0
138.4	36.1	243.2		98.2	**375.3**	58.8	5.0		72.5	56.6	182.4
144.7	0.1	89.8	50.6	38.0	**1,335.5**	1,041.3	90.3	85.6	64.1	321.4	53.9
36.1		73.6	30.4	12.8	**199.7**	116.2	6.2	0.1	11.1	56.1	10.0
701.9	36.2	483.4	100.6	136.2	**2,019.5**	1,200.9	95.3	108.2	141.6	540.6	253.9
174.5	36.2	316.8	30.4	111.0	**575.0**	175.0	11.2	0.1	83.6	112.7	192.4
1,609.4	196.2	391.8	588.8	395.3	**2,639.7**	1,049.9	366.5	161.3	319.1	495.2	247.7
60.5	0.4	80.7	34.9	106.5	**432.5**	270.6	25.7	7.5	90.2	60.8	65.0
564.2	256.2	433.3	512.2	285.2	**2,154.9**	889.0	242.9	152.1	306.7	360.7	203.5
32.1	1.4	53.7	17.2	84.4	**379.0**	247.9	37.1	5.6	38.9	31.1	72.9
1,846.7	253.6	571.2	616.9	466.8	**3,541.6**	1,405.6	502.7	230.5	517.1	546.4	339.3
76.0	1.9	106.8	44.7	136.6	**684.4**	378.8	64.4	12.7	116.3	73.8	102.9
2,548.6	**289.8**	**1054.6**	**717.5**	**603.1**	**5,561.2**	**1,840.8**	**531.6**	**275.7**	**611.6**	**850.7**	**553.6**
250.5	**38.0**	**423.6**	**75.0**	**247.6**	**1,259.4**	**468.8**	**75.6**	**12.7**	**199.8**	**186.6**	**295.3**

Table D.7

Official Development Assistance to Basic Education in Sub-Saharan Africa, by Donor, 1998–2000
(commitment basis, millions of current U.S. dollars)

Donor	1998	1999	2000
International Development Association			
Total education	1,201.5	534.8	468.7
Africa education	372.3	194.1	159.7
Africa basic education	218.3	131.0	58.8
Other multilateral development banks			
Total education	1,274.7	773.7	1,335.5
Africa education	868.9	309.5	1,041.3
Africa basic education	28.2	110.6	116.2
Development Assistance Committee countries			
Total education	4,459.2	5,014.3	3,541.6
Africa education	2,328.4	1,259.2	1,405.6
Africa basic education	422.2	418.4	378.8
All donors			
Total education	6,935.4	6,322.8	5,345.8
Africa education	3,569.6	1,762.8	2,606.6
Africa basic education	**668.7**	**660.0**	**553.8**

Note: The World Bank (IBRD and IDA) reports flows to "primary education," whereas the DAC reports flows to "basic education." DAC and African Development Bank regional classifications cover continental Africa and not Sub-Saharan Africa, as reported by the World Bank. Therefore the regional totals are approximate.

Sources: World Bank Business Warehouse; OECD DAC Database.

Table D.8
....
IDA Disbursements for Primary Education, by Expenditure Type and Region, Fiscal Years 1999–2002
(millions of current U.S. dollars)

REGION	FY99 Capital	FY99 Recurrent	FY99 Total	FY00 Capital	FY00 Recurrent	FY00 Total	FY01 Capital	FY01 Recurrent	FY01 Total	FY02 Capital	FY02 Cecurrent	FY02 Total
Africa	42.2	115.7	157.9	47.2	59.5	106.7	35.9	52.5	88.4	40.0	75.8	115.8
East Asia and the Pacific	3.8	1.6	5.4	2.1	0.9	3.0	0.5	0.3	0.8	0.6	0.4	1.0
Europe and Central Asia	1.2	2.7	3.9	2.3	3.5	5.8	2.4	4.7	7.1	1.8	4.7	6.5
Latin America and the Caribbean	3.0	6.0	9.0	4.8	18.8	23.6	2.8	11.3	14.1	2.6	7.6	10.2
Middle East and North Africa	6.4	2.7	9.1	5.4	2.3	7.7	4.0	1.6	5.6	2.9	1.4	4.3
South Asia	66.5	119.9	186.4	43.1	99.0	142.1	48.8	138.4	187.2	27.3	74.9	102.2
Total	**123.0**	**248.6**	**371.7**	**104.9**	**184.0**	**288.9**	**94.4**	**208.8**	**303.2**	**75.3**	**164.7**	**240.0**

Table D.9
....
Proportion of IDA Primary Education Disbursements for Capital and Recurrent Expenditures, by Region, Fiscal Years 1999–2002
(percent)

Region	FY99 Capital	FY99 Recurrent	FY99 Total	FY00 Capital	FY00 Recurrent	FY00 Total	FY01 Capital	FY01 Cecurrent	FY01 Total	FY02 Capital	FY02 Recurrent	FY02 Total
Africa	27	73	100	44	56	100	41	59	100	35	65	100
East Asia and the Pacific	70	30	100	70	30	100	62	38	100	60	40	100
Europe and Central Asia	31	69	100	40	60	100	34	66	100	28	72	100
Latin America and the Caribbean	33	67	100	20	80	100	20	80	100	25	75	100
Middle East and North Africa	27	73	100	70	30	100	71	29	100	67	33	100
South Asia	36	64	100	30	70	100	26	74	100	27	73	100
Total	**37**	**63**	**100**	**46**	**54**	**100**	**42**	**58**	**100**	**40**	**60**	**100**